THE BOOK OF GUYS

Garrison Keillor is the bestselling author of *Lake Wobegon Days*, *Happy to Be Here*, *Leaving Home*, *We Are Still Married* and *Radio Romance*. He is the host of 'American Radio Company' on public radio and a contributing columnist to the *New York Times*.

THE BOOK OF GUYS

Garrison Keillor

faber and faber
LONDON · BOSTON

First published in 1993 by Viking Penguin,
a division of Penguin Books USA Inc.
First published in Great Britain in 1994
by Faber and Faber Limited
3 Queen Square London WC1N 3AU
This Open Market Paperback edition first published in 1994

Printed in England by Clays Ltd, St Ives plc

© Garrison Keillor, 1993

"Lonesome Shorty," "The Chuck Show of Television" (as
"The Chuck Show"), "Al Denny" and "Zeus the Lutheran" first
appeared in *The New Yorker*. "Christmas in Vermont" (as "A
Christmas Story") and "George Bush" (as "How the Savings
and Loans Were Saved") appeared in slightly different
form in *The New Yorker*. "That Old Picayune-Moon" was
first published in *Harper's*.

Garrison Keillor is hereby identified as author of this work
in accordance with Section 77 of the Copyright,
Designs and Patents Act 1988.

A CIP record for this book is
available from the British Library

ISBN 0–571–17324–1

2 4 6 8 10 9 7 5 3 1

TO MY SON, A REAL GOOD GUY

*A thousand thanks to
Veronica Geng for
her editing and to
Jenny Lind Nilsson
for her reading
of this book.*

G.K.

CONTENTS

THE BOOK OF GUYS

ADDRESS TO THE NATIONAL FEDERATION OF ASSOCIATIONS CONVENTION, MINNEAPOLIS, JUNE 12, 1993

MADAME CHAIR, MEMBERS OF THE CLERGY AND JUDICIARY, DISTINGUISHED GUESTS, MEMBERS OF THE LEGISLATURE, REPRESENTATIVES OF THE SKILLED TRADES, MY FRIENDS IN THE PRESS, FELLOW ARTISTS, LADIES AND GENTLEMEN, CHILDREN OF ALL AGES:

A few years ago in a poker game I won a membership in a club called The Sons of Bernie and last January, late one night, I drove my truck deep into the woods near River Falls to attend the annual Bernie campfire and drunken orgy of song and self-pity, standing arm in arm with other S.O.B.s around a bonfire under the birches, in a raw wind at twenty below zero, the snowbanks up to our waists, and there, under the Milky

Way and a nearly full moon, we ate chili out of cans and drank bourbon whiskey and sang mournful songs like "Long Black Veil" and "Old Man River," and complained about women until six o'clock in the morning, when we retired to our homes to recuperate.

There were about thirty of us, and when I arrived and saw them, I said to myself, "Let's get out of here. You were *had* in that poker game. This membership isn't worth *half* the five hundred dollars you gave him for it, the big cheater." It was not my crowd. They were the sort of desperate low-lifes who will tell you a long story for a five-dollar loan, guys who everything unfortunate has happened to, cruel fathers, treacherous friends, abject poverty, rejection by women, dust storms, prison, tuberculosis, car wrecks, the boll weevil, and poor career choices, all the disasters familiar to fans of the great Johnny Cash. Men peak at age nineteen and go downhill, we know that, but, I tell you, they looked so much older and sadder than you want people your own age to look. One glance at those beat-up faces and you could not imagine women loving them at all and I was by far the soberest and handsomest one in the bunch. "Well, perhaps I will stay for a while," I thought, "and gather impressions of them so that I can someday write about these poor guys so that they will not be completely forgot." As the night wore on, however, I came to feel more brotherly.

You had to stand close to this fire to get any warmth from it. The smoke got in our eyes, hot coals flew into our hair, but we didn't mind. We stood, left arm over the shoulder of the man to our left, right arm free to pass the bottle, and we sang and sang.

We sang "Hard Times Come Again No More," "Abilene," "It Ain't Me, Babe," "Take This Hammer," "Streets of Laredo," and recited poems, such as "When in disgrace with fortune and men's eyes I all alone beweep my outcast state," and then someone recited, "There was an old sailor named Tex who avoided women and sex by thinking of Jesus and terrible diseases and spending the night below decks."

It was not a tasteful or reverent occasion, and yet it was satisfying in some respects. A person can drink quite a snootful of whiskey in subzero temperatures and still keep floating, and while it isn't an experience that you want to base a lifetime on, nevertheless you would hate to come to the end of your life and think, "I never ever once got drunk in the woods on a winter night with a bunch of guys who all knew the words to 'I Ride an Old Paint.' "

We sang about Old Paint and Frankie and Johnny and somebody recited:

Whenever Richard Cory went down town,
The women on the streetcar looked at him:
He was a gentleman from sole to crown,
Clean shaven, and he used expensive aftershave.
And he looked very elegant in a suit.
And he was always friendly when he talked;
He certainly made the heads turn en route
To his office at the First National Bank.

And he was rich, a man of style and grace,
And married to a beautiful woman named June.
And yet none of us wished that we were in his place.
We knew June and she was a bitch.
And one calm summer night, under a beautiful moon,
Richard Cory put a bullet through his head.
No big surprise, not if you knew June.

We got to feeling awfully close, hooked together, the fire blazing away, the whiskey doing its work. After the poem, a guy said, "I don't want you to take this the wrong way, but I'm glad there aren't any damn women here." (LAUGHTER) Sorry, but that's what he said.

Another guy stepped forward and said: "I have worshipped women all my life, especially pregnant women, and then the other day, a woman I know, she looked like she had a basketball under her dress, she told me that she felt *great* when she was pregnant, that she *enjoyed* it, had more energy, felt sort of high, and it just makes me wonder if maybe women have gotten more mileage out of motherhood than they should've and if maybe we could stop bowing whenever one comes in the room."

A ripple of excitement passed through the circle: Guys were Speaking Out! Us! Saying things we wouldn't dare say in polite society (i.e. women).

A guy with snow-white hair stepped into the circle. "Listen, you pineapples. Damn women writers write absolute drivel and dreck and people fawn over them. Women win blue ribbons even though they didn't come in *tenth*. They get hired for jobs they're barely mediocre at. Affirmative action sounds good in theory, boys, but any time you promote incompetence, you are dragging society down, I don't care what your motives are."

A guy said, "I ain't no misogynist or chauvinist but I got to say, women are getting awfully impossible to please these days. I've been busting my butt for years trying to keep women happy, and they're madder at me now than they were before I started trying so hard. I quit playing softball and deer hunting and took up painting delicate watercolors, still lifes mostly, and tossing salads, and learned how to discuss issues and feelings and concerns and not make jokes about them, and they're *still* angry at me. A guy can't win. Boys, let me tell you this for your own good and it'll save you a lot of time later in life: most women down deep believe that everything wrong is men's fault and nothing you can ever do will change that. So don't worry about it. Live your life." *Oya!* we all yelled.

A great big bearded guy stepped into the circle. "I sort of *miss* communism. When the Soviet Union fell apart—I don't know—it seemed like everything went slack. There was no point anymore. Guys lost interest in baseball, guns—guys quit messing with cars. My son *never* gets under a hood. Instead he tries to get in touch with his feelings, tries to understand his girlfriend and keep a nice close peaceful relationship. Something doesn't add up here. We're selling out our manhood, bit by bit, trying to buy a little peace and quiet, and you know something? it won't work. Self-betrayal never works! I say, nuts to sensitivity. Go ahead and fart. Go ahead." So we did. All at once. The fire flamed up blazing bright. It felt good.

I realized right then, standing in that circle, that I know many more women than men. Women are easier to talk to. So I go have lunch with a woman at, say, Le Domicile de Daphne restaurant, and we talk and talk about various things that intrigue us, and suddenly I lean forward across the plate of ziti and sun-dried tomatoes and whisper, "Bozo alert," and nod toward a guy in a dumb T-shirt (HELP ME. I'VE FALLEN AND I CAN'T REACH MY BEER) and a blue satin team jacket, his cap turned backwards, who has lumbered into the restaurant searching for a toilet.

For more than thirty years, I have been nudging women and pointing out dopey men to them so that women would know that I am no bozo. And here I was arm in arm with the very sort of guys I had always made fun of. I felt ashamed.

I stepped forward and sang them a song:

There was once a shy young man who left his country home
And moved to the city to be more free,
For in the city no one cared if you stayed out half the night
And people didn't notice every time you bought a new pair of
pants.
So he enjoyed a carefree life amongst the Broadway crowd
And attended shows they did not have in Minnesota,
And the only thing that worried him was what if he got sick
And fell down in the street, would anybody notice?
He decided to find out, so he laid down in the gutter,

And right away a woman came and knelt down by his side,
And it was Gladys, his old neighbor, who was in the city vis-
iting her niece Denise,
And she said to him, "Jim, I always knew that you were no
good."

"That's right," they said. *Oya.*

A large guy (I would say about a size 62) stepped into the circle. He was blinking back the tears. He had a hank of hair falling down in his eyes that he tossed back with his head. He blew his nose and said, in a soft voice, "I have never been in a group of men before, and it's hard for me to say what I have to say." We shouted our support and manly encouragement. "Thank you," he said. "I had a chance to become a girl when I was in the fourth grade. We all did. You could check a box marked *F* on the Iowa Basic Gender Questionnaire, but they never explained it to me very well, like most things about sex, so I checked *M* instead, but some of the girls in my class checked *M,* and they got changed a few weeks later—in those days, it was referred to as 'having your tonsils out'—and a tiny penis was implanted and two testes the size of hailstones—*and those girls grew up and became extremely successful, happy, and well-adjusted men,* the sort of guys who are easy with their masculinity and get along just fine. And sometimes—" and here his voice shook—"sometimes I wish I had become a girl."

Several guys gave him big hugs. He flinched and tried to squirm out but they had him like a chicken in a vise. (LAUGHTER)

And then the head man of the S.O.B., the Big Burner himself, stepped into the circle, to talk about Bernie. He had been Bernie's best friend.

Bernie was a good guy who married a great girl, Jackie, who then became a feminist, but that was okay by Bernie, and he supported her in all that she did as she flew around to women's conferences and seminars, gave speeches at dinners, was on the boards of NOW and NARAL and the ACLU and ACT and WARM and WARN and YES, and seldom was at home there in Minneapolis, but that was okay, she was happy and if she was happy then he was happy. They had four daughters, Susan B., Elizabeth Cady, Willa, and Betty. Bernie was a good dad and good husband, and the rest of the time he was a cement contractor. He had fourteen trucks pouring concrete. One winter when the concrete business slacked off, Bernie thought he'd maybe go ice fishing for a week with his buddies, play poker and tell some stories, have some laughs—though Jackie thought it was dumb beyond belief and gave him a hard time about him wanting to go off with those rednecks and said, "I thought you *got it,* but obviously you don't"— and then, the day before he was to leave, he ran into the Big Burner on the street and told him how wonderful it would be to see the guys again. "I haven't gone ice fishing in fifteen years, but finally I got Jackie to let me go," he said, "and boy, am I looking forward to it. Well," he said, "I gotta cash a check before the bank closes." And he turned and two seconds later he was rubbed off the face of the earth by a runaway gravel truck.

"Bernie was wearing a red-plaid flannel shirt, an orange down vest, rubber boots, overalls, and long johns, and he had a Vicks eucalyptus cough drop in his mouth and Old Spice aftershave on his face. I can still smell him and I'll always remember how much he looked forward to being with us. He was one of us, a hard worker, not a loafer, a northerner, a trucker, a faithful husband, a good buddy, and here is to him."

We drank a solemn toast.

"She got the house, the concrete business, everything, all that he'd worked so hard to build up, and you know? she didn't share much of it with those daughters either. She sold the company for six million dollars to some jerks who then ran it into the ground and she built herself a big house on Barbados and bought an apartment in New York where she entertains liberals and artists and feminists by the truckload. That's what happened to the life and hard work of Bernie, boys. It went to feminism and he never got to go fishing."

We all leaned forward and spat on the ground.

"He was a loser, boys, and the world loves winners. People used to love their losing teams, but no more. The owners are in it for the money and the fans are in it for the victories. If you lose, you're shit. Well, boys, we are all losers like Bernie—you, me, we're drunk, confused, sad, and we smell like dead trout—but I loved him and I love all of you.

"Here's to that trip he never took and the fun he never had. He wanted to get out of line for a few days, hoist a few, tell some jokes, be with the boys. So let's do it. Here's to Bernie. Let 'er rip."

And we drank a long toast and gave six long whoops, *Eeeeeee-ha!*

By four a.m. there was little left to say and nobody in condition to say it. So about six, I went home. (AP-PLAUSE)

* * *

It is hard to put your finger on, but guys are in trouble. Guys are gloomy. We try to cheer ourselves up, we go down to the Lost Hombre Saloon and hoist a margarita with some sad guys from the Sanitation Dept. and we tell them, "Hey, tomorrow's a new day." So we put on our pants in the morning and think *A Hum babe c'mon babe hum babe, attaboy, let's go, babe, play from within yourself babe, good as ya wannabe babe, let's go, babe, hum babe, a hum it in there babe, focus babe, center yourself babe, c'mon babe, hum babe, hum babe, feel good about yourself babe.* Or we say the prayer of St. Geoff: "Breathe deeply, relax, let go of all stress and anger, and be here within yourself in the universe where you are truly welcome— really." Or we go to a steam room and cook, or we go to a ballgame, or we go to a Unitarian monastery in New Hampshire. The rule there is complete silence but if you think of something really good you can go ahead and say it. So one day, eating our silent lo-cal lunch, we turn to the abbot, a former psychiatrist, and say, "I keep racing and racing, I live life fifteen minutes at a time,

10

I'm stretched thin, and inside I am empty." And then we see the hollowness in his eyes, poor man. In America, you don't have to know what you're doing in order to do what you're doing. You become a holy man by learning to act holy. The furrowed brow, the shambling gait, the vacuous modesty, the blissful dumbness, the maundering, the weird verbless speech, and Abbot Bob has mastered the act beautifully, but one look in his eyes tells you that nobody is home, he is a vacant shrine.

Years ago, manhood was an opportunity for achievement, and now it is a problem to be overcome. Plato, St. Francis, Michelangelo, Mozart, Leonardo da Vinci, Vince Lombardi, Van Gogh—you don't find guys of that caliber today, and if there are any, they are not painting the ceiling of the Sistine Chapel or composing *Don Giovanni*. They are trying to be Mr. O.K. All-Rite, the man who can bake a cherry pie, go play basketball, come home, make melon balls and whip up a great soufflé, converse easily about intimate matters, participate in recreational weeping, laugh, hug, be vulnerable, be passionate in a skillful way, and the next day go off and lift them bales into that barge and tote it. A guy who women consider Acceptable.

Being all-rite is a dismal way to spend your life, and guys are not equipped for it anyway. We are lovers and artists and adventurers, meant to be noble, free-ranging, and foolish, like dogs, not competing for a stamp of approval, *Friend of Womanhood*.

Back when our gender was running on all eight cylinders, women died for the love of us (e.g. Carmen

11

stabbed to death, Butterfly *self-stabbed,* Tosca *self-hurled from parapet,* Brunnhilde *self-burned,* Aïda *self-buried,* Ophelia *swam after mealtime*)—those days are over. Now women watch us and monitor our conversation for signs of bad attitude, they grade us daily, and, boys, *we are in the wrong class.* Men can never be feminists. Millions have tried and nobody did better than C+.

Here's what they won't tell you in class—

• Girls had it better from the beginning, don't kid yourself. They were allowed to play in the house, where the books were and the adults, and boys were sent outdoors like livestock. Boys were noisy and rough, and girls were nice, so they got to stay and we had to go. Boys ran around in the yard with toy guns going *kksshh-kksshh,* fighting wars for made-up reasons and arguing about who was dead, while girls stayed inside and played with dolls, creating complex family groups and learning to solve problems through negotiation and role-playing. Which gender is better equipped, on the whole, to live an adult life, would you guess? (APPLAUSE, SHOUTS) Is there any doubt about this? Is it even *close?*

• Adolescence hits boys harder than it does girls. Girls bleed a little and their breasts pop out, big deal, but adolescence lands on a guy with both feet, a bad hormone experience. You are crazed with madness. Your body is engulfed by chemicals of rage and despair, you pound, you shriek, you batter your head against the trees. You come away wounded, feeling that life is unknowable, can never be understood, only endured and sometimes cheated.

• Women know about life and social life and how to get along with others, and they are sensitive to beauty, and at the same time they can yell louder. They know all about guys, having been exposed to guy life and guy b.s. since forever, and guys know nothing about girls except that they want one desperately. Which gender is better equipped to manipulate the other?

The father of a daughter, for example, is nothing but a high-class hostage. A father turns a stony face to his sons, berates them, shakes his antlers, paws the ground, snorts, runs them off into the underbrush, but when his daughter puts her arm over his shoulder and says, "Daddy, I need to ask you something," he is a pat of butter in a hot frying pan. The butter thinks to itself, "This time I really am going to remain rectangular," and then it feels very relaxed, and then it smells smoke.

• Men adore women. Our mothers taught us to. Women do not adore men; women are amused by men, we are a source of chuckles. That's because women are the makers of life, and we aren't. We will never be able to carry life within our bodies, never breast-feed. We get more than our share of loot and we are, for some reason, incredibly brave and funny and inventive, and yet our role in procreation basically is to get crazy and howl and spray our seed in all directions.

• So we carry adolescence around in our bodies all our lives. We get through the Car Crash Age alive and cruise through our early twenties as cool dudes, wily, dashing, winsome, wearing white socks and black loafers, saying incredibly witty things, shooting baskets, the breeze, the moon, and then we try to become caring men, good husbands, great fathers, good citizens, despite the fact that guys are fundamentally unfaithful. (AUDIENCE REACTION) A monogamous man is like a bear riding a bicycle: he can be trained to do it but he would rather be in the woods, doing what bears do. Nevertheless, we learn to ride that bicycle for the sake of women, and we ride it darned well, considering, and we live a pleasant, if sometimes cloying, life shopping at the Food Shoppe and Wine 'N Stuff and taking the kids to the Wienery-Beanery, attending planning meetings, writing thoughtful letters to the editor, eating bran flakes, supporting the right things, and we accept restrictions and limits, no smoking, jackets required, No Left Turn 4–6, and then, with no warning, we wake up one morning stricken with middle age, full of loneliness, dumb, in pain. Our work is useless, our vocation is lost, and nobody cares about us at all. This is not bearable. In despair, we go do something spectacularly dumb, like run away with Amber the cocktail waitress, and suddenly all the women in our life look at us with unmitigated disgust.

Spectacular dumbness is a guy type of gift. (APPLAUSE) We are good at great schemes and failed brilliance, and some eras seem to encourage this. The seventies was a time when people could do dumb things and nobody gave them a hard time about it. You'd go to see improvisational theater and the actors were climbing naked through piles of tires waving flashlights and reciting numbers at random, and afterward you thought, "Well, life is like that sometimes, I guess," and then a few years later there were strict new rules: everything had to Add Up, as if life were a term paper. People kept turning around and explaining themselves, even people for whom there was no explanation—everyone was seeking plausibility.

I once was interviewed on a daytime radio show whose host wore a tiny pink bathing suit, although she was in fact a normal-sized woman. We sat together in a studio the size of a walk-in closet, and I avoided mentioning her bikini on the air, but she didn't leave out anything when it came to me.

"You seem like a nice guy with a lot of dirty underwear," she said. "Let's talk about it. I've heard it said that you drifted into manhood with the charm of a claims adjuster and a withering sense of guilt due to a good upbringing. That in high school you tried to escape your unworthiness by affecting a sort of wispy bohemianism, writing your name in lower-case letters and composing dippy poems with titles like 'Soliloquies for Stringless Guitars,' and eventually you ran away from home when you were twenty-four. People who know you well have described you as moody and inarticulate, a guy with cold green eyes and a ratlike smile who suffers good fortune with ill humor, which has left you virtually friendless, isolated, adrift, out of touch, and that you have lost approximately thirty-two points of IQ in the past twenty years and were only average to start with. But that's not my question. My question to you is: does loss of brain function justify persistence in the face of, shall we say, a certain *pointlessness* to one's life? A lot of people are asking this question about you. What do you think, Gar?"

I will be honest—through most of her rather long question I was concentrating on her breasts, which were prominently displayed, particularly the left one, which was nearer to me. (AUDIENCE REACTION)

"I don't think that's true about my IQ," I said. "I don't think I've dropped *that* far." I smiled.

She said, "And yet my question remains: is reduced mental capacity the clue to your career or should we look for other explanations?"

I had to admit that I have made some boners in my day. I wasn't about to confess them all but I did tell a few stories on myself, about situations involving cars, in which I had attempted to solve problems through brute force. She seemed genuinely amused by these anecdotes.

"Thank you," she said. "That's all the time we have." And the show was over. "I hope you don't feel I was too hard on you," she said. She put on a brown wool skirt and white blouse and a green blazer, picked up her briefcase, and left.

Her honesty drove me to take a closer look at myself and I made a list of my abilities and inabilities.

A. Useful Things I Can Do

Fix decent meals and serve them.

Be nice.

Make a bed.

Dig a hole.

Write books.

Sing alto or bass.

Read a map.

Drive a car.

Talk on the radio.

Wash and iron clothing.

Clean.

B. Useful Things I Can't Do

Chop down big trees and cut them into lumber or firewood.

Plant a field of corn or any other crop.

Handle a horse, train a dog, or tend a herd of animals.

Handle a boat without panicking the others.

Build a frame structure larger than a birdhouse.

Do simple algebra or mathematical computations of any kind.

Fix an internal combustion engine. Or an external one.

Remember the laws of physics.

Make an intelligent bet on a horse.

Invest money wisely.

Teach electricity, grammar, the Reformation.

Play guitar.

Throw a fastball, curve, or slider.

Load, shoot, and clean a gun. Or bow and arrow. Or
use either of them, or a spear, net, snare, boomer-
ang, or blowgun, to obtain meat.
Defend myself with my bare hands.
Keep my mouth shut.

Maybe it's an okay report card for a *person* but I don't
know any persons, don't know what they can do and
can't do. For a guy, it's not good. A woman would go
down the second list and say, "What does it matter if a
guy can handle a boat? Throw a curveball? Bag a deer?
Throw a left hook? This is 1993." But that's a womanly
view of manhood. (LAUGHTER)

Miss Woofenberg, our second-grade teacher, worked
hard to instill a womanly view of manhood in us boys.
She taught us that it was manly to be quiet and be nice,
to be neat, to share and yet give a slight advantage to
girls, to be studious and listen and do as she said. These
traits, which she believed that girls innately possess,
Miss Woofenberg urged us boys to learn, and she made
us repress our urge to push ahead, to grab, to fight, to
struggle, to press forward in man's relentless quest for
superiority and world domination.

A man achieves world domination every time he does
something awfully well. A guy who has a good fastball,
or knows physics like his own backyard, or can pick up
a .22 and pick off a pine cone at a hundred yards knows
this.

Guys need this feeling if they're going to survive.
Guys know that we are going to lose some, maybe lose

a whole long string, maybe get our butts kicked for *years*, but we have to be No. 1—sometime, somewhere, if only for ten minutes—or else we sag inside and become sad and careful, a guy who when he stands up you hear the tinkle of broken dreams.

Miss Woofenberg created a problem for us when she catechized us in the theology of submergence in the group.

"We want what is best for everybody," she said, which sounds good until you strive for it for a while and realize that, like the horizon, the common good recedes as one draws near. The only way to approach it is to live in a deep canyon.

A fastball travels ninety miles an hour or so, and if it isn't thrown by guys, it isn't going to be thrown, babes.

We go around with a sense that our gender peaked in the eighteenth century. The King, the Court, the Church, Knighthood, Guilds—all of that worked for guys: in paintings by the Old Masters, guys looked good, whether boy or burgher, hearty and flush, good-humored, bold, prosperous, Guys at Their Best. After that, guys vanished from art, except for troubled self-portraits. Now our gender supplies all the major criminals and all the major candidates for high office; the female gender supplies the goddesses of light and mercy. What went wrong?

I haven't seen the S.O.B.s since that campfire and I don't expect to, and if I did see them, I don't know

what we would say. Because *guys don't talk to each other.*
We paw up dirt, we bang antlers, sometimes we graze
side by side, but we seldom talk.

You can fly off to the rain forests of Rawalpindi and
attend the Tribal Gathering of World Men and dance
around pounding your tom-toms, chanting ancient guy
chants, grunting guy grunts, painting your body with
guy markings, squatting around the fire and telling ancient guy myths, but the biggest myth of all is that men
can open up to each other and share their secrets. *Oya.*

You go to the Guy Pride lunch and hear a talk about
All for Oneness and afterward you confide in a fellow
guy that you are going through a hard stretch right
now, and he says, "I can sure sympathize, Jim. Listen,
let's get together soon and do some bonding. Really."
And he checks his watch, glances around for someone
else to talk to, *he can't get away from you fast enough.* He
goes off and talks to other people and he says, "Look out
for Jim. He strikes me as unstable. A liability to the
team. How can we ease him out of here?" Men are capable of this. *You should hesitate to tell a guy you feel bad. It
may embarrass him and he won't talk to you for months. Or
it may excite him and he will think of ways to get your house
or at least some of your savings.*

Men need women to talk to and tell the truth to.
This is a main feature of sexual life, where guys are concerned.

Guys know that we should free ourselves from
women, stake out our own turf, and stop trying to be so

wonderful to them. Let women deal with their own lives and solve their own problems. Stop feeling guilty, as if we could make it up to them. (AUDIENCE REACTION)

Guys know that we ought to get together with other guys and drink whiskey with our arms draped around each other and sing "Old Paint," and tell our ripe rich jokes.

But we keep coming back to women.

They can't take over the world fast enough for me. (APPLAUSE) I mean that. Let them run everything. (APPLAUSE) They should take over business and government and manage society and finance and let guys be artists and hoboes.

We are delicate as roses in winter and need to be wrapped in warmth or else we die. (LAUGHTER) I don't know why I said that, except that it's written down here and also it's true. (LAUGHTER)

Women can rule the world, fine, but we need them to love us again, or else it's no good.

"Why is it so important to you to be as wonderful as you are?" a woman asked me one night as I lay sobbing into a pillow, having made a cherry pie that tasted like some old sparrows had been baked into it. "Why can't you just be yourself?"

I am trying to do that, my darling. I am going to go be myself right now. Thank you very much. (APPLAUSE AND AUDIENCE REACTION)

LONESOME SHORTY

The summer before last, I was headed for Billings on my horse Old Dan, driving two hundred head of the ripest-smelling longhorns you ever rode downwind of, when suddenly here come some tumbleweeds tumbling along with a newspaper stuck inside—I had been without news for weeks so I leaned down and snatched it up and read it trotting along, though the front page was missing and all there was was columnists and the Lifestyle section, so bouncing along in a cloud of manure I read an article entitled "43 Fabulous Salads to Freshen Up Your Summertime Table" which made me wonder if my extreme lonesomeness might not be the result of diet. Maybe I'm plumb loco, but a cowboy doesn't get much fiber and he eats way too much beef. You herd cattle all day, you come to despise them, and pretty soon, by jingo, you have gone and shot one, and then you must eat it, whilst all those cattle tromping around on the greens takes away your taste for salads, just like when you arrive at a creek and see that cattle have tromped in the water and drunk from it and crapped in it, it seems to turn a man toward whiskey.

I thought to myself, Shorty, you've got to get out of this cowboy life. I mentioned this to my partner, old Eugene, and he squinted at me and said, "Eeyup."

"Eugene," I said, "I've been cowboyin for nigh onto two decades now. I know every water hole between Kansas and the Sierra Nevada, but consarn it, I miss the company of my fellow man. Scenery ain't enough for me, Eugene, nor freedom. I'm sceneried out, pardner, and freedom is vastly overrated as an experience, if you ask me. I got to be with people. I'm a *people* cowboy, not a cow cowboy."

A few miles of purple sagebrush drifted by and a hawk circled high in the sky.

"Do you hear what I'm sayin?" I inquired.

He said, "Eeyessir."

I said, "*Give me a home where the buffalo roam?* It don't follow, Eugene. Buffalo have nothing to *do* with home, nothing at all. And I'm sick o'deer and antelope, Eugene. I'm sorry if this sounds like a discouraging word, but animals do not make for a home, Eugene. Not on the range nor anywhere else."

I continued, "And whoever wrote *The air is so pure and the breezes so free, the zephyrs so balmy and light* never spent time driving cattle, I can tell you that."

He grunted.

A few miles later, I said, "You ever think of just calling yourself Gene, Eugene? Gene is more of a cowboy name. Eugene is sort of a bookkeeper's name. How about I call you Gene, Gene?"

He thought this over for a few miles as we jangled along, eating dust. Then he said, "You do that and I'll lay for you and jump you and gouge your eyes out and bite off your ear."

"You'd rather be Eugene, then?"

"Eeyup."

We rode along for a ways. "Is there some topic you have a desire to talk about, Eugene?" I inquired.

"Nope."

A taciturn sidekick is like buying a ticket to see the sun set. Who needs it? You go humping along the trail, you would like some conversation, but no, Eugene could no more think up things to say than he could sing *La Traviata*.

That night, I was feeling low. The wood was wet and the campfire smoked, the beans were cold and the pork half raw, the mosquitoes descended in a cloud, and then it took hours to get the cattle bedded down, and as I was fetching a camp stool from the saddlebags, Old Dan accidentally stepped on my foot and about broke it. I hopped around on the good one and swore a blue streak, but none of it woke up Eugene. He was wrapped in his blankets, dead to the world. I sat down and listened to Dusty Joe on night watch, slowly circling the herd and singing "Tenting Tonight on the Old Campground," but all he knew was the chorus, and he sang that over and over.

I approached him where he sat on his horse on a little rise and asked him if he could not vary his performance.

"The cows like it," he said.

"That may be so," I replied, "but you are drivin me crazy. Why'n blazes can't you sing somethin else? Sing 'Bury Me Not on the Lone Prairie' for Pete's sake or 'The Night Herding Song.' Lay off the tenting tonight—it ain't even a cowboy song, for cryin out loud."

He said it was the only song he knew.

I remarked that it was a poor cowboy indeed who couldn't make up some songs of his own. "Just sing *I ride an old paint, I lead an old Dan, I'm goin' to Montan to throw the hoolihan,* and then keep making up new verses."

But of course he was stubborn and wouldn't do it. I got back to camp and I hear the damn tent song start up again, and of course the wind carried it right back to us.

To distract myself, I sat down and drew up a list of pros and cons on the back of a picture of my mother.

Reasons to Be or Not to Be a Cowboy
Freedom to be your own man. *The awful loneliness of doing so.*

Most beautiful country on God's green earth to look at. *No home, nowhere to sleep but on the cold ground. You get a bad back, pretty soon you're too bent over to look at scenery.*

Good old Dan—what else can he do but ride the trail? *You can't live for your horse, especially not one who steps on you.*

Love to be with my pals. *Those cheating lying gin-soaked idiots? They all moved to town a long time ago.*

The West must be won for the White Man. *I done my part.*

The chance to be a True Cowboy, who stands up for what's Right and Fair. *Fine, but it's time to settle down and start building up equity. You have got nothing to show for your hard life, nothing.*

So it was an even draw, six of one, half a dozen of the other, but my foot hurt me so bad, I couldn't sleep. I dosed it with a few slugs of whiskey and only managed to give myself a sour stomach, and I kept hearing, "Tenting tonight, tenting tonight, tenting on the old campground," and when morning came I announced to Eugene and the other boys that I was packing it in.

I said, "The problem is I don't drink enough water and I don't eat right. That pork last night was full of fat, for example. And riding a horse, you never get the cardiovascular exercise you need. I've got to think about my health." Well, you'd a thought I'da put on a dress and high heels the way they laughed and carried on. I said: "I quit. I'm a cowboy no longer. It's a rotten lonely life and I'm done with it." And I jumped on Old Dan, who luckily was right there, and I rode away.

I headed into a friendly town named Pleasant Gulch, having read in the paper that it offered a healthy climate, good soil and water, good schools and churches, a literary society, and "all the adornments of advanced civilization." *That's for me,* I thought. I became deputy to Sheriff Dibble, a full-time job with a decent pension plan, and bought a condo over the saloon. The realtor, Lefty Slim, had a four-bedroom ranch house with great views for cheap—"Must sell, owner is wanted for murder," he said—but I had seen all I wanted of ranches, so I bought the condo. Partly furnished with a nice walnut bedroom set and dining-room table and carpet, and I could move in right away because the previous owner had been shot.

I bought sheets and towels and hung up blue dotted-swiss curtains. You miss curtains so much on the trail; there's really no way to hang them. (I know. I've tried.) And I bought myself a set of china. A cowboy gets sick of the sound of his fork scraping a tin plate, and this was the first *good* china I ever owned: four place settings with salad bowl, soup bowl, cup and saucer, dinner plate, and dessert plate, plus two platters, two serving bowls, gravy boat, teapot, and soup tureen, in the Amaryllis pattern.

The truth was, I didn't know three other people in Pleasant Gulch well enough to invite to dinner, but I felt confident I soon would because the town was perfect, its lawns and porches and street lamps so welcoming and warm compared to rocks and buttes. I hiked around town twice that first evening, just to absorb the beauty of it, and then returned home and fixed pork and beans, but they looked like cassoulet on my Amaryllis.

I had eaten exactly two bites when shots rang out and some cowboys whooped and bullets tore through my curtains and one busted two teacups, and another one hit my good serving platter and blasted it to smithereens. I was so pissed off, I stalked downstairs and out into the street, which was deserted except for a cowboy lying face down in the dirt.

"What in the Sam Hill is going on around here?" I yelled.

He said he had been shot clean through the heart and was done for.

I knelt down by him and yelled, "You busted my Amaryllis china, you dink! I came in off the trail to get away from your ilk and here you are messing around in town. Well, not for long."

He asked me to take a letter to his mother in Pittsburgh.

"Your mother has no interest in hearing from you, so don't even think of it. You're nothing but a filthy savage and death is too good for you," I said. And then he died, presumably. At any rate, he didn't have any more to say.

Next day, I went back to the General Store to replace that serving platter, and they were plumb out of Amaryllis. And that night, the old couple next door banged on my door and said, "You're gargling too loud in there, Mr. Shorty, it's driving us nuts, and you twirl your rope and jingle your spurs, and your yodeling is a pain in the neck. No more *yodeladihoo* or *whoopitiyiyo,* okay?"

I told them that it was my home and I would yodel in it as I pleased.

So they called the sheriff and he said, "Sorry, Shorty, but they're right. We have a yodeling ordinance here and also one against gargling after ten p.m."

I got so dagnabbed mad, I stomped home, put my Amaryllis into saddlebags, climbed on Old Dan, and left town at sundown. I was burned up. I yelled at them, "Okay, I'll show you! You can take your damn piddling laws and ordinances and regulations and stuff em in your ear!" And back out on the range I went. Frankly, I'd left so many towns by then that I was used to it and didn't get nearly as mad as in the past. Leaving town is what cowboyin is all about.

You find a nice place and it's wonderful and then suddenly you can't stand it. So you drift off down the trail and get wet and miserable and lonesome till you can't bear it for another minute, so you gallop into the nearest town and are overwhelmed by the beauty of society— cheap floozies, old coots, preachers, lunatics, hoboes, schoolteachers, old scouts with their sunburned faces and their voices raised in song, the jokes and gibes and yarns, the barn dances, the woman who invites you to stay the night—*people are great when you haven't seen any for a few months!*

So you find a job and an apartment, settle down, get comfortable, think "This time it's for real"—and two minutes later you are brokenhearted, mad, miserable, and back in the saddle again. This is the basic cowboy pattern.

From Pleasant Gulch me and Old Dan headed for Dodge, with all the china, and ten miles beyond the Little Crazy River, a rattler sprang at us and Dan shied away and I slid off and we busted a gravy boat! And one morning a grizzly came into camp and I reached for something to throw at him and I tossed my teapot—it was the worst trip, and the next night, two cougars snuck in and stole my pants as I slept and it was snowing and I headed for a little town called Pit City. Rode along in my underwear, cold and soaked to the skin, and a woman waved from a porch, people smiled at me, and a nice lady cried out from a white frame house: "My brother Dusty is just your same size, mister—if you need a pair of pants, you can have one of his. And if you haven't eaten I'll rustle you up a plate of grub. And if you care to set and talk a spell, why, that'd be just hunky-dory."

The Andersons. Euphonia and Bill Anderson. Kindest people you'd ever meet.

I sat in their toasty warm kitchen by the coal stove and gabbed for three hours and told them everything about myself, personal stuff, and it was satisfying.

"Your problem is that you never found the woman you loved enough to make you want to come in off the range and settle down," said Euphonia. She introduced me to their daughter Leonora, a beautiful redhead who worked at the Lazy Dollar Saloon—"as a bookkeeper," Euphonia emphasized.

Leonora treated me like the lover she never had. She and I went for long walks out across the prairie to the ridge above the town. I sang to her, "Mi amor, mi corazón," and she liked that pretty well. We got close. She did my laundry and saw the name tags on my shirts and started calling me Leonard, which nobody had done since I was a child.

"You're a gentle person, Leonard. Not like other cowboys. You like nice things. You ought to live in town," she said, lying with her head in my lap in a bower of prairie grass.

I told her, "Leonora, I have tried to live in town, because the cowboy life is a hard, wet, miserable, lonesome life, so town is wonderful, but doggone it, you go there and two days later, somebody kicks you in the shins and it's back in the saddle again. A guy can't live with people and he can't live without them. And besides, I am a cowboy and have got to be on the range." I spat on the ground to emphasize this.

"When you fixin to go?" she inquired.

"Tomorrow. Mebbe Tuesday."

"For long?"

"Six months. Mebbe longer. Depends."

"Six months is a long stretch of time to be away from a relationship," she said.

"Sometimes it is," I said. "And sometimes it's just long enough."

"Well, Shorty, you just go and do whatever you're going to do, because that's what you're going to do anyway, makes no matter what I say. I know cowboys," she said.

I cried, "Well, if I don't cowboy, tell me—what would I do for a living in town?"

"You could write a western," she said.

So I started in writing a western novel with lots of hot lead flying and poetic descriptions of western scenes:—"The setting sun blazed in the western sky as if a master painter had taken his brush to the clouds, creating a multihued fantasy of color reflecting brightly off the buttes and mesas." That night I showed it to Leonora. "Not what you'd call a grabber," she said.

I sat there with my face hanging out and wished she'd say *Well, it ain't all bad, actually some is rather good, Shorty, and I loved where the dude cuts down the tree and the bear bites him in the throat,* but of course a sweetheart isn't going to tell you that, their critical ability is not what attracts them to us in the first place.

She was the prettiest woman I ever knew in my life, the sweetest, the kindest. I discovered that Amaryllis was Leonora's china pattern too. She had four place settings, as I did. Together, we'd have eight. It was tempting to consider marriage. And yet she had a way of keeping me on a short rope—she'd look at me and say, "What are you thinkin?" Nuthin, I'd say, nuthin in particular. "What is it?" she'd ask. *I don't care to talk about it,* I'd say. "Silence is a form of anger," she said. "A person can be just as aggressive with silence as they can be with a gun."

Oh for crying out loud, dear God of mercy, I cried, and jumped up and went straight to the barroom, not the Lazy Dollar but the Dirty Dog Saloon, and sat in a dim corner and had a stiff drink and then another to keep the first one company, and by and by, who should mosey in but Mr. Higley, author of numerous western songs, including "Goin Back to Colorado" and "How I Miss the Old Missouri," so I bought him a drink and me one too and said, "Tell me how it is that you love it so out here on the plains. You write poems about the beauty of the land and the goodness of the folks—what am I missing, pardner?"

He said, "I have not set foot in Colorado in forty years, nor seen the Missouri for thirty-seven. Does that answer your question, L.S.?"

We hoisted a number of drinks then, and I staggered back home about midnight and slept on the porch swing, the door being locked, and the next morning Leonora and I had a tiff. She said, "How come you go do a dumb thing like that, Leonard? Can you imagine how it makes me feel? Or do you think I don't notice that you got drunk and were walkin around this town singin and whoopin and ropin street lamps and laughin like an idiot at two in the morning? Do you think that decent people don't *talk* about this and wonder why you're not home here with me? Don't you see that it makes me look like a fool?"

I said, "If I have got to ask permission to take a drink, then let me out of it. I quit."

She said, "Don't you see there's a pattern in your life,

Leonard? You're someone who avoids conflict. It's what makes you a cowboy." "You're mad at me, aintcha," I said. She was mad.

"I'm not mad. Only concerned. We have a dysfunctional relationship, that's all."

"You're mad and you're always *going* to be mad," I said.

She said she had read an article in the Emporia *Gazette* that said male restlessness may result from a hormone imbalance caused by an eating disorder.

"That's the westward impulse you're talking about, Leonora! That's what brought us here!" I cried. She said it wasn't an impulse, it was an imbalance. She said, "Maybe you should get help. The schoolmarm is a therapist part-time, you know."

Okay, I said.

Doggone it, I did everything I *could* to please that woman.

Twice a week for eight weeks, I lay down on Mary Ellen Henry's parlor sofa and told her everything about myself. She used cats as a medium. (She explained why, but I forget.) A cat lies on your chest and you talk to it, and she listens, e.g.:

ME: Boy, I sure feel confused, Puff. I'm so sad and mixed up I could go get drunk and jump off the roof. But with my luck I'd probably miss the ground.

HER: Puff, you tell that nice man to tell you more about when his mama left him at the train depot and went off with the drygoods salesman.

It felt dumb but I did it. Lay on the couch, cat

stretched out on my chest, Mary Ellen sat in the rocker, I talked about Mama to the cat—"My mother was the saintliest woman who ever trod this earth, Puff, and my daddy was the meanest sumbitch ever drew breath"— and Mary Ellen said to the cat, "Puff, I want you to tell Lonesome Shorty that some people might say that riding the open range is a cowboy's only way of keeping that powerful mama at a distance. You tell him that, Puff, and see what he says."

"Why, Puff, I believe that is the biggest crock of horse poop I've heard yet," I replied.

"Puff," she said, "remind Shorty of how his mama ran his daddy off so she could control her boy better."

"Lies, Puff. You're lying, ya miserable cat."

And on it went. I gave it my best shot but was no good at therapy, and one morning I said, "I've decided that you've probably done as much for me as you possibly can, Puff, so this will be my last visit. Thank you."

Mary Ellen was stunned, as if I had slapped her. Her eyes welled up with tears. "How can you *do* this to me?" she cried. "Don't you realize that you're my only client? You're important to me, Shorty! How can you walk away from me like I was just your hitching rail?"

This was much too complicated for me. So I saddled up and without a word to Leonora I rode off down the trail toward the Bitterroot, feeling dumber than dirt. Couldn't bear to be alone, couldn't bear the company. Thought it might be due to a lack of fluoride. Or it could be genetic—it's hard to tell. My daddy left home when I was two. If we had any fluoride, he took it with him.

Rode seven days through Arapaho country and was full of loneliness and misery, thinking only of Leonora, her touch and smell, until finally I began to sing "Mi amor, mi corazón," and burst into tears and turned around and rode back to Pit City. A bitterly cold day, windy, snow flurries, and me without shoes—I'd forgotten them at a campsite—and I was a sorry sight but when Euphonia saw me she said, "Welcome back, honey, and come in and let me get you a pair of Bill's shoes."

I took a shower, and the towels were soft and smelled lemony. You miss that softness, that cleanliness, on the trail. Had split-pea soup and Leonora came home and hugged me and cried, and the next day I got a job at the stagecoach office as assistant director of customer service and group sales, and the next few days went along like a song. Euphonia made my breakfast and Leonora made my bed and I bought six new place settings of Amaryllis, and we made plans to marry.

Then the Chautauqua put on a play called *The Secret Forest of the Heart* that Leonora had a big part in, so I went and I hated it, it was the dumbest sheepdip show you ever saw, about good women who nurture and heal and men who rob and control, and Leonora held out a magical garland of flowers and vines and herbs and celery and sang, "Know the quiet place within your heart and touch the rainbow of possibility; be alive to the gentle breeze of communication, and please stop being such a jerk." People with big wet eyes stood and clapped and a stagecoach driver named Gabby turned to me and said, "I could sure use a big hug right now." I got out of there as fast as I could.

I told Leonora, "You hate me 'cause I walked out on yer dagnabbed play and you're going to give me my walkin papers, aintcha?" and she said, no, she wasn't, she didn't expect me to like the play, she knew me well enough to know *that,* and I said, "Oh there you go again, just like always, you never stop finding fault with me, so I might as well go be bad, there's no percentage in being good," and she said I was crazy. "Well, to hell with you," I said, and I got so mad, I went in and robbed the bank. Pulled my hat down low and went in with six-guns in hand and yelled, "Everybody face down on the floor! Nice and easy, now, and nobody gets hurt."

They said, "Why are you doing this, Shorty? You're a wonderful guy and have a good job and you're blessed with the love of a wonderful woman."

"If that's what you call blessed, then I'd like to try damned to hell for a while."

"What do you have to be mad about?" asked the lady teller.

"Doggone it, I can be mad if I want to be. If I say I'm mad, I mean I'm mad."

"You'll never get away with it," someone yelled as I rode away with thirty-four thousand dollars on me, and as it turned out, they were right, but I didn't know it yet.

I headed off across the sandy flats on Old Dan toward the big mesas, rode hard for a week, then lay back. I was rich, and lonesome as an old galoot. Wanted to hook up with a partner but then thought of the trouble involved and decided against it. Made up a song as I rode along, "Livin inside/I'm dissatisfied/Guess I'm qualified to ride." Rode to Big Gap. No family took me in, no woman offered me comfort, and I sought no solace in the church. I paid with cash. A man in a saloon said he knew my old partner Eugene. "He got bit by his horse and was laid up with gelding fever and had fits and hallucinations and talked a blue streak for a month before he died, mostly about economics," he told me. I was sorry I had not been there to see it.

I rode on. I tried not to think about Leonora but I missed her terribly.

I wished I knew how to patch things up but there's no way. The love between two people is fragile and one false move can break it like fine china, and when it breaks, it's broken. I rode on, but I rode slower, and after a while I felt sick. I was so lonely. I lay down in the dirt and wrapped myself in a blanket and lay shivering all night and woke up in the morning and—I was about thirty feet from the Colorado Trail! All these wagon trains were going by and now and then a pioneer or a gold prospector'd call over to me—"Howdy! How are you doing over there yonder? You headin west too?"

And I'd answer: "I feel like I'm coming down with something. I don't know, I got a headache and chills and I feel weak and listless. You got a thermometer with you? Is saltpeter supposed to be good for this? You think maybe I should bleed myself?"

And they'd lope over near me and ask if I had a fever. "You're supposed to starve a fever," they said. "Just lie there and rest and don't eat anything and pretty soon you'll feel better."

And I did that, and three days later I died. The vultures came and feasted off me and the dogs fought over my bones and some old bum came and took the thirty-four thousand dollars in twenty-dollar bills out of my saddlebags and stomped on my china set and pretty soon what was left of me lay bleached and white on the lone prairie, but I didn't care because I was in heaven. I assume it was heaven. It was like Brown's Hotel in Denver, a suite, with a bathtub eight feet long, and a canopied bed, and an angel to bring me my breakfast.

It's a good breakfast: fresh biscuits and butter and two strips of thick crisp bacon and two eggs soft poached and fried potatoes and all of it on a beautiful pale-blue Amaryllis plate. But it does not vary from day to day, and neither does the angel, who sings beautifully but always the same song.

It is perfect here and a person should be grateful, I reckon, but I am about fed up with it and ready to move on to the other place, if only I could think of something bad enough to say that would get me sent there, and, being a cowboy, I suppose, that won't be a problem. Something will come to mind.

THE CHUCK SHOW
OF TELEVISION

Monday

MULDOON (10 A.M.): NEARSIGHTED GUYS DISTURBED BY THE BLUR WHO WENT BERSERK AND KILLED AGAIN AND AGAIN

AGNES ERSKINE (10 A.M.): DEALING WITH LOVED ONES WHO SMELL BAD

HECTOR (10 A.M.): THE FATTEST FOLKS YOU EVER LAID EYES ON—WE HAD TO BUY A SPECIAL COUCH FOR THIS SHOW!

ELAINE TIBBY POMFRET (10 A.M.): KIDS FROM NICE HOMES WHO EAT FISTFULS OF DIRT

HAROLD DERN SHOW (10 A.M.): PLEASE DON'T WATCH THIS IF YOU WEEP AT THE SIGHT OF CRUELTY!

Chuck (10 a.m.): Parents from District 18 Discuss Bus Transportation

It was the week after Flag Day, a slow time for morning talk shows. The week before, Muldoon had led the pack with five shows on young Wall Street executives who suddenly cut loose and became primitive herdsmen in the Adirondacks, living in yurts and subsisting on currants and elk milk, and now, on Monday, the pack was off again, Muldoon with men whose poor vision had sent them down the trail toward multiple homicide, and Agnes probing the problem of family members who smell like wet dogs, and who, if you tell them this, may never speak to you again or, worse, may suffer such loss of self-esteem they lose their careers and take up drugs—last week, she had done people who try to deal with their anonymity by writing a book about it and going on television. Hector was doing obese male exhibitionists who enjoy putting on organdy tutus and dancing to the "Waltz of the Sugarplum Fairy" in public and were pleased to do so on his show, and Elaine Tibby showed dirt eaters, and Harold Dern ran around the studio with a pickax and did $150,000 worth of property damage as the studio audience cheered.

Meanwhile, on *The Chuck Show of Television* on PCN (the Pedersen Cable Network, Minneapolis), you saw four parents discussing the fact that the school had canceled the late bus, which made it necessary to drive all the way into town every afternoon and pick up the kids after field-hockey practice and choir rehearsal. "I don't want to make a big thing about it, and all I'm saying is that it would've been nice if the process had allowed for some input from the parents," one parent said.

The next morning, Chuck's producer, Big Al, hit the ceiling. "You guys are dumber than dirt! Gosh, for boring! I'd rather watch a man paint a house. What a bunch of dummies! Whose dumb, dumb, dumb, dumb, dumb idea was this bus show anyway?" he screamed, when he saw how bad Chuck got beat in the overnight ratings. "A zero point six! That's as low as you can go and still be talking English." In fact, Chuck got beat out even by Miklo Pstachek's talk show, which is in Latvian. Mik had a woman guest who picked up and threw three spinet pianos fifteen feet and then lowered her head and busted through an oak door and ran down the alley with her clothes off. Mik got a one point two.

By the time Big Al saw the overnights and had calmed down enough to sit the *Chuck* staff down for a meeting, however, it was Tuesday already.

Tuesday

MULDOON: MYOPIC EXECS WHO BECOME HERDSMEN RATHER THAN MURDER THEIR WIVES AND KIDDOES

AGNES ERSKINE: AUNTS WHO STINK—SHOULD YOU SEND COLOGNE FOR CHRISTMAS?

HECTOR: BIG BLUBBERY GUYS IN POOFY DRESSES (ONES WE DIDN'T SHOW YESTERDAY, AFRAID YOU'D BE OFFENDED)

ELAINE TIBBY POMFRET: THEY EAT DIRT AND TOUCH THEMSELVES IN BAD PLACES AND WHAT DO PARENTS DO? NOTHING

HAROLD DERN SHOW: HE WILL RAGE AND FOAM AND SCREECH AND POUND—HE WILL RIP HIS CLOTHES TO SHREDS AND SHAKE THE BARS OF HIS CAGE UNTIL THEY ARE SO LOOSE YOU ARE SURE HE WILL JUMP OUT IN THE AUDIENCE AND WHOMP YOU

CHUCK: WHAT'S NEW THESE DAYS IN VOCATIONAL COUNSELING IN AND AROUND BROOKLYN PARK?

"Who is killing this show by booking guests who are dumber than stumps?" inquired Big Al when the whole *Chuck* crew assembled in his office at PCN's long, low cinder-block headquarters on Cheyenne Drive, next to the Wal-Mart, on Tuesday afternoon. Big Al's office is full of stacks of pornography (research for an unfinished master's thesis) and they had to scootch in tight, Eliot and Melody and Fielding and Shazzaba and Bob, all of them afraid they were about to be fired, each with a clipboard, a cup of coffee, and a stopwatch.

None of them said, "Al, those are exactly the guests whom your predecessor producer, Mary Ellen Hare, would have described as *really neat people.* Okay, so you were brought in from Chicago three weeks ago to shake things up, but don't blame us if it takes a while to get out of PTA-mode and into mud-wrestling." Nobody said that.

Big Al closed the office door and locked it and stood in the middle of the room and roared like a buffalo.

"Fess up and tell me which one of you dumbbells is stiffing this show by hauling in dead meat and dumping it on Chuck's couch. What's the deal? This is a show, not a civics class! We need the elephants and acrobats and instead you dumbheads are booking a bunch of librarians!" But in fact it had been the Chucker himself who booked those two shows. Those guests were all Friends of Chuck (FOC). And here in the swamp of paper on Big Al's desk was a Chuck memo saying they ought to do a show on recycling. Chuck's wife, Marge, is a lifelong recycler, a fanatic who carries a garbage bag to other people's parties and collects cans, bottles, paper, and recyclable plastic, and one of Chuck's big interests at Pedersen Cable is recycling: he's the one who persuaded President Bill T. Pedersen to put a recycling bin next to the soda machine.

But none of the staff cared to point out the obvious: the host himself, a pleasant man and lifelong Minneapolitan, was dragging the show to the bottom.

"One problem is that here in the Twin Cities it's hard to find that many freaks—at least, any who care to come on TV and talk about it," said Fielding. "We don't have a reliable supply of cross-dressers, hermaphrodites, eunuchs, or geeks. We have plenty of alcoholics, but how interesting are they? They don't *remember* anything. This is Minnesota, we're a journalistically challenged state. I mean, when was the last time a band of Lutherans holed up in a compound with automatic weapons? We don't have that here. We have a few fatties, but nothing like you see in New York or L.A. I was in New York once and I saw a man as wide as the whole sidewalk. He was driving himself along on a forklift and singing in a sweet, high-pitched voice and lifting up his T-shirt to show his belly button. I'll bet Hector has him booked for Friday."

They discussed some combos who might be fun to have—alcoholic execs who abused their elk, obese cross-dressing grandmas who eat dirt as a way to erase memories of childhood trauma—but could *The Chuck Show* afford the airfare? Probably not.

"Anyway, no more of these Dumb Dora guests or I'll throw you all out the window," said Al. "We got to have some sad weird people—some people who make you go, *Whoa-oa-oa-oa*—or else I'm going to start kicking fanny around here. Now, go work the phones."

Ironically, Al was a potential guest himself—forty-seven, unable to read or write, terrified of cats, addicted to sugar, chronically depressed because of a rare disease called Phelps, trying finish a master's-degree thesis on masturbation—but of course as the show's producer he needed to be in the control room, not sitting on the studio couch sobbing over the bum hand that life had dealt him. Though Big Al could have cried plenty about his dad, who abdicated the parental role and married Big Al's beautiful Aunt Nick and thereby became Al's uncle, a kindly but distant figure who sat on the porch chuckling and spitting but never giving the boy a smidgen of discipline. *Growing Up with Dads Who Are More Like Uncles.* But was that the reason Big Al was illiterate? And did it matter? Loneliness was Big Al's major bugaboo.

He felt like the only person like himself in the whole world. There were no books about his ilk, not even a color brochure. His problems were apparently so unspeakably vile that nobody dared talk about them. Was that why he always ran around the Pedersen offices yelling and waving his big arms—to cover up his uniqueness? "What's the matter with you people!" he said. "How come you can't think? You want this show to go down the toilet?"

The Pedersen Cable Network
   Their exciting showcase productions:
   Championship Spelling! (Boys vs. Girls!)
   Science Fairs! featuring *hundreds* of exhibits!
   Thrilling Piano Recitals by Artists of all ages!
   Professional Trolling Tournaments!
   Bob's Cavalcade of Furniture Refinishing
   Demolition Derby
   Bowling for Prizes
   The Chuck Show of Television

THE MEETING CONT'D: "I don't think it's just guests. The star has been looking a little peaked since the show started to cool off," said Bob. "We need him looking fresh and eager again, like when we had the barking spiders on the show."

True, said Melody. Eliot smiled. That spider segment had been good. Six months after Chuck went into syndication, he had four Girl Scouts on the show, and one of them, a spider hobbyist, owned three rare barking spiders, and it was fascinating to see the tiny hairy insects and hear their unmistakable woofing and arfing. It got Chuck in papers from coast to coast, and the next day 2.2 million Americans tuned in—

"What???" yelled Al.

Their all-time best audience tuned in the show the next day, thanks to big spider word-of-mouth.

"What happened?"

Chuck's guests that next day were four old coots who sat and reminisced about Days Gone By and grumped about high property taxes and the cost of prescription drugs.

"You finally got yourself an audience and you blew it on old farts—how could you be so dumb?"

But the old farts had been booked for weeks; it was the only day they weren't busy at the senior center; they were looking forward to being on TV. So Chuck couldn't bear to cancel them.

"If I had been producer then, I woulda taken them geezers and heaved them out the door and I woulda signed those barking spiders back for a week!" cried Big Al.

He beat his fist on the desk. "Animals!" he said. "Go out there and bring back live animals!"

Wednesday

MULDOON: $500,000-A-YEAR GUYS WHO QUIT AND GO TO THE WOODS AND BANG AWAY AT ELK BUT MISS, BEING NEARSIGHTED

Agnes Erskine: How Do You Tell Your Dad That He Has Badger Breath?

Hector: Will Guys This Fat Bounce If We Drop Them? Will They Roll? What Do They Look Like Hanging Upside Down?

Elaine Tibby Pomfret: Parents Who Sit and Watch Kids Stuff Fistfuls of Dirt in Their Mouths

Harold Dern: He Escapes from His Trainer! He Leaps into the Crowd of Innocent Bystanders! He Has a Small Child in His Hands and Is About to Crush Its Head Like a Beer Can!

Chuck: Rabbits Copulating in Cages

The rabbits belonged to Melody's brother Donald, who had a hobby farm in Chanhassen, three males and three females in heat. The males mounted the females and pumped fast and furiously for six seconds like furry pistons and then fainted and toppled over and lay on their backs twitching, with their legs sticking up in the air, and then awoke and jumped up and remounted.

The PCN crew did some fantastic camerawork— slow-mo and stop-action and split-frame—and the minute Chuck went off the air all three major networks were calling and begging for footage. All three evening newscasts ran a story on it, deploring the depths to which television now descended and the implications of this for literacy and the arts, and that night Big Al took the *Chuck* staff out for prime-rib Angus at Harry's Cafe. The big guy was so happy and so drunk that he almost stood up and said, "I'm illiterate, sugar-dependent, catophobic, Phelps-infected, and a self-abuse abuser, and every day I feel sadder than you'll ever know, but I still love you so much I could hug you to pieces!" Anyway, that's how he felt.

They all whooped and laughed and chowed down on oysters and Martinis and the twenty-four-ounce portions of Angus, and then flaming fudge sundaes for dessert. Chuck wasn't there—he and Marge had their Amnesty International meeting on Wednesday nights, when they and their friends sat and listened to Paul Winter albums and wrote protesting postcards to totalitarian regimes— but Chuck sent a chocolate cake with green icing that said "CONGRATULATIONS TO A GREAT BUNCH OF PERSONS!" Chuck was happy about the rabbit show—he felt it would open the door to a greater frankness in sex education in the schools.

"The bunnies were fabulous, and the dumbest thing we could do would be to sit on our keesters at this point and coast," Big Al said. "We've got our work cut out for us now. The hardest thing is to stay on top!"

Thursday

MULDOON: THOSE EXECS AND THEIR ELK—WHAT ELSE MIGHT BE GOING ON THERE?

AGNES ERSKINE: PEOPLE WHO SMELL RIPE NEED TO DEAL WITH IT SO THEY CAN MOVE ON

HECTOR: MUCH FATTER PEOPLE THAN THE ONES WE

SHOWED BEFORE. THOSE WERE JUST THE TIP OF THE ICE-
BERG

ELAINE TIBBY POMFRET: MOTHERS WHOSE KIDS EAT
DIRT. OFTEN THEY ARE GROUND-FEEDERS TOO

HAROLD DERN: THE CHILD WEEPS COPIOUSLY, THE PAR-
ENTS SCREAM IN TERROR, BUT IT'S TOO LATE—IN AN-
OTHER SECOND, THE MADMAN HOST WILL RIP IT TO
SHREDS

CHUCK: HYPNOTIZING CHICKENS

Bob's brother learned about hypnotizing chickens
when he was in 4-H. You hold the chicken gently in the
crook of your arm and murmur "Cheese chips, parsnips,
and Charlie" over and over and stroke its beak until the
bird's eyes cross and it goes limp as a pillow. Then you
can set it down on the ground (chickens' knees lock
when hypnotized; nobody knows why) and it'll stand,
motionless, its white feathers riffling in the breeze, the
eyes focused on the tip of the beak, until suddenly it
falls over on its side. Or you can prop it against a stake.

The PCN crew shot some footage of hypnotized
chickens on location at several egg ranches in the area,
including the controversial segment in which a chicken
under hypnosis is beheaded with an ax and tears around
in circles for a full fifteen seconds, blood pouring from
its neck. Some stations cut that segment from *The Chuck
Show,* and then all three networks did stories that
showed the execution segment—on *MacNeil/Lehrer,*
three psychologists agreed that the sight could have

been traumatizing to small children and do damage that might not show up until they were in their late fifties. The PCN switchboards were jammed all day, and Thursday night the radio call-in shows were full of it, and Friday morning there were big newspaper stories, and the overnight ratings showed Chuck with the highest numbers ever recorded by a daytime cable talk host.

Phenomenal!

Big Al burst into Chuck's office laughing and screaming like a maniac, waving the survey, jumping up and down as he danced around and around, singing, "We did it, we did it, we did it, we did it!" and what did Chuck say? He glanced at the numbers and said, "This is great. You know why? Because it gives us a platform to say some things about urban planning. I think the Reagan-Bush years left us with huge urban problems—we turned our backs on the cities and left them to drown in garbage—and now we need to decide if we have the national will to invest in our cities, and if so, what they should be like. We have a chance to set the urban agenda in this country for the next fifty years. It's an incredible opportunity."

Big Al felt sick to his stomach. "That's interesting, I'll have Bob work up a proposal on that," he muttered, but he thought to himself, "You dumb Norwegian, we beat our brains out and make you the king hell maneating champion of the white race and all you can think about is urban planning. Man, now I know why Mondale lost."

Big Al went to his office and got a sawed-off shotgun

out of his desk drawer and came back to Chuck's office and stood in the doorway with the muzzle pointed at his own head and told Chuck the truth. "I cannot read or sign my own name, I am dying of Phelps, I drink three six-packs of Coke every day, my cat terrifies me at night, and I masturbate in unnatural ways. This show is the only bright spot in my life. If you want to be high-minded and pretentious and pompous and ruin this show, I am going to blow my head off right here and now."

Chuck offered to obtain professional help for Big Al. "I don't need professional help, Chucker. I need to win. We got to go out tomorrow and kick their butts off the air." He put down the gun and walked over to Chuck and kissed him on the lips, hard, a big wet smacker. "Chuck honey, if it meant higher ratings, I'd make love to you in slow motion, and, Chuck, you aren't even attractive."

Friday

MULDOON: I WILL QUIT MY SHOW, DRINK ELK'S MILK, AND DON FEMALE APPAREL IN FRONT OF MILLIONS!

AGNES ERSKINE: FOUR TOPICS I USED TO REFUSE TO DISCUSS ON THIS SHOW, INCLUDING BESTIALITY, PHONE CALLS FROM THE DEAD, RUMORS ABOUT NUNS, AND MY RECENT OPERATION TO HAVE MUSK GLANDS REMOVED FROM MY LOWER BACK

HECTOR: OBESE PEOPLE INVOLVED IN SECRET SATANIC-

CULT RITES? (EXTREMELY VIVID PHOTOGRAPHS, NO CHILDREN, PLEASE)

ELAINE TIBBY POMFRET: YOU WERE RIGHT, VIEWERS, I WAS WRONG! MILLIONS OF YOU TOLD ME, "DON'T KNOCK IT IF YOU HAVEN'T TRIED IT!"—SO TODAY I WILL! A WHOLE BIG BUCKET!

HAROLD DERN: LOOK! A DOG RUSHES IN! HE BARKS, "DERN! DERN!" AND BIG TEARS RUN DOWN THE ARCHFIEND'S CHEEKS AND HE RETURNS THE CHILD UNHARMED TO ITS PARENTS! IT IS HIS BOYHOOD DOG, CHIPPER, WHO RAN AWAY AND NOW HAS COME BACK! THE CHILD IS SAVED AND THE MONSTER REDEEMED BY THE LOVE OF A PET!

CHUCK: MY PRODUCER AND A GUY I'M PRIVILEGED TO CALL A FRIEND, BIG AL

Big Al knew that his guest appearance was a mistake the minute the "On Air" light flashed, but what could he do? Too late. He told everything in five minutes, and it was nothing. Masturbation—big deal. Adult illiteracy. Sugar addiction. Cat fear. Depression. Phelps. It was old hat. Noise. He wished so badly that he'd listened to the staff—the great stuff they'd gone out and found. The world's tiniest horse! A cow with two heads and two separate udders with a total of ten teats! A pig with a wooden leg who dives and swims and attacks on command!

The Big Al segment was lame. Al was even more depressed afterward, and locked himself in his office, and stared listlessly at pornographic pictures for an hour. But he cheered up later when the weekly ratings came in and *The Chuck Show* finished the week on top, followed by Agnes, Muldoon, Hector and Harold tied for fourth, Elaine Tibby dead last. E.T. promptly issued a press release decrying low standards in television and said she would devote two weeks to showing clips from the most disgusting TV shows of the past year.

There was quite a bit of soul-searching around the *Chuck Show* office in the Pedersen Cable Network building that afternoon. Chuck was gone—he and Marge were spending the weekend at a conference on American policy toward Canada—and basically what Big Al said was, "My fault, guys. I let you down. Autoeroticism isn't what got us here. We gotta get back to basics."

Bob reported that Hector was planning a whole week on capital punishment, comparing the merits of hanging, electrocution, firing squads, lethal injections, stoning, and pressing under heavy weights, and Muldoon was going to do grandmas hooked on methadone and nobody knows it except they seem sleepy in the afternoon, and Agnes was going to do death itself and her guests would be terminally ill persons hovering on the edge who could go at any moment, and Elaine Tibby would have a week on sex in car pools, and Harold Dern would go berserk and rave and foam as usual.

"Don't worry about them," said Big Al. "We're going to play our game and do what we do best. Otherwise you'll all be fired and hurled naked into a vat of acid."

By three o'clock that afternoon, they had worked up a tentative schedule:

MONDAY: Snakes eating live rats, and lizards eating the snakes, and giant horned toads eating the lizards

TUESDAY: Pigs vs. horses (IQ)

WEDNESDAY: Transvestites wrestling alligators

THURSDAY: Various pets from tiny towns near nuclear testing sites who look exactly like different celebrities, such as William F. Buckley, Jr., Joan Collins, and David Letterman

FRIDAY: A hundred-foot-long white whale, named Ruby, captured from the North Atlantic, who swallowed several men (perhaps six or seven) who are thought to be still alive inside, at least doctors listening with powerful infrared stethoscopes hear what sounds like English emanating from the behemoth's lower digestive tract

"The gigantic creature will be carefully anesthetized and opened up on Friday morning at ten-thirty," said Big Al. "Ambulances will be standing by to take the survivors, if any, to the hospital. No expense will be spared to rehabilitate these men and restore them to a useful role in society."

"How is this whale going to get to the studio?" asked Eliot.

Big Al said she would be flown by Federal Express in a special tanker plane from Bedford, Massachusetts, and would be kept in a large plastic tank outside the PCN building. After the operation, she would be returned to Bedford.

"Why don't we do the show from Bedford?" asked Shazzaba.

"Because we're here," Big Al explained. "People expect the show to come from the Midwest. You take Chuck east and people will think we're putting on airs."

Melody wondered if they shouldn't try to extricate the men from the whale right away and then have them as guests when they recovered.

"No," he said. "We're going to wait and cut the whale open on live television. Otherwise we get scooped. We'd wake up Monday morning and there they'd be on *Today*."

Fielding was troubled. "We could put exclusive-interview contracts into spitproof cylinders, make the whale swallow them, get the men to sign them, and recover them from the other end, and then open her up tonight and out they come."

Big Al screamed *"No!"* He pounded his fist and stamped his feet: *No no no no no no no no no!* He locked his office door and he tore all the pictures and awards from the walls and stomped them to bits! He cursed and he screeched! He hurled heavy objects out the window and onto the parking lot!

"We're not going back to the old days, never, never, never, never, never! We worked hard to get us a king hell man-eating shin-kicking daytime TV show and we are not going to wimp out—hear me?"

Melody pointed out that there could be negative publicity if the whalectomy revealed the limp lifeless bodies of sailors recently expired, sailors who could have been rescued had the TV folks called 911—"You ever hear of third-degree manslaughter?" she said.

"You ever hear of losing your job?" he replied.

"What if there *are* no guys inside that whale?" cried Fielding.

Al looked around the room. "I personally guarantee you that there will be at least one man inside, and two if we can manage it. Don't ask me how I know. I know. I'm paid to know. That's how I know. Money makes me smart. Two guys in that whale and neither one of them is going to speak English. We'll need translators. Can you translate from the ancient Aramaic, Fielding?— good, I'm glad."

Fielding, who hadn't known of his Aramaic fluency until that moment, looked at Bob, and Bob looked at Melody, and Melody looked at Shazzaba, and Eliot looked at his shoes. None of them said a word, only sighed. There would be no sleep for any of them the next week—they could see that. Four big shows to produce (and where were they ever going to find transvestites willing to get in a pit and wrestle with gators?), and then the whale story—good gosh, the headaches— they could feel a tightening in their temples—and then what would they do the week *after* next?

THE MID-LIFE CRISIS
OF DIONYSUS

Dionysus, the god of wine and whoopee, the son of Zeus and Semele, Dionysus the eternal party animal, to his great surprise one sun-drenched afternoon suddenly turned fifty years of age as he reclined on a languid young woman in his temple on Mount Cithaeron in Boeotia. He was dipping his finger into a very fine 1925 B.C. Pinot Noir and swabbing it onto her lips, and he was fussing about the orgy scheduled for that evening, saying that he had laid in six gallons of extra-virgin cold-pressed olive oil—"You think that's too much or not enough?" he asked—"All depends," she said, licking the wine off her lower lip with her rough pink tongue. He said he hoped that nobody would use Roquefort salad dressing at the orgy, it was hard to clean the cheese out of his ears, and then he heard the unmistakable clip-clomp-clomp of the sensible shoes of the Muse of maturity, Gladys, clambering up the steps, clipboard in hand, knapsack on her back, wearing a frumpy brown dress with sweat stains under the arms. She blew a hard tweet on her whistle and cried, "Climb off that girl, Gramps, and put down the beverage. And brace yourself for a major news item," and then she broke it to him hard. He was fifty. Fifty years old.

Dionysus sat up—*"What?"* he said, letting go of the supple young woman. *"Fifty.* Ha! I'm immortal! Ageless! You can look it up!"

"Everybody gets just so much immortality and then it's time to grow up," said Gladys in her deep horsy voice. "You were young for thousands of years, like everybody else, and now you're fifty. Better face the music and learn to dance to it."

But acceptance was not part of Dionysus' godly nature. He was the god of revels, the god who resisted dull care and deadlines and the long grim slide of mortality, the one who always shouted, "Play, gypsy fiddlers, play! Dance on, you fools! Throw the theologians in the cellar and bring us more oysters and more hot sauce! More young women! And make them even younger!" He wasn't ready to sit in a sunny corner with a knitted comforter on his lap and chuckle to himself over geezer news in the newspaper.

He looked at her, dumpy Gladys! and laughed his big

careless laugh, *haw, haw, haw,* and tossed his raven tresses, which suddenly felt—what? *thin? his* hair? *Dionysus'?* He touched it delicately. The hair was there, sort of, but it felt stringy, not flowing as before, not flowing fluidly and bouncing. It hung like dry dead moss.

The young woman squirmed away and put on a robe. She kissed him nicely on the cheek, said "Thanks, lover," and wandered off to find a toothbrush.

Dionysus strode to the edge of the reflecting pool and looked down. His hands looked old, mottled, with big ropy veins, the skin wrinkly and raspy as a lizard's. Big tufts of hair poked from his ears, and his jawline felt poorly defined, his chin seemed not so much to thrust forward as to be a lump atop his neck, and his chest had descended about five inches. "Who did this to me?" he asked. "Whose handiwork is this?"

Gladys shrugged. "You don't look that bad, mister. Your back looks youthful. And your prostate's okay. So far. Slightly enlarged but good for another two or three years anyway. Your brain function seems fairly sound, considering. Health's good, considering. You're no gem but you're in good shape. You should live well into your senility and beyond."

Dionysus called up the nymphs and satyrs, the madwomen and bull-roarers and wild swine, and called off the orgy, told them he wasn't in an orgy mood, that he felt stiff and achy and blue and wanted to be alone. To the last orgiast, they told him that a good orgy was exactly what he needed to restore his spirits—enjoy a skin of good wine, strip naked, feel the oil trickle down his thighs, feel the heat of golden down-covered young women writhing upon and around and under him moaning and crying out his name, their proud young breasts, their taut brown bellies, their limber shanks, their—no thanks, he said, he'd just stay home and work the crossword with his wife, Ariadne.

He returned the olive oil to the store, and the manager, a solemn fellow with a nose like a chisel, said, "It didn't feel right? Too slick? You want something with more texture, like a basil vinaigrette or honey mustard? Myself, I find that mustard irritates the privates, but maybe you're into that, I don't know. You interested in molasses? Or we have this new strawberry body jam." The leer in the man's voice seemed dreary and disgusting.

He drove slowly home, through the leafy suburbs of Boeotia. A flock of dark birds poured out of a poplar tree, skimmed the ground, and wheeled, their undersides flashing brilliant silver, like a burst of rockets.

Ariadne had fixed poached grouper for supper, not his favorite, and the potatoes were burnt and covered with a cream sauce. And there was a papyrus salad, rather dry to the palate. Dionysus put down his fork and reached for the wine. Ariadne leaned across the fish and took his hand, her eyes large with compassion. "Dio, we need to talk about your drinking," she said.

Dionysus rolled his eyes. "Look," he said, "I'm the god of wine, okay? I'm not the god of iced tea. I am the god of revelry, a crucial element of the fertility process. The dancing and drinking and whooping and wahooing is what makes the wheat grow, babes. That's what gives us the corn crop. Why am I telling you this? You know this."

Nonetheless, she said, she was concerned about his health. She had read an article that said most people drink to build up self-confidence and compensate for low self-esteem. She thought he needed to see someone.

"I have no lack of self-esteem!" he cried. "I'm a god!"

"Are you?"

"Of course I am! What do you mean, *are you?* What do you mean by that? Of course I'm a god." Dionysus leaned forward. "Aren't I?"

"You're fifty," she said. "To me, fifty spells *m-o-r-t-a-l.*"

He held out his hands. "I'm the same beautiful guy with the same flowing locks as when you married me. Look." And he touched his hair, and it was still limp. Was he using the wrong conditioner?

"Drinking too much wine is hard on your hair, honey. And it causes loss of memory. And it makes you flatulent," she said.

He looked at her, confused. *Memory loss!* What memory loss was she referring to? When?

"You're still my dreamboat," she said. "But grow up. And get help."

The next morning, three satyrs knocked on his door and announced that they had gone ahead with the orgy on their own, it had been *va-va-va-voom zing-zing-zing* all night and now the orgy had recessed for vomiting and baths and would resume at ten-thirty with a wild-boar brunch. They cried, "Sixteen young virgins are arriving from Macedonia, the tenderest and prettiest ones! Fresh as dewdrops on spring roses! Shy and freckled and peach-soft skin! Big brown eyes and long black hair! Or blonde! Take your pick!" Despite the long night of partying, they hopped around on their hairy legs, their goat feet tapping, their eyes burning diamond-bright, their long ears twitching. Satyrs know no sexual restraint except that imposed by their natural cowardice—they are terrified of confrontation, darkness, nonelective surgery, loud noises, and long-term commitments; but once liquored up, they can go for days, humping like bunnies. Dionysus winced at the odor of their musk. "Look. Guys—short-term, I'd love to join you, but I got to think long-term now. I've got a mortality problem I've got to deal with."

That morning, he flew to Mount Olympus to visit Zeus, and instead of forty minutes, the trip took four hours; Air Parnassus bumped him off the first flight—"I'm a god!" he cried, but the woman pointed out that his deity card had expired the day before and put him on standby, and finally he got the last available seat on the four-fifteen, a middle seat in the last row, next to a fat man who perspired heavily and who asked him what line of work he was in. "Wine," said Dionysus. "Oh," said the fat man, "that's a coincidence. I'm in the beer business." He seemed to think that beer and wine were closely allied, like cheese and crackers, or philosophy and philately. Dionysus took a cab to the temple, where Zeus kept him waiting another hour. When

Dionysus finally was ushered into the sacred office, Zeus—his own dad!—shook his hand stiffly, smiled officially, and said, "I've decided to make a change. Latromis is going to become the god of wine, and you're going to be the chairman of wine. He'll do the revels and orgies and lie around with the nubile young women and you can form a wine board, organize wine programs, formulate wine goals, that sort of thing. Maximize wine. Whatever. And by the way, congratulations on turning fifty. I meant to send a card, but anyway, here's your birthday presents." He pointed toward a marble pedestal.

There was a sack of fruit such as you'd buy in a supermarket, and a pound of blue cheese, and a T-shirt with a picture of a cow saying "Fly Me to the Moon," and a photograph of Zeus in a silver frame, signed, "Yours sincerely, Zeus," as if Dionysus were only a fan.

"Dad," he said. "Why am I fifty? Why did my divinity expire? You never told me this would happen."

Zeus feigned surprise. "You? What are you talking about? You still look pretty darned divine to me!" he said, chuckling in a dry, insincere way as he steered Dionysus to the door. "But if you think there's a problem, I'll look into it. First thing next week. I'll get back to you," he said. "Bye!"

It was a bad time for a guy who had been a god, now suddenly mortified, degraded, pitied, and abandoned, and Dionysus thought he would drop in at the orgy and see how it was going. It was going wonderfully! An all-girl band played in the nude, including a fabulous ram's-hornist and a blues harpist who plucked handfuls of strings and cried "Oh yes! yes!," and a naked lady poet leaped around and shouted at Dionysus—*O your body my body somebody and the liquid light leaping into the howling arroyos of the boyish soul, you yoyo!*—and Janis Idol the pop star and blonde strumpet was lurking in the corner of the room, throwing smoldering looks over her shoulder, and nubility was in full flower and pliancy and suppleness and some women are meant to be bare-breasted, that's all, and a young virgin named Grace Huggins turned out to be not only supple and pliant and delicious but also a tremendous Ping-Pong player, and after long slow dizzying triumphant love she beat him two out of three games, her sarcastic young breasts bouncing, faking him out, as her topspin serve rocketed off the table and her backhand spinners hooked the corners and her slop shots handcuffed him with their little dips and flutters, and then more love, and some wine, and love again, and she looked up at him dreamily and said, "Oh wow," and her simple sincere *Oh wow* was what cured his blues. To make love and hear a woman say "Oh wow"—it was all a fifty-year-old needed, to know that he was still impressive. "I love when you look over your left shoulder like that," she whispered. Dionysus said, "Thanks, babe," and reached for a glass and drank it down, and the next he knew, she was gone, the afternoon sun blazed down, he was crawling buck-naked through a cornfield with the glass in his hand, his head felt like a lag bolt was screwed in the side of it, and overhead, immense black buzzards slowly circled, shrieking. Something dangled from his mouth that felt like the tail of a small rodent. Just the same, he felt no regret. Her *Oh wow* was worth it. He slumped down in the dirt and the sharp stones, his poor old body hurting, his back raked with scratches, his lips dry and crusty, the taste of sorrow in his mouth—*and yet,* he thought . . . *and yet.* Oh wow.

When he dragged himself home, Ariadne took one look and gave him an ultimatum: "Get help or get out."

He tried to explain. "Life is a celebration," he whispered, his cracked lips hurting. "In order to grow, we need to enjoy who we are. In order to get to tomorrow, we have to fully enjoy today."

"Tell it to a therapist," she said.

Theros, the Muse of caring, ran a treatment program on Mount Aesculapius especially for gods, demigods, and ex-gods, and when Dionysus walked in and sat down on her couch, she said, "I'm not surprised one bit to see you. Do you want to know why?"

He did not. He was tired of the knowingness of women.

Theros had a tight mouth and big legs. She crossed them, licked her lips, and opened her notebook. She said, "Tell me about your parents."

"You *know* about my parents," he said. "Dad was God, of course. Zeus. Fell in love with Mom and then his wife Hera got jealous and came to Mom in disguise and said, Hey, congratulations, but if you want a *really* good time, tell him to bring his thunderbolts, it's a real charge! So Mom did, and it was too much—she burst into flames. But Dad snatched me up from her burning body—out of the ashes—and sewed me up in his thigh and I spent my prenatal period there, next to his gonads.

"My nurse was Mom's sister Ino, who Hera drove mad so Ino ran around in a frenzy, spit dripping from her lips, a terrible babysitter, and she jumped off a cliff into the sea. Then Hera had me torn into shreds and boiled in a cauldron. I was rescued by my grandma, but death and destruction made a big impression on me. Maybe that's why I invented wine, as an escape from the violent disapproval of my father's wife. I don't know. I often have dreams in which I have been locked in a chest with my mother and put out to sea and we drift for months, then she dies. I lie in the dark, starving, mad, next to her dead body, rolling on the ocean waves, and then I am found by kindly fisher folk and brought to a green island paradise where I run naked in the woods, and one day, wild swine with bloodstained tusks and tiny red eyes come charging at me through the tall booji grass and I run and run and run, panic-stricken, and fall off the edge of the mile-high cliff and wake up soaked with sweat, trembling, the sheet wound around my neck."

"What kind of chest?"

"You know. A sort of trunk," he said.

She squinted and pursed her lips. "With drawers?"

"I don't know. Maybe."

"Like a cabinet or cupboard?"

"No, I don't think so. I don't know."

"Why don't you know?"

This was the maddening thing about Theros, he discovered: you told her a great story and she got wrapped up in one dumb little detail, like when you described your first orgy, even though the whole point of the story was mindless ecstatic sex, she leaned forward, pencil in hand, and said, "Let's go back to those little smoked-herring sandwiches. *Why herring? And why curried herring?*" until you groaned with frustration, remembering that pile of glistening naked young bodies, that ocean of passion, and she said, "And those celery sticks with cream-cheese spread in them. Were there pimentos in those, too?" As a therapist, she was an awful bore.

"As I understand wild revelry, it is a celebration of life," Dionysus told Theros, patiently. "Before we can create new life, we need to enjoy the life we have and to defeat sullenness and lethargy and depression, the withering of the spirit. So we take our treasure and spend it lavishly, inspiring ourselves with happiness, we get drunk, we sing, we fling food at each other, and the next week the fields grow rich, fertilized by wild song, and the grain outlasts the heat and drought of the Dog Star, and the land pours out a bounty of wheat and corn. And from this, we make more beer and whiskey."

"You're avoiding mentioning the celery sticks," she said. "Why?"

Dionysus wearied of therapy. His spirit sank every day as the appointment approached. He hated sitting in that dim dry room and trying to be a patient, trying to feel needy, when, in fact, his life seemed to him powerful, thrusting forward, drawn by a powerful wind. So one day he quit. "I don't have you down for next week," she said. "Good," he replied. He kissed her goodbye on the lips, a lingering kiss to give her something to think about.

Instead of therapy, he tried a new brand of bran flakes, which included flecks of birch boughs. He did push-ups and he climbed chairs. His hair improved slightly, when he switched to a shampoo with extra oil to compensate for not attending orgies.

And he cut down on wine, limiting himself to only the best varieties and only on special occasions. No more glugging, just sipping. And no more young Macedonian women.

It was a dreary business, middle age. He missed those nymphs, doggone it, and even the satyrs with their hairy legs and odor of rut. Say what you will, they are the right sort of disreputable people, and when you drape your arm around them and all sing "Waltz Me Around Again, Willie," those nymphs and satyrs sing the dirtiest verses *loud,* no sheepish looks as if Mom might be watching, they let the lust and gluttony and hairy grunting beast of bad taste hang out all the way, and now, as world chairman of wine, he found himself more and more among people with the emotional range of Lucite, earnest men indistinguishable from other earnest men, serious women who shrank from any sort of playfulness, people who said *How pleasant to see you* when there was not a crumb of pleasure within a hundred feet. He had lived thousands and thousands of years, but it wasn't until he reached the age of fifty that he realized how desolate life could be.

"How are you?" Ariadne asked him.

"I am fine," he said.

"We're having the Whipples over tonight," she said. "And the Snaffles. And Jim and Judy Woofle." Dreadful people, all of them, people who could bore the shoes right off you. Their idea of a big time was to sit around and complain about schools and traffic congestion. "Good," he said, "I'm looking forward to it. That'll be real fun." In reduced circumstances, one must show generosity and elegance of spirit, he knew. He tried to smile. He stared out the window. Long stone houses lay half-hidden back among the olive and fruit trees across the sweep of clipped sward, and he could see sunlight flickering on distant pools in which he had swum at midnight, naked, the pool crowded with happy women splashing and laughing—*there had never been a bad party for him*—always there had been boring men, yes, with voices like handsaws, but the young women turned instinctively toward him when he rose dripping from the pool and the party rose to a higher pitch and the tide of music and laughter rose and carried the celebrants off the stony shoals of life and career and family, even sometimes the boring men, and for all the parties he had enjoyed, he wanted *more,* many many more.

He trudged into his study and plopped down at the desk. Piles of work lay there, a sheaf of papers relating to the upcoming conference on Meeting the Wine Needs of the Nineties and a sixteen-page speech on

"Promoting the Total Wine Experience" that he himself must stand at a dais and deliver the following day, a real stink bomb. There was a stack of bills, from the dentist, the phone company, the chiropractor, and a curt reminder that he owed four hundred drachmas for a shipment of olive oil.

Dionysus picked up his pen. "Dear Hatchet Face," he wrote in a bold hand. "You have some nerve demanding payment for a jar of rancid oil that made me smell like an aging buffalo and that had so much grit in it as to make concupiscence an uphill climb."

He balled the page up and flung it toward the wastebasket and cried out as the ball fell short. After thousands and thousands of years without pain of any sort, now, at the age of fifty, he had a backache.

BUDDY THE LEPER

My mother believed that if you go out of your way to be friendly to people, they will take a liking to you, but this philosophy did not work for me, because I was a leper. I contracted the dread disease at the age of twelve, living with my parents, Pastor and Mrs. Sorenson, in the tiny village of Masabam in the African Congo, a collection of mud-and-plywood huts with corrugated tin roofs clustered around our white three-bedroom rambler with a big green lawn and patio and basketball hoop on the garage. My mother and dad were Methodist missionaries, and Dad also played saxophone in a dance band called The Whiteman Orchestra that performed for large safari groups and at the Ramada Masada Inn. During his twelve years in Africa, Dad had moved up the missionary ladder and become a regional coordinator of missions, and we could have lived in the city where his office was, but Dad wanted me to have the benefit of a small-town upbringing, the sort he had had in South Dakota. Instead, I caught leprosy.

I caught it from using a toilet in a bus depot. Mom and I were on our way to the witch dentist, whose office was a hundred miles from Masabam. Mom was terrified of drills and needles, and she found that the witch dentist, who sprinkled a circle of sand around you and put pebbles in your mouth and then danced around shaking rattles and crying "O-hi-yeeeeee, O-hi-yeeeee," actually did a better job of preventative dentistry than dentists in the States. We traveled to see him for our six-month checkups, riding on a bus full of Africans with crates of chickens and ducks, black mamas packed in with their babies, bouncing around the mud roads, and when we made a rest stop, all of the others simply made a beeline for the bushes.

I needed to go, bad, and was about to squat by a tree when Mom cried, "No! Buddy! We have to set an example! Use the toilet in the depot!" The depot was a long, low, poorly ventilated shack that stank of disease and decay, but Mom insisted, so I went, and I picked up the leprosy. From a sense of Methodist obligation, from the toilet seat. They say you can't get it from a toilet seat, but I'd like to see them say it to me. I got it. Mom was spared because she has a bladder of steel.

It was strange, of course, to live in such a nice clean house as ours and be a leper. Mom and Dad worked hard to make our home as nice as any in the States—we had a beautiful ceramic-tile shower and a powerful toilet, a lovely breakfast nook, a carpeted living room and dining room with a chandelier, a new piano, Mom's collection of salt shakers, a coffee table with *Time* and *Life* and *The Family of Man* on it—but there I was, a leper in the ointment. In fact, Dad couldn't believe it was leprosy, he thought it must be a nutrition problem, and then after vitamins failed to clear it up, he thought it was eczema and sent for creams and gels, and then he decided it was psychosomatic. "We'll get you treatment, Buddy," he promised, and he tried, but psychiatry was primitive in the Congo at that time. The common treatment for an adolescent boy was to send him into the bush alone to hunt a lion.

"No, he's not ready," Dad told the headshrinker. "He's only twelve."

"He's a big tall boy and he'll never *be* ready unless you're willing to let go of the strings and let him grow up," the shrinker replied. He was squatting in front of our coffee table, a tiny jet-black man with paint daubed on his chest and red chalk dust in his hair.

"He's terrified of the jungle," said Dad. "And he's never harmed a living creature in his life. He'll die if we send him out there."

"He'll die if you keep sheltering him as if he were a child. A boy has to become a man. That's the problem with you Americans. You shrink from necessary pains. You want life to be like television." The shrinker looked down at the plate of cheese and crackers that Mom had set out. He took a slice of mild cheddar on a Hi-Ho. "We'll give him a spear and a knife, a sack of dried fruit, and we'll set him down in the lion blind, next to the watering hole. He will wait there for the lion, and if the lion comes, the boy will try to kill him. Maybe he will, or maybe the lion will run away, or maybe the lion won't come at all and the boy will only sit for a week and wait. But in that week he will become a man. This is the truth. I have spoken. As for the leprosy, there are drugs that keep it under control very nicely." And he got up, bowed, and left.

So my dad put me on antileprosy drugs, which handled it okay. Nevertheless, as a leper, I was shunned in the village and had to remain at home. I sat in my bedroom with the dark-green-plaid wallpaper and maple desk and bullfighter poster and read magazines and played solo Parcheesi and listened to the phonograph. Mom was a big Doris Day fan and I listened to "Que Será Será (Whatever Will Be, Will Be)" a thousand times, and I read *National Geographic* articles about pygmies and elephants, though the pygmies were only five hundred feet away.

"I think humor is so very important, Buddy," Mom told me. "It's so crucial to be lighthearted. Don't let this get you down. I'd like to hear you laugh more." She told me jokes but Mom couldn't tell a joke well and kept telling the same one. It was about a dog who went in a bar and ordered a vodka sour.

One day, I found a man sitting on our patio whose body was covered with open putrid sores. I called for Mom to come. His name was Joe, he told us, he was in agony, but he was used to it. He begged for bread. Mom went in and made him a sandwich.

"Have you seen a dermatologist?" I asked, trying to make small talk.

Joe groaned. "Everything I had is gone. Destroyed. My home, my wife, my children, everything. I was happy and then suddenly everything went up in smoke." He looked me deep in the eyes. "Touch my sores and you will be healed," he said softly.

"I don't know what you're talking about," I said.

Mom brought out a tuna-salad sandwich, a glass of milk, and a Rice Krispie marshmallow bar. As he ate, groaning, she mentioned that she had heard that ashes were good for those putrid open sores. Not charcoal ash, but wood ash, and you should sprinkle them on the sores and not rub, and not use too much ash, because open sores need to breathe.

"Thanks for the tip," he said. He said to me again, "Touch my sores and you will be healed."

I said that I would rather not.

A few months later, Dad was transferred by the Methodist church back to Sioux Falls, South Dakota, to be a regional director of family counseling and professor of New Testament ethics. He would also be joining the

Carl Welk Orchestra, playing his sax. "Music is so primitive in Africa," he said. "It'll be nice to get back to playing more waltzes and sambas." We left our African home and flew to America.

My leprosy had put my mom under a lot of pressure. She blamed herself for it, which was okay, because it was her fault. She lost her appetite and she ground her teeth in her sleep, with terrible force. The witch dentist had recommended sacrificing a chicken or goat, but Dad wouldn't allow it. So Mom ground her teeth down to tiny nubbins, and by the time we settled in Sioux Falls, her speech was so awfully slurred, people naturally assumed she was sloshed, even after she got her teeth capped. Mom began drinking mixed drinks at about that time.

Meanwhile, word got around that I was a leper. It was Dad's fault. He took me to Bible camp in July and suggested that I stand up at the fellowship campfire and share the story of my leprosy and how God had given our family the strength to deal with it.

Like a fool, I stood in the fellowship circle, next to the campfire, and said, "My name is Buddy and I am a leper," and right then, I noticed people edge away in revulsion. "I look on leprosy as an opportunity for grace," I said, but of course leprosy is a disease, not an opportunity, and everyone knew it. Nobody wanted to be anywhere near me after that. Sometimes, when their parents were watching, they pretended to, but not for long.

Within days, everyone in South Dakota was aware of my leprosy situation, and that fall, in school, I got the nickname "Leppie." Boys followed me in the halls, limping and jerking spasmodically—apparently making fun of my condition, though I didn't jerk any more than other fourteen-year-olds. Nobody ever sat next to me of their own free will. Nobody said hi in the hallway or stopped by my locker to shoot the breeze. Nobody made eye contact—I became invisible—except for boys who saw me, started twitching and convulsing, rolled their eyes, gasped, and pretended to die. Everybody else considered this rather hilarious.

"Be friendly and try to smile. Return their taunts and jeers with good-natured replies. Learn to poke fun at yourself. Be outgoing," advised Mom. But the smile a person tries to make when people are so hostile is not an attractive one.

A pretty girl named Phoebe liked to line up all her classmates on the playground and go down the line saying, "You're my first best friend, you're my second best friend," and so on. I was always her two-hundredth best friend, dead last, though I had gone out of my way to be friendly with her. One day, I presented her with a valuable African coin from my collection, and she glanced at it and shuddered. "I don't want that. You touched it," she said. "If I accepted, I'd be known forever after as a girl who took money off a leper. No man would ever touch me. I'd be obliged to leave Sioux Falls and go to Minneapolis and lead the lonely life of a cashier in a cafeteria and live in a room over a drugstore and spend my evenings reading movie magazines and I'd become a withered spinster in a print dress smelling of lilac talcum, with my big watery eyes behind my pop-bottle glasses, taking vacation tours of the Black Hills on a bus. Do you want to see my life blighted because I once took pity on you and became your friend? No? Then why did you ask me?"

Her hostility was not untypical. Once I was chased through the park by three boys who jumped out from behind the jungle gym waving softball bats. I tore off down the hill and through the trees, where I used the old low-lying-limb trick that Roy Rogers used so often—swung myself up and into the leaves and waited for them and then jumped down on top of them. My face brushed against the face of one of them and he screamed and rolled around like a bee had bit him, and the others ran off.

I could see that redemption was impossible in Sioux Falls, that I would have to grow up and move away before my life could begin. Often, a person so persecuted will turn out to be a genius like Hans Christian Andersen or Tennessee Williams, but aptitude tests showed that, among the bright stars in life's galaxy, I was a small dim moon. A moon without a planet to orbit around, a moon adrift in the cosmos, a leper moon.

There were a reporter and a photographer from the Associated Press who were nice to me, though. They visited me often. I was one of only two lepers in America who would give interviews, and the other one was a grumpy geezer in Coral Gables who only wanted to talk about the national deficit and rant and gibber about

Congress. I was willing to talk about my disease. "You don't have to," Mom told me. But I wanted to, in order to create better public understanding of leprosy, I said.

But that wasn't the real reason. There were only a few of us in the country; how much public understanding do a few people need?

I did it hoping to make my classmates guilty and also because Skip and Doug were friendly guys and I was starved for company. They came, shot a picture of me smiling and showing my coin collection, did the interview—"How do kids treat you at school?" asked Skip, and I said, "They treat me just great. They have taken me into their hearts and given me love and support beyond anything a leper could dream of. They are always there, cheering me up, inspiring me, making me feel wanted. This is the greatest place in America. I love South Dakota"—and then we sat in the backyard and talked, off the record.

"Kids treat you like shit, I'll bet," said Skip.

I said, "You're not kidding."

"You know what might be a good idea for you?" he said. "Take a shotgun to school and blow away a couple of them. You're fourteen. You'd be sent to a reform school for a few years, get a good vo-tech education, it might be a good experience for you."

I told them that, as the son of missionary parents, I would find it hard to take a shotgun to school and kill classmates. They said they could understand that.

"Maybe a .22 then," said Skip. "Twenty-two is a good

number. It's the number of letters in the Hebrew alphabet. In the I Ching, the twenty-second book is the Book of Grace. Did you know that?"

I did not.

"And," said Doug, "it might be good for you to express the anger inside you, rather than repress it and screw up your life."

Skip said he thought that any jury would find me innocent and I'd be sent somewhere for treatment.

"Wouldn't it be hard for a kid my age to get his hands on a gun?"

No, Doug said. Not necessarily. In fact, he thought it would be easier for me to find a gun than to find a girl.

It was nice to have homicide as a possibility. When classmates looked at me with loathing, as if to say, "What are *you* doing here, you piece of garbage you, you're blighting our teenage experience with your extremely depressing presence," I looked at them real cool and thought, "You should be more careful with your contempt. I could bring a gun tomorrow and put a hole in you the size of a pieplate. You would die with evil thoughts in your heart and go directly to hell. Isn't that a big price to pay for treating a classmate so bad? Big clumps of your hair stuck to the wall, your blood spattered on the floor, and the rest of you under a sheet, and you in hell and God scowling down at you and saying, *Huh-uh. No way.* Wouldn't it have been easier to invite me to your birthday party?"

Mom kept telling me, "Don't complain. The reason kids aren't nice to you is because you don't smile,

Buddy. You don't go out of your way. Forget about leprosy and just be *you,* and people will be friendly. You
wait and see." Mom was drunk as a skunk most of the
time. She figured that as long as her dental problem
made her sound drunk anyway, she might as well have
the pleasure, so she drank a raft of vodka gimlets in the
morning and screwdrivers in the afternoon. I knew that
Mom would never be of any help to me again the rest
of my life. And Dad was too busy teaching ethics and
supervising family-counseling programs and playing
dances. I went to the Sioux Room at the Dakota Hotel
once to see him and perhaps have a word, but the band
breaks were only ten minutes long and a number of his
ethics students were there and he yukked it up with
them while I sat alone in the corner. My portly dad
playing "Bésame Mucho" and candles flickering and
stale potato chips on the table with plastic cups of
whipped cheese and glasses of warm grape pop. A bad
scene.

At the doctor's office once, I saw a magazine ad: "AT-
TRACT WOMEN TO YOU EVEN IF THEY DON'T WANT TO BE—
EASY! IN LESS THAN 60 SECS.!" A picture of gazellelike
women in thin cotton garments, their thick pouty lips
parted slightly, their garments soaked with perspiration
and pasted tight to their bodies. "Learn the ancient secrets of hypnotic conversation and send subliminal erotic
messages that hot babes are powerless to resist. Talk
about sports, weather, hobbies, etc., and in *one minute*
you can focus her unconscious sexual desires on *you!* Hot
babes have NO IDEA what's happening, only that they

lust for your body and feel revulsion for ALL OTHER MEN! After an hour, they're TAKING OFF THEIR CLOTHES and yelling, Do it! Do it! Or your money cheerfully refunded."

I was tempted to send $24.95 for the booklet and cassette and learn those hypnotic conversational techniques. The worst part of being a leper is to be shunned, to see people turn away and avoid touching you. A person needs to be touched. South Dakota is not a touchy place even under the best of circumstances, and if you are a leper, you can go for months without a caress or a pat on the back. I was a missionary child, and sending subliminal erotic messages went against my upbringing, but I sent for the materials. I gave the name William Rehnquist in case the FBI tried to trace the recipient.

"You're lucky," said Mom, sauced as usual. "Look at lepers in India, they have to stand and beg in the streets, and all their fingers fall off. You have parents who love you, you live in a nice home and sleep between clean sheets and eat good food, and you're on a very good-flavored medication. Quit your bellyaching." But a person's misery is never diminished by the greater misery of others, you know. And the food *wasn't* that good. Breakfast was cold cereal and bad sweet rolls, with Mom sitting there drinking vodka, or "potato juice," as she called it, and by nightfall, she was leaning badly as she cooked our dinner, sometimes hanging on to the cupboard door to keep vertical. She fixed veal chops, which I couldn't bear to eat because the poor calves are chained in dark fetid stalls knee-deep in excrement and also because she burned the meat to a crisp. The vegetables were burnt and the mashed spuds were full of lumps the size of golf balls and everything was covered with melted cheese. Garbage au gratin.

Dad couldn't see what was happening. "Mary, what's wrong with you? These string beans are inedible," he complained. "And they have dirt and twigs in them."

I told him that Mom was bombed out of her gourd. I said, "Our family is falling to pieces. You're a minister, Dad. Do something."

"Don't speak so of your mother," he said. "She's only tired because she works hard taking care of us. I'll hire a girl to help."

She arrived a week later. Lulu Rivera. She arrived on the day after my hypnotic conversation tape and instruction booklet came in the mail. "Who's William Rehnquist?" asked Mom. I read the booklet and listened to the cassette that evening; it was written and narrated by a guy named Sandy, who suggested that hot babes could be yours for the asking if you learned to talk *slow.* "Guys get excited by a babe's you-know-what and the hot hungry look in her eye and pretty soon they're yapping like sled dogs," said Sandy. "But babes go for guys who go slow, if you know what I mean. Leave long pauses—use few words—be deliberate—focus—maintain eye contact but don't push, don't lean—draw her to you with silence."

Lulu Rivera had long black hair and wore a red satiny dress, and smelled of flowers and earth and rainfall. South Dakota women smelled of chalk dust and laundry starch, but she smelled of precipitation. I stood close to her, downwind, and exhaled off to my left, afraid I might have bad breath from the au gratin. She carried all her possessions in two paper sacks, except for her guitar. She moved into the guest bedroom, next to mine. I liked her a lot. I kept thinking, *Here's someone who doesn't know that I have leprosy.* I rubbed my forehead to make it hot so I could stay home sick from school, because she would come and sit on the side of my bed, put her hand on my forehead, sometimes rub goose grease on my chest. I did not say much to her and what I did say I said slowly.

Late at night, through the bedroom wall, I could hear her softly strumming her guitar and singing "Come to my arms, my darling, sleep in my arms, my love," a song about love so powerful one cannot resist:

> *The sight of your face,*
> *The touch of your hand,*
> *The sound of your voice*
> *I am helpless to withstand*
> *The feeling that comes over me*
> *Like the mighty sea*
> *Beats against the land.*

It was hard not to take this as an invitation.

I drilled a tiny hole through the wall, and saw her naked left shoulder once. Then she moved a dresser in front of it.

She brought me tomato soup in bed when I stayed

home from school. She wore flipflops and when I heard her walk down the upstairs hall, *flipflip-flipflipflipflip*, all the juices in me rose. Mom passed out around noon every day and slept until dinner. Lulu sat on the side of my bed, talking to me in a normal way about the future and about being happy, new topics for a leper boy. I almost told her, *Hey, you know what's so great about you? You don't know I'm a leper! Can you imagine what that's like? No, probably you can't. Let me tell you. It's the greatest feeling in the world, that's what.* But I remembered Sandy's advice. I said, "Not everyone is meant to be happy, Lulu." But I was thrilled by her. To be normal in the eyes of one person! After years of wearing the badge of LEPER around my neck. And I loved looking down the front of her dress. She had beautiful little brown bazookies.

She told me, "I'm here to help for a while, but this is only a pit stop for me. I'm on my way to California, where I understand a person can go around buck-naked if she wants to. People are freer there. A woman she can do what she wants to, when she wants to, with whoever she wants to do it with. I like you really a lot. Did you know that? Eh? I do. I wish I could make you so very very happy. So tell me. What makes you happy, Buddy?"

Evidently, conversational hypnosis was working. "I don't know, except—" and I paused for a long moment—"a man can't be happy alone. But—I don't have broad parameters when it comes to happiness. Happiness always seemed accidental to me. It comes and it goes."

"I'm an ethnic person, and to us ethnics, happiness is no accident," she said. "Happiness is written into the deal. It's part of the plan."

I was helping her make my parents' bed as we talked, and I was having a hard time getting a good tight corner on my side. Evidently, my silence excited her. "I want to experience life with you," she said softly.

She came over to my side of the bed to help me, and suddenly her hand was roaming the front of my shirt. I said, "I don't think happiness is—it's not like going to the store for a—a quart of blueberries. If it were, then it—it wouldn't be so special." I was really getting the hang of the long pause.

She unbuttoned my shirt. Nobody had ever done this to me before. "It's *exactly* like getting a quart of blueberries," she said. "You just happen to come from a place that has no blueberries."

She pressed her body against mine. "My dress has a ripcord, right under my left breast," she said. "It's an ejector dress, developed by U.S. Navy pilots. Pull this little string and tiny explosive charges will fling my clothes off like you'd shuck an ear of corn."

I laughed. "You'd never guess to look at it that—it was an explosive dress. It sure doesn't—look like it's loaded."

"Pull my string," she whispered, her lips inside my ear.

"Does it make a—big bang?" I asked. "I'm kinda—leery of explosives. I'd hate to—pull that string and—have your dress blow up in my face."

"Don't worry," she said.

I held the string lightly between my thumb and index finger. "Maybe we ought to—stop right now before somebody gets hurt," I said, as a missionary child should say.

And then she threw me onto the bed and there was a *poom-poom-poom,* and the red dress fell apart into four separate streamers and her naked body fell on top of mine, and she had her way with me. I forgot all about my other chores. I did what she wanted me to do. I felt as if I were in a car racing through great stands of primeval trees, and through tunnels and thick forests of ferns and past steaming lakes where flocks of herons rose from the water and then to a natural geyser that blew millions of gallons of water a half-mile into the sky, and I was in the back seat of the car. She was at the wheel.

Afterward, I said, "Not bad. Am I—supposed to—get used to that?"

"You're so nice, Buddy," she said. "I think I could learn to like you. You're young but you have a sweet sadness about you that I find so attractive."

We did it again and again, day after day, and every day, I worried that she'd talk to the milkman or the mailman or the meter-reader from the gas company and the truth would come out, the terrible word "leper" would be spoken, and then I would be cast out in the cold again.

"You're so unhappy. You cry in your sleep at night. You talk in mournful tones. I hear you through the wall," Lulu told me.

"What do I say?"

"You talk about schlepping peppers with a girl named Debra, I think, or perhaps you are escaping from leopards across the sea. I don't know."

I told her that I was unhappy because I was afraid of losing her.

"That makes no sense," she said. "Here I am."

And she took me in her arms and led me into bed and exploded.

She told me that the world was mean to me because people can be destructive, especially when envy gets hold of them.

"People envy *me?*" I said.

"You have a sly inner beauty that shines through. You're not thick and dumb like them. You're smooth and lean. You are the attractivest man I know."

This was news to me.

Lulu became like a member of the family. Even Dad noticed how nice she was. Mom included Lulu in our Scrabble games. In her lucid moments, Mom was a fierce player, one who could dig down into the rattiest collection of letters and root up incredible winning words like "etytylic" or "zumbrist" and then, when challenged, go to the unabridged Webster's and, bango, there it was, the exact word, meaning "that which pertains to the indehiscent fruit of the buckwheat," and of course her word hit Triple Word Bonus and the Z landed on Triple Letter, so she rang up a hundred points with one word and left you no openings except a "but" or an "aunt" or "tuna" and she would rub her hands and gloat. "Skunked you there, Buddy. What's your problem? Hormones getting you down again?"

"Hormones are acting up, Mom," I chuckled, looking at Lulu. Her cutoffs were cut off as high as cutoffs can be cut without becoming a belt, and her halter top didn't hold much back. I was dazed by her beauty. So generous. Lavish even.

Dad sensed what was happening with me and Lulu, I guess, and he took a sudden fitful interest in me. "You haven't been to church for a while, Buddy. Months. Hope you haven't given up on us guys. You need a little spiritual component in your life, you know. If it's the *church* you don't like, did you know you can take communion at home now, using a Methodist modem? I can get one for you—" I told him, No thanks.

And then, one night, Mom put down the word "therapy" in Scrabble and scored thirty-six points and looked at me and Lulu and said, "That's it. No more booze." She joined a group called Alamom, they met twice a week and sobbed into their coffee cups and sighed and smoked cigarettes and heaved their bosoms, and Alamom convinced her that she needed to confront her family with the truth about her feelings.

So she did. She sat us down around the kitchen table one afternoon and she told Dad that he was a jerk but that she loved him anyway. She told me that she had never wanted me and that I had ruined her life. "It's time I started thinking about myself," she said. "You've been hanging on me like dead moss for years, Buddy. I'm an alcoholic because I felt guilty about not wanting you. Now I don't feel guilty about it anymore."

I staggered up to my room as if poleaxed and cried into the pillow for an hour and finally Lulu came in and sat on the bed. "Let's go west," I said. "I'll steal the car and we'll drive to California and find us a cabin in the woods. A log cabin with a barrel stove and a lot of plants and us in a big bed, naked, making love and then running naked down to the pale-blue sea streaked with pink and diving in and swimming and running back to the cabin and jumping into bed and drinking coffee and eating goat yogurt with honey and oranges, and making love again—what a happy life, Lulu. Let's do it. Let's go to California." I said all this in a torrent of words, breaking all the rules of hypnotic conversation. I yipped like a dog. "Please, Lulu. Please. Say you will."

She looked at me long and mournfully and held my fluttering hand in hers. She said softly, "You're trying to find love and happiness, but in the woods you must find it within yourself, and, Buddy, I don't think you have it in you. Maybe that's why I don't love you."

"You don't?"

She said she didn't. So she couldn't come to California with me. She had a job to do. She couldn't walk away from it. She hoped I would understand.

"Why?" I asked.

"Don't ask why. You'll avoid a lot of confusion that way."

I told her that if she didn't come with me, I would go

by myself. I immediately regretted saying this. I wished I could stay and continue to blow her dress off and to be whatever I was to her, but she said, "Well, then, you will have to go by yourself. I will pack your clothes and make you a lunch."

I took my sweet time getting dressed, putting on my coat, walking to the Sioux Falls bus depot, hoping that Lulu would run to me and throw her arms around me and tell me to stay. I stood outside the bus until the driver snapped at me to get on board and even then I looked up the street, praying she would make me stay, and then I climbed on and headed west across the prairie for California, there to seduce beautiful women with my subtle techniques and bury forever the terrible secret of my leprosy.

MR. ST. PAUL

Thirty-one waist and sixty-five chest,
Three hundred pounds clean jerked
and pressed,
But body-building is more than phy-
sique,
It's about conceptualizing success and
using all
Your inner self, the way I did last week.
Against eleven other guys, I was
named Mr. St. Paul.
Confidence is the mark of a true
champion:
Before the match begins, you know you've won.
And yet, when I was crowned onstage,
A winner, the best that a guy could wish,
I thought, "Thirty-two years of age:

It'll never be better than this.
No, nothing will ever be as good as in the past
And all you can do is try not to lose it too fast."

Mr. St. Paul was the only good thing to happen all year,
It's been all grief since she walked out,
The only girl I really cared about.
I felt so bad, I wished I could disappear.

Every day, I wish I was walking with my right hand
Around the waist of the beautiful Jacqueline Ann,
Riding on her hips and feeling her long body sway,
Walking in the crowd along the State Fair Midway.
We necked everywhere, in the dark at the Aquarium
And at the movies, and in the summer we'd come
To the Fair and ride the double Ferris wheel
And I would reach up her dress and feel
Her—what a thrill on a summer night,
The feeling that you've absolutely got it made.
Your girl there, dressed in white,
And you knowing how this game is played.

A year later, she is often on my mind.
I keep the picture of her that she signed:
"When the darkest night surrounds you,
Cold and lonely as can be,
Don't give up, just look around you,
You can always count on me.
Lots of love to a great guy. Jackie Ann."
She made me a happy man,

And I love her no matter what my friends say,
And I would take her back today
If she decided to leave that jerk, Everett.
It would be even better than before, I bet.
Just her beside me would give me happiness,
My girl in her cool white summer dress.
And could I forgive her? I would say, yes.

I haven't gone with anybody for thirteen months,
Except on a blind date once
With a sad girl from Minneapolis, arranged by my
   buddy Jim,
Who thought I needed one, and any one would do.
But you couldn't find two greater guys than him
And his brother-in-law Barry.
We've known each other since '82.
We go fishing almost every Saturday
During walleye season, up in northern Wisconsin.
We never discuss money, work, or religion,
And not even women that much, which suits me fine.
So they don't know I think about her all the time.

They think I'm over her and back to my old self,
And sometimes I think so too and yet
A girl like her is hard to forget
When she leaves you for someone else.

Last weekend, in the boat, a big old green fly
Came buzzing around my head. It
Was the kind you see sitting on horseshit.

It lit on me right between my eyes.
And I thought, "It's hard to fool one of them green
flies."

I've felt like horseshit since a year ago.
Felt like I was drowning, dragged down below,
And woke up some nights in a cold sweat,
Unable to breathe,
Thinking of her and Everett
In a bed and her underneath.

I know where they live in St. Louis Park,
Which is miles away, luckily.
And yet once or twice I've driven past and seen the win-
dows dark
And imagined her with him, his big ugly
Face next to hers, him taking off his pants,
Her trembling and beautiful and nude,
And his two big hairy hands
Grabbing her like she was a piece of fruit.

I guess I have got to kill the son of a bitch
One of these days, haul him out of bed
And throw him off the Lake Street bridge,
Either that or accept him living in my head,
Year after year, grinning at me like an ape,
A man I never met
And can't escape,
My true love's lover, Everett.
Maybe shoot him in the pants,

Watch him jump and dance,
See the dark blood run.
That might be fun.

Probably this is why guys used to go west,
To Alaska, or if it was really bad, Australia.
To avoid homicide, they recessed
Into the wilderness, the skunk of failure
On their clothes, and took their broken hearts
To the end of the line, out to the farthest parts,
And settled down where good luck could strike,
Some mother lode of goodness make them well.
And they could drive the golden spike
Into that old story that was too sad to tell.

But I like it in St. Paul. My folks are here.
I don't want to be the one to disappear.
Let him go, not me. Today I bought a gun,
And though I'm not saying I'd shoot anyone,
I believe that tonight I'll go to St. Louis Park.
Load the gun and drive slowly past in the dark
And see what I see, and see what I do.
Get this thing out of the way and go on to something
   new.

THAT OLD PICAYUNE-MOON

To the editor,
The Zenith *Picayune-Moon:*

I grew up among positive-thinking people with seldom an unkind word for anybody and I have tried to be positive too, a founder and builder and cultivator and patron and a medium of light in the world, a philosophy that led me to run for mayor of our city, in which office I have served four terms, as you may know.

Democracy is a tedious business. It tends to attract people who have time to kill, and so a public official spends vast aeons of time sitting and listening to gasbags, but I always tried to remember that public service is a high calling and that bitterness is beneath a public servant. I looked on the bright side.

And then along came that greasy, flabby, small-minded, mealy-mouthed, pasty-faced, and potato-headed daily fishwrap and dog's biffy, the *Picayune-Moon,* edited by that dildo Hector Timmy. (You.) If it had been St. Francis's hometown newspaper there in Assisi, sir, he would have dropped the Golden Rule like a bent pool cue and taught those birds to attack.

My wife thinks I'm wrong. She says, "You wanted to be the center of attention. That's why you ran for mayor. Stop picking on the press."

She has a point. A person does feel sheepish picking on journalists, a class already so richly despised that if a planeload of them crashed in flames, most people would smile from pure reflex. Reporters like to think they are despised because they are brave and dare to tell the truth, but the public smells something else, a little sadism and ghoulishness floating around in the tank. Plus a weak filament in the ole light bulb. Whenever a newspaper reports on something you know about, half the time they get it two-thirds wrong.

I quote my wife now: "You have your health and a good home with lovely children and you have the passionate love of a handsome woman in her early fifties, a woman's erotic peak period. You are a lucky man, in no position to despise anybody. Anyway, if there was ever somebody not worth getting mad at, it's the paper."

Of course she is right, and at first glance the *Picayune-Moon* doesn't look like much, only about the thirty-first-worst newspaper in America, not even a contender, full of blither and blather about the same hundred ditzy celebrities and "lifestyle" stuff about lives so banal you'd be thrilled to be dead and stock photos of tots and pets and athletes caught in silly positions and the obligatory headline puns and a regular brothel of columnists, all of it tricked out in bilious blue and gooseshit green and virulent yellow, and ten minutes later you can't remember a single sentence you read. She's right. What's to get mad at?

Hector Timmy, I suppose. A man who isn't easy to describe in twenty-five words or less, but here's a try:

Airhead, buttface, cretin, dork, eunuch, fungus, guttersnipe, hack, imbecile, jackal, loser, meatloaf, numb nuts, *objet d'merde,* pissant, rummy, scumball, turkey, upchuck, vulture, windbag, yahoo, zero, a real piece of work.

That's you, you weasel.

I laid eyes on you the other night as you sat dining at the Blue Light Cafe with your managing editor Delores Whinny. Her hair was drawn up high on her head, bright orange like the inflammation on a baboon's hinder, so when she scratched her face, it gave me a jolt. And when she poked a fork in it, I almost fell over.

I asked the waitress, "Who is that chinless man with the droopy mustache that looks like he is eating a brown baby rat, Stella?"

"The one sitting with the horse-faced lady? That's Hector Timmy, of course," she replied. "You know him. The one who keeps falling off his chair."

The good woman was right. You had chained your wrist to a bottle of bourbon and were halfway to the bottom of it, slowly turning yourself into a sandbag. *What a gorgeous opportunity,* I thought. My enemy, immobilized—a chance to say something vile and withering and poke him in the snoot. I tried to conjure up an insult so sharp it could penetrate your mind and slosh through the vast fat deposits and find a working synapse and sting you, but someone as viscous as yourself is hard to sting. It occurred to me to stroll over and casually tip the cherries *flambé* into your large lap and pelt you with macaroons. As you may be aware, I did not.

At the moment, it is eleven p.m. I have spent thirty minutes on this letter so far and now my wife, her black hair tumbling over her bare shoulders touched with freckles under the pale-blue gossamer negligee hanging light as a leaf on her pale breasts and her bold etcetera, says, "Quit writing to that bebo and take off your clothes." She runs her fingers through my thick hair. "There is nothing deader than this morning's paper and here you are, strong and healthy and not all that bad-looking, so turn out the light and come to bed and do your homework," whispers the woman who still, after twenty-five years, makes my lips twitch. "In a moment, love," I tell her. She sighs.

I will not bore you here with a list of my accomplishments as mayor, the businesses and organizations I've helped at every turn, the thousands of little favors for ordinary folks, the countless dedicatory speeches (brief, lighthearted) and the endless public meetings at which I have sat patiently and allowed my fellow citizens to rail and screech at me for the mortal failings of city employees. I will not cite these. I doubt that a flabby little guy with a rat for a mustache would be impressed. The man who edits the paper that printed the story "City Hall Renovation Disturbs Cancer-Stricken Gold-Star Moms in Shabby Rooms One Block from Where Trucks Rumble, Power Tools Whine, Making Lavish Suite for Mayor, Including Luxury Shower and Track Lighting" two weeks ago is not going to be deflected by facts.

"Make peace with the man," my beloved Annie told me at the time. "Put on your cheap sport coat and your dumb shoes with the tassels and fill your big brown eyes with warmth and smile your brotherly smile and go to the man's office and grovel." I decided not to, and perhaps I was wrong.

Your story last Tuesday, "Mayor Loads Pants Pockets at City Treasury in Broad Daylight, Leaving Veteran Observers Sad, Disgusted," about the City Council voting a salary increase of eight percent for city employees, including the mayor, did not upset me, and I read with amusement the Wednesday installment, "Fat Cat Mayor Jets Around Country at Our Expense—$130/Day Suites, Cocktails, Shrimp the Size of Your Fist"—and then your Thursday front page ("Mayor Stung by Charges of Corruption, Arrogance, and Deceit") didn't bother me either, nor Friday's ("Limo Liberal Cruises to City Hall While Workers Walk—He Is Hauled in Luxury to the Public Trough While Sick and Blind and Deaf and

Lame Sit on Cold Corners Waiting for Public Transit"),
and when, for the Saturday edition, you sent reporters to
rifle our garbage cans ("First Family Doesn't Clean
Plates—They Waste Steak, Trout, and Dark Things
That Resemble Truffles"), I rolled over and had a restful
nap. It was nothing but that gallant old eye-gouging
spirit of the tabloid that maybe we need a little more of
in this age of marshmallow newscasters. After your Sunday story, "Six Sofas in Mayor's Reception Hall—Could
He Not Donate One or Two to Old Soldiers Home
Where Crippled Vets Who Toppled Tojo Must Squat on
Chill, Dank Concrete?," I actually was moved to send a
fifty-dollar check to the Salvation Army.

No, what burned my bacon was when you assigned
your photographer Burns L. Schaper to follow me in the
streets with a zoom lens.

All week, whenever I bent over or scratched myself or
picked my nose, I could hear Mr. Schaper's camera
ratcheting away like a corn planter. Next day a photo
appeared, 4×6, page one, Metro section, always a lulu.
Now, I never claimed to be handsome, though in por-
traits by reasonable people I look presentable, a tall
clean man who you would not mind welcoming into
your home, but Burns had a knack for sensing when I
felt gassy, or my dogs ached, or a popcorn husk was
caught in my throat. Suddenly there he was, Speed
Graphic in hand, and after a while, just the sight of him
made my face turn to wood. He'd jump out from behind
a parked car and yell, "Hey, fruitcake!," and snap away
and next day in the *P-M*, there I was looking like a box

turtle with a migraine, a basilisk stare, brow furrowed, lip curled, looking straight at the readers as if I wanted to pound them down a rathole. Underneath, it said: "Having fed at the public trough, he refuses to come clean about his financial shenanigans." Or some such. "Guests in his home say his medicine cabinet contains some big surprises. Reports of dirty books, liquor, sexually explicit correspondence, ladies' underwear, you name it—how long will authorities dawdle before action is taken?" But what really squeezed my bunions were the photographs: me bending to tie my shoelace, my face all baggy. Hands to my face, rubbing dust from my eyes, hand in my crotch, easing my shorts. I asked Burns, "Why are you doing this to me? Are we not Christians?"

"Nothing personal, just a journalist's job, y'know, being the gadfly," he mumbled. "I know how painful it is to be in the public eye, but that's what it's like, and I know that a big man like you can stand it, otherwise you wouldn't be where you are today." As he said this, he held his camera low and squeezed off some shots of the hairs in my nose.

The *Picayune-Moon* is a monopoly, like the Ministry of Information in Peking, and though people discount most of what they read in it, the paper carries a big stick in the realm of the visual, what you might call the Power of Propriety. It can print a picture of a guy and label him "civic leader" or it can tattoo the word "controversial" on him, locking him in the zoo with the wackos, and the photograph can be one of him gazing sensitively into the distance like an author on the back of the book jacket, or one of him slightly cross-eyed, mouth ajar, tongue lolling out, his finger in his ear. In a high-decorum city like Zenith, this is no idle threat.

Schaper lobbed peas at me in restaurants, he put mucus on doorknobs, he once crept under the dais and tied tin cans to my ankle as I accepted an award from the Women's Club, and finally he got the close-up he wanted: me, enraged, stricken, lurching at him, hair disheveled, waving my arms, mouth like an open wound, spit dripping, a maniac. The one you printed yesterday.

That was meanness of unusual ferocity, *malice rara,* and so, when I saw you sitting in the Blue Light, napkin wedged betwixt your dewlaps, humming flatly, staring at the blank wall that was Delores Whinny, I felt a civic duty. I stood up and approached your table and was about to hurl you to the carpet and kick you to death, when I had a sharp vision of the future—of Delores Whinny taking over the paper and making it into a joyful celebration of life, the editorial page coming out against ignorance and corruption, the columnists writing about their children and the hope for a better world, and the paper changing its name from *Picayune-Moon* to *This, Our City and Our People* with a big Neighborhoods & Families section, and fiction and poetry, and the Sports section renamed Games & Growth—and I turned and walked out into the gentle night.

It dawned on me then that *a good newspaper is never quite good enough but a lousy newspaper is a joy forever.* These words ought to be chiseled onto every newspaper office wall, right above the urinals.

These are my last words on the subject, because now, at half past one in the morning, my wife has come stark pure naked into the room, glowing pink from a hot shower, her hair damp and glittering, carrying a tray of sliced melon, smoked ham, chunks of Stilton cheese, a toasted baguette, a 1969 St.-Emilion, and a bottle of olive oil. She set the tray on top of this letter and gently removed the pen from my hand and tore off my shirt. "Come to my bed, you animal, and let that poor wilted editor lie moldering in his cups," she murmured, chewing my ear with her perfect little incisors. "The picture of you enraged, charging the camera, has inflamed me. Come, come—I want to devour you with my body—"

She has a point. The beauty of having a *Picayune-Moon* peeing on your shoes is the way that it leaches the anger out of your life and opens the door to passionate love—I grab her like a drowning man and she strips the clothes off me with her left foot while we roll over and over on the floor and, though we try to make the moment last, mindless sexual passion tosses us like a Tilt-A-Whirl as if we were seventeen and now I forget which of us is her and which is me, I seem to be wearing an Acrilan carpet and am lying on my back in the stratosphere looking at the lights of the city far below and now there is a joyful updraft and now I can write no more. My best to you and yours, if any.

MAROONED

I remember exactly when the marriage took a weird turn. I was on the examining table with my shorts draped around my ankles and my tail pointing high in the air and Dr. Miller surveying my colon through a cold steel periscope and making *hmmmm* sounds, his ballpoint pen scratching on a notepad, and at this delicate moment, he said, softly, "Do I strike you as a selfish person?"

"No . . . why?" I asked. The periscope felt like it was about six feet up me and I'm only five-foot-eight.

"I took a personal-inventory test in that book about getting ahead that everybody's reading—you know, the book that I heard you're related to the author of," he said. According to the test, he said, he was rather selfish.

I groaned, feeling the excavation of the Holland Tunnel within me, but of course I knew which book he meant. My dumbbell brother-in-law Dave's book, that's which one.

He told me Dave's book had meant a lot to him. "I never buy books other than science fiction," he confided, "but my partner Jamie gave it to me for my birthday and I opened it up and I couldn't put the rascal down. Heck of a book." Meanwhile, *the periscope was way up there in my hinder, probing parts of me I had been unaware of until now.* "He says that what holds us back is fear, and that fear is selfish, and that getting ahead is a problem of *getting outside yourself*," and he gave the periscope a little nudge for emphasis. "You have to really *focus* on a goal outside yourself in order to succeed. My goal is to open a restaurant. Jamie's a wonderful cook. Chinese and Mexican, what do you think?"

I felt sore afterward. I went home and told Julie that a person as dim as my proctologist was exactly who Dave's book was aimed at, one ream job deserves another, and so forth. I was steamed.

She said, "You've always resented Dave, Danny, and you know why? I'll tell you why. Because your life is in Park and the key isn't even in the ignition. You're totally into negativity, Danny. You stopped growing twenty-six years ago. And how would I know? Because I'm your wife, that's how I know."

* * *

Twenty-six years ago I graduated from the University of Minnesota journalism school with honors, the editor of the Minnesota *Daily*, and got a job as a professional copywriter at a Minneapolis ad agency. Dave Grebe was a clerk in his dad's stationery store, peddling birthday cards. He and I played basketball on a Lutheran church team; that's how I met his sister Julie; she picked him up after the game because he'd lost his driver's license for drunk driving. He was twenty, big and porky and none too bright, just like now. "I'd sure like to get the heck out of stationery, I hate the smell of it, mucilage especially, and the damn perfume, it's like someone vomited after eating fruit," Dave remarked to me more than once.

So I was not too surprised when, one fine day, Dave walked away from his job and shaved his head clean and moved to a commune in south Minneapolis, living with sixteen other disciples of the Serene Master Diego Tua, putting on the sandals of humility and the pale-green robe of constant renewal. "I have left your world, Danny," he told me on the phone.

Julie, who had become my wife, thought that Dave "just needed to get away for a while." I pointed out to her that the Tuans were fanatics who roamed the airport jingling bells and droning and whanging on drums, collecting money to support their master and his many wives and concubines. The Tuans believed that they held the secrets of the universe and everyone else was vermin.

Julie thought they were Buddhists of some sort.

"They could be Buddhists or nudists or used-car

salesmen who like to dress up in gowns, but whatever they are, they're working your brother like a puppet on a string."

She thought that Dave was only doing what he felt was best for him. Subject closed. So I did double duty for a few years—was a copywriter *and* kept the Grebe stationery store going—and Dave went around droning and whanging and dinging and making a holy nuisance of himself.

"We are God's roadblocks," said the Happy Master, Diego himself, "warning the people that the bridge is washed out." His real name was Tim U. Apthed; he chose the name Diego, *Die—ego,* and crunched his initials into a surname, and founded a church for jerks. My agency, Curry, Cosset, Dorn, flew me to Atlanta or Boston or Chicago occasionally, and I'd come running through the terminal to catch a plane and hear the drums and bells and there were the Tuans in the middle of the concourse, holding up their signs, "Your Life Is a Lie," and chanting, "Only two ways, one false, one true. Only one life, which way are you? Back! back! turn away from your lies! And God will give you a beautiful surprise!" and I'd be trying to squeeze through the crowd of shaven men including my blissful brother-in-law and get on board the plane. It was like Run, Sheep, Run.

"Well, when he talks about people being so materialistic, I think he has a good point," said Julie.

Then, fifteen years ago, Mr. Grebe died of a cerebral hemorrhage—clapped his hand to his forehead one morning and said, "Oh mercy. Call Ann and tell her I'll be late," and fell over dead onto the ballpoint-pen rack. The rest of us were living in the felt-tip era but Mr. Grebe never gave up on ballpoints, which worked better on carbon paper, he explained patiently, ignoring the fact that photocopying had replaced carbons. The family was devastated at the loss of this vacuous and bewildered man. They mourned for weeks, during which I was the bulwark, arranging the funeral, paying the bills, ordering stock, and Dave sat in a corner weeping. They never found out who Ann was.

Dave left the Tuans and let his hair grow out and went to work at the Wm. Grebe Stationery Shop. Every few days he'd call up and say, "I don't know how I can ever make it up to everyone for the terrible things I've done."

You get sick of remorse when it becomes a broken record. Dave kept saying, "You've been so great, Danny, and I've been a jerk. I don't know why God lets me live." After a few months of it, I told him that I didn't know either but that he could take his guilt and put it where the sun don't shine. He reported this to Julie. She vindictively canceled our vacation trip to the Bahamas. "I can never forgive you for saying that to my brother," she said, and she was right, she couldn't.

Meanwhile, Dave, who once had renounced material things, took over Wm. Grebe, stocked it with felt tips and expanded into malls and branched out into discount bookselling, got rich in about three years, and became one smooth guy: bought a Hasselblad camera, Finnish furniture, a Steinway, a Martin guitar, four Harleys, a

Peterbilt truck, an original Monet (*Girl with Light Hair*), and next thing I knew he was going around giving pep talks to Kiwanis clubs, and then, he wrote his book about getting ahead, *Never Buy a Bottle of Rat Poison That Comes with Gift Coupons.* It sold more copies than there are rats in Rio (millions). He turned Tuanism inside out and restated it in capitalist terms, and made low cash flow seem like a denial of God's love.

On the same day that an interview with Dave appeared on the front page of *The Wall Street Journal,* I got canned at the agency. Twenty-five years I had labored at Curry, Cosset, Dorn, and on a Monday morning, as I sharpened my No. 2 pencil, a twenty-nine-year-old guy in a red bow tie leaned over the wall of my work cubicle and said, "The folks at Chippy called and cut back on the campaign, Danny, I'm going to have to let you go for a while."

"Are you sure?" That's all I could think to say. A quarter-century with the company—"Are you sure?" He was sure.

I crawled home, bleeding, and Julie was glued to the TV, watching Dave talk about the irrelevance of suffering. It was a videotape, not a live appearance, but even so, she did not turn it off when she heard my tragic news. She said, "That's too bad," and then, "I'm so proud of him. This is one of his new videotapes. He's going to put out twelve of them. He just seems to touch a chord in people, don't you think? People can't help but respond to him. It's a natural gift." She recommended that I study *Rat Poison* to give me the confidence to find a new job and wait for his next book, *How to Find Your Rear End Without Using Both Hands.*

"Your brother," I said, "is one of the world's biggest b.s.ers."

This was when Julie decided that we needed to face up to my problems. "You are a dark cloud in my life, Danny. A small dark cloud," she said.

I don't know what she meant by that. I'm a happy guy who loves life, it's just that I have a moony face. A guy can't help it that his face won't light up. Inside, I'm like a kid with a new bike. Though being flushed down the toilet while your brother-in-law is getting rich certainly puts a crimp in a guy's hose. Dave was hot. I was dead. For twenty-five years, I had been a happy guy who created dancing ketchup commercials, who made high-fiber bran flakes *witty,* who wrote those coffee commercials in which the husband and wife share a golden moment over a cup of java. I brought lucidity to capitalism, and Dave brought gibberish, and he walked off with the prize.

The next day, Julie told me that Dave thought we should go away and be alone and he'd given her fifteen thousand dollars so we could charter a fifty-foot schooner for a two-week cruise off Antigua, where we could try to put the marriage back together.

"Fifteen thousand dollars would come in handy in other ways than blowing it on a cruise," I pointed out. "We could invest it. I'm unemployed, you know."

"Aren't you willing to invest in our marriage?" she said.

"We could *buy* a boat for that kind of money and sail every weekend." She said that fifteen thousand wasn't enough to pay her to get into a boat with me at the tiller.

"Remember the time we drifted powerless down the Mississippi because you put oil in the gas tank? Remember how you tried to rig up an overcoat on an oar to make a sail? Remember how we drifted toward that oncoming coal barge and stood and waved our arms and cried out in our pitiful voices?"

Ten years had not dimmed her memory of that afternoon.

So off we flew to Antigua.

We flew first-class, in those wide upholstered seats, where everything is sparkly and fresh and lemony and candles flicker on the serving cart. A painful reminder of how cheery life can be for the very rich, people like Dave. The flight attendants wore gold-paisley sarongs slit up the side and pink-passion lipstick, they were Barnard graduates (*cum laude*) in humanities, and they set a vase of fresh roses on my table, along with the seviche and salmon loaf and crab puffs with Mornay sauce, and they leaned over me, their perfect college-educated breasts hanging prettily in place, and they whispered, "You've got a nice butt. You ever read Kant?" I knew that they only flirted with me because I was holding a first-class ticket; I wanted to say, "I'm forty-seven, I'm broke, ashamed, in pain, on the verge of divorce, and sponging off a despised relative. I've hit bottom, babes. Buzz off."

We stayed one night at Jumby Bay, dropping a bundle, and headed off by cab to the Lucky Lovers Marina, and there, at the end of the dock, lay the *Susy Q*. I put my arm around Julie, who was shivering despite the bright sunshine and eighty-five degrees.

"Is that a schooner or a ketch?" I said.

"It's a yawl," she replied. It was hard not to notice the frayed rigging and rusted hardware, the oil slick around the stern, the sail in a big heap on deck, and what appeared to be sneaker treadmarks along the side of the hull. But we had put down a deposit of fifteen hundred dollars already, so we banished doubt from our minds.

"Hello! Anybody below?" I hollered. There was a muffled *yo,* and a beautiful young man poked up his head from the cockpit and smiled. His golden curls framed his Grecian-god-like face, his deep tan set off by a green T-shirt that said "Montana . . . The Big Sky." He was Rusty, our captain, he said. "I was just making your bed downstairs. Come on down. Your room's up front!"

This struck me as odd, that he said *downstairs* instead of *below decks,* and I mentioned this to Julie as we stowed our bags in the cabin. "How can you get upset about poor word choice when our marriage is on the rocks?" she asked.

The *Susy Q* cleared port and sailed west toward Sansevar Trist, and she and I sat below discussing our marriage, which I have always believed is not a good idea for Julie and me. My experience tells me that we should shoot eight-ball, sit in a hot tub, go to the zoo, rake the lawn, spread warm oil on each other's bodies, do anything but talk about our marriage, but she is a fan of those articles like "How Lousy Is Your Marriage: A 10-Minute Quiz That Could Help You Improve It" and of course the first question is, "Are you and your husband able to sit down and discuss your differences calmly and reasonably?" *No! Of course not! Are you kidding? Who discusses these things without screaming? Name one person!* So she launched off on a reasonable discussion of differences, and two minutes later we're screeching and hissing and slamming doors so hard the pictures fall off the walls. We simply are unable to discuss our marriage—does that make us terrible people? Our marriage is like the Electoral College: it works okay if you don't think about it.

"Do you love me?" Julie asked, as the boat rocked in the swell, Rusty thumping around on deck overhead.

"How do you mean that?"

"I mean, is it worth it to try to stick together? Marriages have their rough passages. It's only worth it if there's love. If there isn't, why waste time trying to patch this up."

"Do you love me?"

"I asked first."

"How come I'm the one who has to say if I love you or not? Why is it always up to me?"

There was a loud thump above, like somebody kicking the side, and then Rusty let out a cry, "Oh shoot!" I poked my head up out of the hatch. "It's the steering thing," he said. The tiller had broken off and was now bobbing in our wake. I told him to lash an oar in its place and come around and retrieve the tiller, and I ducked back down into the cabin. Julie was sitting on the bunk, her back to the bulkhead, her trim brown legs drawn up.

"I better go up and help Rusty," I said.

"You can't run away, Danny," she said. "It's a simple question. Do you love me or not? What's so hard about that?"

I flopped down on the chair. "Why can't we *converse* about this in a calm friendly way instead of getting into a shooting match over every little thing—"

"A little thing," she said. "Our love. A little thing. Oh right. Sure. Great way to start off a vacation. Our love, a little thing."

There was a loud *cra-a-a-ack* above, like a sequoia falling, and a muffled splash. I stuck my head up. The sail was gone, and the mast. "I was gonna turn right and the whole thing broke and fell off," he said, shaking his head. "Boy, that was something!" He shrugged and grinned, like he'd just burned the toast. "Oh well, we still got a motor." I told him to come about and retrieve the sail and mast and then head for port.

I told Julie that we had serious problems above and maybe we should postpone our talk. She said we had been postponing it for twenty years.

I was about to tell her how full of balloon juice she was, and then I heard the motor turn over, a dry raspy sound, like gravel going down a chute, and I realized the *Susy Q* was going nowhere. Still, it wasn't as aggravating as Miss Priss there, sitting and telling me about my marriage.

"Dave recommended a great book to me and it opened my eyes. *The Silent Chrysalis*. I read it twice. Danny, in some way my love for you is a symptom of my denial of myself, an attempt to make myself invisible."

The starter cranked over once and wheezed and coughed a deep dry cough.

Julie's eyes locked with mine. "We need to change that love from something angry to a *mature* love," she said. "I can't use you as an instrument of my self-hatred."

What is that supposed to mean? I asked.

"Dave thinks you're trapped in a lingering infantile narcissism, like a lot of guys. I don't know. I can't speak to that. Only you can."

How does a stationery-store clerk suddenly become the expert on American men? I wondered, but then Rusty's face appeared in the hatch, a mite taut around the eyes. "We may have to ditch the boat in a minute, you guys. We're coming real close to the reef, I think. The water looks sort of bubbly out there."

Julie grabbed my arm when I got up to go topside. "You're not going to just walk away from this one, Danny. You're going to face up to what's wrong, which is your selfishness. Your selfishness is a *fact*, Danny. Let's stop denying it. Let's deal with it."

Rusty's voice was hoarse. "Come on, folks."

I poked my head up. The Great Navigator had an odd horrified expression on his face, and his chin was aquiver. He wore an orange life jacket. "Want me to take the helm?" I asked.

"No helm left to take, and there's big jagged rocks

up ahead, folks, so if you see a cushion, better grab on to it. This is not a test."

There was a distant roar of waves that was not as distant as before.

I ducked down and told Julie we were about to abandon ship. "If you can't deal with the truth, Danny, then I can't be married to you," said Julie, softly. "I don't want a marriage based on a lie."

I was just about to tell her that she wouldn't have that problem much longer, when there was a jagged ripping tearing crunching sound from just below our feet, and the boat lurched to a dead stop. Water began boiling up from below. I grabbed Julie and hoisted her through the hatch, grabbed a carry-on bag and a couple cushions, and took Julie by the hand, and we jumped into the water. Rusty was already on shore, waving to us. It was shallow, all right; the water frothed around our feet on the jagged coral, but it wasn't too hard wading in to shore, a beautiful white sandy beach that curved around and around a very pretty island— uninhabited, we soon discovered. "Well," said Rusty, "looks like you guys may get a little more than two weeks. Nice place, too." And he glanced down at Julie. Her T-shirt was wet from the surf, and her breasts shone through. He looked at her a long time, I thought.

We made a hut from palm fronds and the jibsail. Julie had brought her purse and suntan oil and four books about marriage and communication, and I had dragged in our suitcase and a bottle of Campari, and Rusty had salvaged the oregano, sweet basil, rosemary, chives, coriander, cayenne pepper, paprika, orange zest, nutmeg, cinnamon, pine nuts, bay leaf, marjoram, tarragon, caraway, and saffron.

"The boat sinks and you rescue the spice rack?" I cried. "You're the captain and your boat goes down and you come ashore with the spice rack?"

Rusty looked at Julie. "Just because we're marooned on an island doesn't mean the food has to be bland and tasteless," he said.

She nodded. "It's no dumber than bringing a bottle of Campari. You don't like Campari," she said. "You only like beer."

And an hour later, Julie had made beds out of pine boughs and Rusty had carved a salad bowl from a stump and tossed a salad in it—"Just some ferns and breadfruit and hearts of palm," he said. He had also baked a kelp casserole over an open fire. Julie thought it was the best salad in salad history. Actually, it was okay. "And this casserole!" she cried. "I have never tasted kelp that tasted like this kelp tastes. What's the secret?"

"Paprika," he said.

Julie couldn't get over it. She said, "Danny couldn't even boil an egg. I kept offering to teach him, but he never wanted to learn."

It was hard not to notice that she was talking about me in the past tense.

"No, Danny couldn't have made a salad like this in a million years. Are you kidding? Not him," she chortled. "No, no, no, no, no."

We sat under the palm tree as the sun went down,

and Julie and Rusty talked about the American novel, how they didn't care for Updike, who had never written strong women characters and was hung up on male menopause and had no ear for dialogue.

"No ear for dialogue?" I cried.

"No ear for dialogue," she said.

"John Updike? No ear for dialogue? Are you kidding me? Updike? That's what you said, right? Updike? His dialogue? No ear?"

"He has none," she said.

"None. Updike."

"Right."

"I can't believe this," I said. "You're sitting here under this palm tree and saying that John Updike—*the* John Updike, who wrote the Rabbit books—that he has no ear for *dialogue?* Tell me something. If John Updike has no ear for dialogue, then who do you think *does* have an ear for dialogue?"

Rusty looked at Julie. "Maya Angelou. Alice Walker. Doris Lessing," he said.

"Doris Lessing," I said.

"Yes," she said. "Doris Lessing."

"An ear for dialogue," I said. I stood up. "You know, I must be going deaf, but I could swear you just said Doris Lessing. Or did you say Arthur Schlesinger?" I kicked a little dirt toward Rusty.

"I said, Doris Lessing," he said.

It was the first of many discussions where I was in the minority. One morning, over a dried-seaweed breakfast, Julie said she thought there is such a thing as a "masculine personality" and that it is basically controlling and violent. Rusty agreed. "But some of us are working to change that," he said. Julie felt that men are inherently competitive, i.e. linear, hierarchical, and women are circular, i.e. radiant. "I never thought of it that way before," said Rusty. Julie and Rusty started meditating together every morning, sitting on the beach facing the east. "Hey, mind if I sit in?" I said, cheerfully.

Julie squinted up at me. "I think you'd block the unity of the experience," she said.

Rusty nodded.

"Well, far be it from me to block anyone's unity," I said, and walked away.

That night, Julie and Rusty were cooking a bark soup and she looked up at me and said, "Rusty is such an inspiration. I'm glad this happened."

I grabbed her arm. "This numbskull who ran the boat onto the rock is an inspiration?"

Rusty confronted me later that night, after Julie went to sleep. "I've decided to take Julie away from you," he said. "You two do nothing but fight, and she's obviously attracted to me, so if she and I paired up, at least there'd be two happy people on this island. It makes more sense that way. Two out of three isn't bad. So why don't you go and sleep in the jungle someplace. This tent is for Julie and me."

I said, "Okay, you're right," and I turned and bent down and picked up my Campari bottle and then whirled and swung it straight up into his nuts and he staggered back and I threw a handful of dirt in his eyes.

He bent down, blinded, and I kicked him as hard as I could in the gut, and he went *whooomph*, like a needle sliding across a record, and down he went, and I picked him up and threw him into the ocean and suddenly the water was whipped to a froth by thousands of tiny carnivorous fish and the frenzy went on for a half a minute and subsided and whatever was left of Rusty sank bubbling to the bottom.

It wasn't the Zen way but it got the job done.

Julie was distraught in the morning. She dashed around the island screaming his name. "What have you done to him, Danny?" she shrieked.

"He fell in the water and the fish ate him," I said.

"You killed him!"

"Nothing ever dies. He is at one with the fish."

Two weeks later, when the big cruise ship saw us and anchored a half-mile to leeward and sent in a launch to take us off, Julie had calmed down and was almost ready to talk to me again. I could tell. I yelled up to her where she sat on the ledge of the rocky promontory, "You know something? I think the secret of marriage is that you can't change the person you love. You have to love that person the way he or she is. Well, here I am!"

"You got that out of a book," she called back. It was the first time she'd spoken to me in two weeks.

A man in officer whites with big tufts of hair on his chest was on the launch. He said, "You the couple who went down with the *Susy Q?* Where's the captain?"

"He drowned," I said. Julie said nothing. She still has said nothing about Rusty to me at all, and nothing about our marriage, but we have had sex more often than any time since we were twenty-four. It has been nice. I definitely think there is a vital connection between anger and an exciting sex life.

When we got back to the States, I saw a newspaper in the Newark airport with a picture of Dave on the front page glowering at the photographer and trying to stiff-arm him. He had been arrested for fondling a couple of fifteen-year-old girls in his swimming pool at his birthday party and was charged with six counts of sexual assault. I chuckled, but it was a low chuckle, and Julie didn't hear it. We were back two days and a publisher offered me $50,000 for a book about our "desert-island" experience. "Nah," I said, "nothing happened. Worst part was having to go around in a wet bathing suit." Since returning, I have done little except be a help and a support to Dave and Julie and the whole Grebe family. I have been a monster of pity and understanding and quiet strength. I have been there for them every moment in their terrible suffering. Dave sat weeping in our kitchen and told us, "I've been under so much stress, and it was like it was somebody else unfastening those girls' straps, and I was only watching." I said, "Don't feel you have to talk about it." He told me that he didn't know what he would ever do without the strength I gave him in this awful crisis. "It's my pleasure," I said, sincerely.

DON GIOVANNI

Tonight!

Marriage takes too much out of a man, says the old seducer through a cloud of cigarette smoke. Marriage is an enormous drain on a man's time and energy, it produces continual deficits, it reduces him to silliness and servility, it is the deathbed of romance. Figaro, my friend, a man owes it to himself to stop and consider the three advantages of the single life.

One, if you're single, you can think. Two, you can act. Three, you can feel. Probably there are other advantages, but those three surely are important, yes?

Think about it. There is never a substitute for freedom, and there is no prison so deadly as a life of unnecessities, which is what marriage is. A woman takes over a man's life and turns it to her own ends. She heaps up his plate with stones, she fills his bed with anxiety, she destroys his peace so that he hardly remembers it.

But even a married man knows what he should have done. You should find a cheap place to live—who needs a mansion? You put your money in the bank and you furnish your place as you please, with your own junk and great bargains from auctions. You come and go, you eat when you're hungry, you stay up late, you get drunk as it pleases you, and you have two or three terrific lovers who visit when you invite them and stay about the right length of time.

Enjoy yourself. That's what we're here for.

Some men should have two lovers, some three, it depends on the man, said the Don. Never limit yourself to one: monogamy leads to matrimony, and marriage, my boy, is pure struggle. Of course the single life has problems—having two lovers is a scheduling problem, and three is a real test of a man's organizational ability, and yet those are the very problems a man hopes for, Figaro. Living alone in a cushy old apartment with your friendly Jamaican housekeeper coming on Fridays to put a shine on things, the corner laundry delivering clean clothes on Wednesdays, and your girlfriends dropping in on various evenings, each of them crazy about you, anxious to please—you know how accommodating young women can be when they want to be. Think of having three like that at once, their eyes alight at the sight of you, their lips moist, the flush of desire on their cheeks. Sound good? My, yes. The Don smiled at the thought.

"No woman would accept such an arrangement. You would have to lie to her," said Figaro.

Yes, certainly, said the Don.

"To lie to three women at once? To keep inventing stories about where you went? Is that nice?"

The girls who share my bed want to share my life, said the Don, and that would leave me no life at all.

"But to be so selfish—what if everyone were? What if your parents had been?"

I am selfish, Figaro, because I have a larger capacity for pleasure than other people do. Pleasure is only a hobby to them and to me it is a true vocation: the joy of eating a sumptuous meal in the company of a sharp-tongued woman who secretly adores me—who argues with me and ridicules my politics and my ideas, the things I don't care about, and who, in a couple hours, will lie happily next to me, damp and drowsy, smiling, this is to me the beauty of the male existence. As for my parents, what they did wasn't my responsibility.

Figaro had dropped in to see his old friend at the Sportsman's Bar in Fargo, where the Don was engaged for three weeks to play the piano. Figaro had moved to Fargo with Susanna shortly after their marriage, and he had not laid eyes on the Don since he had attempted to seduce Susanna on their wedding night—one of those cases of mistaken identity in dimly lit places, so Figaro bore no grudge.

The Sportsman was an old dive near the Great Northern yards where the switching crews liked to duck in for a bump of whiskey on their coffee breaks. It was not a place you would bring a woman, Figaro thought, and any woman you might find in there you wouldn't want to know better. The little marquee out front said, "BBQ Beef S'Wich $1.95 Happy Hour 4–6 Two Drinks for Price of One D G'vanni in Hunters Lounge Nitely." When Figaro stepped into the gloom, the cloud of beer and smoke and grease, he heard someone playing "Glow Worm," and recognized the Don's florid glissandos, the tremors and trills, the quavers and dips, the big purple chords rising, the mists, the Spanish moss, the grape arbor in the moonlight, the sighs, the throbbing of the thrush. The Don sat all big and glittery at the keyboard in the rear of the deserted room, in an iridescent silver jacket that picked up every speck of light from the sixty-watt spotlight overhead. The silver threads went nicely with the Don's flowing bleached-blonde hair and the gaudy rings on his fingers, chosen for maximum sparkle. Six rings and six chunks of diamond, a ruby-studded bolero tie, a silver satin shirt with pearl buttons, and silver-and-turquoise earrings.

He looked much the worse for wear, Figaro thought, as if he had been living in these clothes for a number of days, including some rainy ones, but he was full of beans, as always. He told Figaro he would soon be back in New York, where a big recording contract was in the offing, a major label, large sums of cash that he was not at liberty to disclose—he rubbed his fingers together to suggest the heavy dough involved—the people were secretive types, *you* understand, said the Don.

"And you? How are you? Have you found a wife yet?" asked Figaro.

The Don laughed. It was their old joke.

Marriage looks very appealing until you are in the company of married people and then the horrors of the institution cry out to you, said the Don. Marriage is for women, Figaro, ugly women. It makes no sense for men. It never did.

The married guy has to have an airtight explanation for everything he does by himself. If he wants to go for a *walk around the block* alone, he has to invent an excuse for not taking his beloved with him. To get up out of his chair and go into the kitchen and run a glass of tap water, he has to announce this to his wife, like a child in the third grade, or else she will say, "Where are you going? To the kitchen? For a glass of tap water? Fine. Why can't you say so? Why do you *always just wander away without saying a word?* You wouldn't treat anybody else that way. How do I know if you're going to the kitchen or going to New Orleans for a week? And it would've been nice if you'd offered to bring *me* something from the kitchen. If you loved me, you'd think of these things. But no. You just get up and walk away. I could be sitting here dying and you'd never notice." And then she bursts into tears, grieving for herself and her future death. This is marriage, Figaro.

A single guy can walk around without explaining it

to anyone. He can also go to New Orleans. This gives a man a dignified feeling, knowing that you could, if you wanted to, drive somewhere. Or drive *nowhere,* just cruise around with the top down soaking up rays and laying down rubber. Married guys can't go nowhere. There always has to be a plan, a list of errands, a system, a destination. Alone, your life is intuitive, like poetry. With a woman, it's a form of bookkeeping.

"So—how long are you in town?" asked Figaro, trying to change the subject, but the Don had more to say.

A home belongs to the oldest woman inhabitant, no matter what. Every day, a man has to get her permission to come in, to use the toilet, to draw oxygen from the air, to keep his things in the closet. The permission is always conditional, and some of her rules are never explained: some secret rules (No Loitering, No Unnecessary Conversation, No Putting Things There, No Whistling, No Guests, We Reserve the Right to Change the Terms of This Agreement) are kept for emergencies.

And a married guy is responsible for *everything,* no matter what. Women, thanks to their having been oppressed all these years, are blameless, free as birds, and all the dirt they do is the result of premenstrual syndrome or postmenstrual stress or menopause or emotional disempowerment by their fathers or low expectations by their teachers or latent unspoken sexual harassment in the workplace, or some other airy excuse.

The guy alone is responsible for every day of marriage that is less than marvelous and meaningful.

"Why don't we ever make love anymore?" That is the No. 2 all-time woman's question in the world. No. 1 is: "Why don't we ever talk to each other?" Now, there's a great conversational opener. You're ensconced on the couch, perusing the funny papers, sipping your hot toddy, feeling mellow and beloved, and she plops down full of anger and premenstrual uproar, and says, "Why don't we ever talk to each other? Why do you treat me as if I don't exist?"

You take her hand. "What do you want to talk about, my beloved?"

"You and your utter lack of interest in communicating with me, that's what," she snaps, yanking her hand back.

"My love, light of my life, my interest in you is as vast as the Great Plains. Please. Share with me what is in your heart so that we may draw close in the great duet of matrimony."

But she didn't want to converse, of course, she only meant to strike a blow. "Humph," she says, standing up. "I know you. You are only saying that."

That is marriage, Figaro. A boy's constant struggle to maintain his buoyancy.

"Some of what you say, I suppose, is true," said Figaro, "but a guy needs a wife, someone who cares if you've collapsed in the shower with your leg broken."

Well, your chances of collapsing in the shower are

sharply improved by being married, the Don said. Helpless rage is a major cause of falls in the home.

No, marriage is a disaster for a man, it cuts him up and broils his spirit piece by piece, until there is nothing left of him but the hair and the harness.

An unhappy man with heavy eyelids appeared in the doorway to the Lounge, hands on hips, chewing a mouthful of peanuts. He appeared to be an owner or manager of some sort. "You on a break right now, Giovanni? Or is the piano busted?"

The Don turned with the greatest disdain and said, "Oh. Cy. I *thought* it was you."

"I hired you as a piano player, Giovanni, not a philosopher. I'd like to hear less thinking and more tinkling. A word to the wise." The man turned and disappeared.

The Don looked down at the keyboard, plunked a couple notes, got up from the bench, and motioned to a table in the corner. "We can sit there," he said.

"A life without a woman is the lonesomest life I can imagine," Figaro said with a sigh. "I would be miserable without Susanna."

Life *is* lonesome, said the Don, and lonesome isn't bad, compared to desperate. But of course a man should not live without women. Luckily, marriage is not a requirement. Nobody needs monogamy except the unenterprising. Hungry women are everywhere! Lonely housewives who advertise on recipe cards pinned to a bulletin board in the Piggly-Wiggly—wistful ladies at the copier, putting flesh to glass, faxing themselves to faroff officedom—fervid women sending out E-mail invites—hearty gals working out on the weight machine who drop a note in your street shoes—cocktail joints along the freeway, wall-to-wall with women whose lights are on and motors are running!—Figaro, they're out there! Free. No legal contract required. What could be better?

Figaro shook his head. "The life of a libertine ends badly," he said. "You get old, your teeth turn yellow, you smell like a mutt, and you have to pay women to look at you. Much better to marry, to be faithful, to build a deeper partnership that will hold together through the terrible storms of old age."

My dear Figaro, seduction is an art, to be learned, practiced, adapted, and improvised according to the situation, and, like other arts, it will not desert you late in life.

"Seduction is a lie, and as we get older, we get tired of lies," said Figaro. "We know them all and they're not amusing anymore."

Seduction is a sweet story, and if the listener wants so much to hear it, then it is no lie. Seduction is a mutual endeavor in which I conspire with a woman to give her an opening to do what she wants to do without reminding her that this goes against her principles. A woman's principles and her desires are constantly at war, and if there were no one to seduce a woman, she would have to figure out how to do it herself. Her principles call for her to remain aloof and uninterested until she meets a man who makes her faint. Her desires are otherwise. She wants to say, "That man, there. Unwrap him and send him over here so he can love me." She cannot say this. So I try to help her. I say, *Zerlina, I would like to hold your hand for two minutes and then you can shoot me and I will die a happy man.*

She laughs, but she does not turn away. She rolls her eyes. She says, "Oh, phoo." She gives me her hand.

I say: *The greatest tragedy is to be cut off from intimacy, from touch, which is the most human of languages, Zerlina, and the most honest. There is no lie in a touch, a caress, never. The language of the body is a language of the purest truth.*

She is amused. I put my other hand on her shoulder. She turns and leans against me. "You're something," she says.

Zerlina, I say, *there's a bottle of champagne waiting on ice at the Olympia Hotel, and a couple dozen oysters. When we get there, we'll order up a big salad in a wooden bowl, with basil and spinach and fennel and cilantro and radicchio, and we'll have it with olive oil and vinegar and pepper and garlic. Then a steak tartare, with chopped onions and an egg yolk. And then we'll undress quickly without shame, as adults, and jump into the big bed and amuse each other as only adults can do. And afterward, we'll eat an omelet. And then do it again.*

Her hand twitches in mine, and I guess that I have touched a chord—"This is the best time of year for oysters," I say in a low voice, "and one should never eat them without erotic plans for later."

She tells me to be real, but even so, she is reaching for her purse, putting on her coat, checking her lipstick. "You're outrageous," she says, and now we are almost to the hotel, and then in the room, she says, "I can't believe I'm actually doing this." But she is. She is. A wonderful occasion, Figaro. The sort of evening that someday, as you lie dying, you will remember and it will bring a smile to your lips.

"You *slept* with her? Zerlina? But she is married to Maseppo," said Figaro. "I can't believe this!"

I may have slept with her, I may not have slept with her, I only mention her as an example. Zerlina, Marilyn, Marlene—what's the difference? A *woman.*

"Having an affair is not the same as marital happiness," said Figaro.

You are right. Marital happiness is briefer and it has a sword hanging over its head. The happiness in marriage is fitful, occasional. It is the pleasure one gets from the absence of the pain of not conforming exactly to the wishes of your wife. A married man walks into the room and his wife looks up and smiles—he is dressed and groomed exactly as she has trained him, his gait is perfect, his personality is champion quality, and he is prepared to converse on topics of her liking, a neat trick it took her years to teach him—and for the duration of her smile, he is happy. But her smile is brief. She spots the flaw: the spiritual emptiness in his eye. She has warned him against emptiness, but there it is. "Why are you looking at me like that?" she hisses. "You look as dim as a dodo." And his happiness is now over for a while. He must think of a way to fill up his spirit.

The man with the heavy eyelids reappeared in the door, an envelope in his hand. "Time to go, Giovanni," he said, setting his big hand on the table. "Yer outta here. You broke the deal. Yer history. The job's over. Move it."

The Don sneered. What a relief to get out of this mausoleum, he said. I am, he said, the greatest romantic pianist of all time. But a romantic pianist in Fargo is like an All-Star shortstop in Paris. Not a priority item.

"Go to hell," said the man, and he stamped his foot on the floor. Figaro looked down. The man had hooves instead of shoes.

The Don stood up. *Gladly,* he said, *it would be better than looking at your ugly face.*

The man strode to the back door by the piano and opened it, and Figaro saw the orange glow of flames in the basement, fingers of flame licking the doorsill.

"Stop!" he cried. "No! Giovanni! Repent!" He took the Don by the arm. "It's not too late. *Repent!*"

The Don put a hand on Figaro's shoulder. "Believe me," he said, "it's easier simply to go. And compared to marriage, it isn't that bad. Farewell, *mon ami.*" And he took off his great silver jacket and gave it to Figaro and walked to the stairs, put his hands on the door frame, and then, with a mighty cry, plunged down into the fiery abyss.

"Your hair smells of smoke," Susanna said to Figaro when he arrived home. "Where were you? In a bar? You stopped in a bar on your way home? I thought you had outgrown that, darling. And what are you going to do with that hideous jacket? My gosh. You can put it in the garage. It reeks of shellfish. I don't want it in the house. Go on. Take it out of here."

So he did. He put the silver jacket on a hanger and hung it on a nail next to the rakes and shovels, and it stayed there for years. Twice she threw it in the trash and twice he retrieved it.

ROY BRADLEY,
BOY BROADCASTER

I t's your broken heart that qualifies a man for broadcasting, but of course Roy Bradley couldn't know that, growing up in Piscacatawamaquoddy-moggin, a scallop-fishing village on the rock-swept coast of Maine. He had aimed toward a radio-broadcasting career ever since he won the Maine Pronouncing Bee in 1952, when he was ten. Radio seemed to be in the cards for him all right. He was pleasant and kind and even hard words like "sagacious" and "hermaphrymnotic" tumbled off his tongue like drops from a faucet. Clear enunciation was a skill prized by most Piscacatawamaquoddy-mogginites, who considered themselves the finest speakers of English on the Eastern Seaboard. "People in Bangor talk like they were choking on potatoes," said Roy's mother, a schoolteacher.

When he was thirteen, Roy joined the Boys' Broadcasting Club, Box 1421, New York City, and quickly rose to the rank of Golden Tone. The registration form was on the back of every jar of Pebble Beach Brand Peach Preserves, but only boys who had "demonstrated a superior aptitude for effective, correct, and pleasant speech, distinguished by correct pronunciation and natural inflection" qualified for advancement, and Roy wore his gold medallion with the *BBC* emblazoned above the silver lightning stroke proudly.

The BBC Handbook contained The Boy Broadcaster Oath ("I swear to be of service to others, to prefer that which is wholesome and pure, and to speak the truth at all times, except when it might compromise national security") and The Boy Broadcaster Law—"A Broadcaster is always punctual, well prepared, friendly, in control of his emotions, attentive to women and children, alert, law-abiding, loyal, helpful, obedient, clean and neat of dress, and adept at radio sign language." And there was a "Reflection on Radio" by the BBC Chaplain W. Ranston Leed:

Always live your life as if each moment were being broadcast to a large unseen audience of your family and friends. When you speak, imagine that your mom is listening—invisible to your companions but known to you. Imagine that your grandma and grandpa are sitting and watching your every deed.

That is what we mean when we say, "Broadcasting Is the Key to the Good Life."

It was the mid-fifties and radio shows were dying every week: Jack Benny, Bob Hope, Fibber McGee & Molly, Amos & Andy, George & Gracie—all fled to television, leaving nothing on Roy's big Atwater-Kling receiver except the afternoon serials on WBE, Bangor, such as *Dean Davis, Teen Investigator*, and *Florence Beebe, Chow Pilot*, sponsored by Johnson Frosted Chocolate Cherries, the story of a brave aviatrix who flies the uncharted Yukon territory, bringing wholesome well-balanced meals to lonely trappers, and Roy's favorite show, *Avis Burnham, Frontier Librarian*, sponsored by Thompson Tooth Tinsel for brighter, more festive teeth, and by Drexel, makers of Durite.

Avis was a woman who brought learning and beauty to the lawless towns on the Kansas frontier: she was beautiful, indomitable, physically fearless, standing up to the cowhands and sheepherders who tried to break the strict code of library borrowing. Avis was Roy's ideal. The men on the Kansas frontier were surly, often violent, inarticulate, liable to fall to pieces, but she was a gem, that Avis, wisecracking, tough, and yet with a heart of gold. Roy knew that if he ever met Avis, they would be friends.

Roy's only true friend in Piscacatawamaquoddymoggin was his girlfriend, Royell Dobbs. They had been pals since first grade, and when he and she were sixteen, they became secretly engaged and exchanged rings, a big relief to Roy, who was afraid he would grow up to be old and eccentric like Bobo Doodad, a scallopman who lived in a run-down bungalow with his sad wife, Sandy, and walked around town talking to himself. Royell was small and beaky, with limp black hair, a tiny torso, and big-mama hips, and some boys called her "Squeaky" for her tiny piercing voice. Nevertheless, it was good to have these things settled. He would marry her, and save himself trouble. When you go into radio, you have to devote yourself, you can't be messing around with women. And Royell's cousin was in radio, Brad Beale, the Voice of the Bangor Buffaloes, on WBE. So she understood the uncertainties of the profession.

Roy's dad was dead set against him going into radio. Doc Bradley had been a successful radio playwright, then a serious and unsuccessful one, and he had come to see that ambition is but vanity. Anyone could be happy if they simply put on hip waders and stood in the crash and tremor of the sea, breathing the raw salt air, and cast into the surf for bluefish and lived a simple commonsense life, doing what needs to be done, including making yourself happy, he believed. The Bradleys' ramshackle house stood on a sandy bluff above a vast curve of stony beach. Doc lived off his annuities, lived a low-maintenance life, fished whenever the temperature was above freezing, and every Friday night he fried up a mess of fresh scallops and opened a bucket of Old Marblehead beer and got down his ukulele and sang:

There is a place where I'm longing to be,
Back in the state of Maine.
Where the wind and clouds seem to beckon me
Through the driving rain.
When I'm tired of downtown noise
I stand up and tell the boys:
"Let's grab our hats and use our noggin
And go back to Piscacatawamaquoddymoggin."

Doc Bradley told Roy, "You're no more cut out for radio than I am to do brain surgery. Ambition is not conducive to happiness, son. To be successful in radio, a man has to live in the city and learn to cheat and lie. We Bradleys are not New Yorkers. We don't think that way. Here in Piscacatawamaquoddymoggin, a Bradley can breathe fresh air—in New York, you inhale and get air that's been breathed and exhaled by three other people and gone through a diesel engine and in and out of a Greek restaurant and through a taxi with a whore in it smoking a cigarette and wearing a turgid cologne and through a fleabag hotel where old shoe salesmen lie around in pee-stained shorts and cut some ripe ones and then you get to breathe it for a while, and when you're so far down on the air chain, it makes you as crazy as a rat in a coffee can. You lie and cheat so you can get out. Well—*you're out already. You were born in the place New Yorkers would kill to be from. You're here! You've reached your goal without knowing it!*

"You'll never be happy anywhere but here, Roy."

That sentence rang in Roy's head as he plowed

through the grades at Piscacatawamaquoddymoggin High and was elected president of the Audio-Visual Club, and was chosen to operate the public-address system at all school events. His mother encouraged him to aim for a radio career. "I would be so disappointed if you stayed in this town and became a bum like your father," she told him.

Roy graduated in 1960, winner of the Ruth W. Clarion Memorial Enunciation Scholarship (thirty-five dollars), and spent the summer operating a roadside fresh-bait stand. Doc lent him money to get started and to purchase a large leghorn hen trained to shell a peanut in two seconds. Roy put up a sign on the road, "See the Chicken Shell a Peanut—500 yds. Bait for Sale," and he was amazed at the number of cars that pulled over and paid a nickel to see a chicken do that. *Most of them also bought bait,* although they didn't appear to be fishermen. They appeared to be city slickers out for a drive. *They wanted to see the chicken but they didn't want to appear interested only in the chicken.* So they strolled in and bought bait and then glanced at the chicken and said, "Oh, is that the chicken who shells peanuts?" Yes, said Roy, want to see him do it? And the people shrugged and said, "Well, as long as we're here, I suppose we may as well." And the chicken shelled the peanut, the people drove off, and down the road a ways, they heaved the bait out of the window.

Roy felt he had made a great discovery: the secret of marketing. He trained the chicken to do pistachios also, and then installed a hotplate under the floor of the cage and advertised "See the Dancing Nut-Shucking Chicken—500 yards—Bait for Sale."

"When are you going to do something about radio?" his mother inquired in November.

"I have sent off dozens of applications. I'm waiting for word," he said, testily.

"You don't get anywhere waiting. Your father is proof of that."

"All things come to him who waits," he reminded her.

"God helps those who help themselves," she added.

What she didn't know was that he was salting away money, thanks to the chicken, and could afford tuition at the best radio schools, whenever he felt ready.

Royell was wondering when the marriage would take place. She had found work as a babysitter, but had plenty of time to hang around and pester him with queries. When is the wedding, where would they live, what style of silverware should they have, modern or antique, and white or colored sheets and pillowcases? Did he like wicker chairs, and should they be dark green or white? The china pattern: traditional or contemporary? Aluminum or cast-iron cookware?

"You decide all that," he said. "I don't plan on being home all that much."

"I want you to be happy," she said.

He did not know how to tell her that he was now about as happy as he knew how to be. He was happy enough.

Of course he would marry her. A broadcaster does not

lie. But he was noticing that fifteen minutes a day of Royell was enough for him, thirty at most.

Then, one night, the chicken suffered a stroke. The corn Roy fed it was seed corn, treated with mercury. The chicken had to be put to sleep. Bait sales fell off and Roy closed the stand. He got a job as cabin boy on the Piscacatawamaquoddymoggin Packet, which carried salt and nails and whiskey and roofing to the coastal islands, and then Roy got seasick; he went to work at the Piscacatawamaquoddymoggin Puzzle Plant, working the jigsaw, making the curvy lines through the Winslow Homer seascapes, cutting through the big waves pounding the rocks, carving out the five thousand pieces. One puzzle per day—cutting it in the morning, a break for lunch, and assembling it in the afternoon.

"What happened to your wonderful dream of radio?" his mother asked him pointedly one night as she and Roy and Royell ate supper. Doc was out fishing.

Radio had changed, he explained. He had hoped to become a radio news analyst, only to find out that the age of news analysis was over—newscasts were now three minutes long, interrupted every twenty seconds by a half-minute commercial for a hemorrhoid cream, a pimple pump, an enema pack you could carry around in your pocket. What should he do? be a shill for a lot of junk he'd be ashamed to be associated with?

"There's public radio," she said.

He shook his head. "Public radio, it's nothing but a cult, like Christian Science—it denies the reality of human nature. Public radio believes that if everyone only wore sensible shoes, there'd be no more suffering. Crazy."

Roy sighed. "There's no place in radio for an honest man," he said sadly.

"Why not talk to my cousin Brad Beale?" said Royell.

Brad often drove up to Piscatawamaquoddymoggin in his red T-bird with a beautiful babe named Sugar to pick up fresh scallops and stroll along Main Street wearing his mirror shades and a snappy white beach outfit and be admired by the locals. Roy had always been too shy to approach him, and *The BBC Handbook* made it clear—"Never impose on the privacy of a famous man in order to gain a personal advantage."

Brad was visiting for Thanksgiving, Royell said. "You could come over for dessert," she told Roy. "He is a nice person, not at all stuck up."

"Okay," said Roy. Secretly, he wondered if Brad could introduce him to Avis Burnham, the frontier librarian, a WBE star whom Roy kept a picture of in his sock drawer, a snapshot from *Radio Mirror* magazine of a slender shadowy woman with bobbed hair and a cool lopsided smile.

And on Thanksgiving Day, there he was, sitting down at the Dobbs table next to Royell, across from Brad Beale, a real *radio man.*

Royell didn't wait a moment. "This is my fiancé, Roy, Brad—he is a broadcaster himself, or will be as soon as he finds a job. Do you know of any openings for a real steady worker?" Roy blushed.

Royell's dad cleared his throat. "Some say that radio is on the way out," he noted.

Brad said he would gladly inquire about openings at WBE and put in a good word for Ray if an opening came up.

"Roy," said Royell.

Later, Roy cornered Brad by the refrigerator and obtained not only Avis Burnham's address—Number 7J, Dalemoor Apartments, Bangor—but also her home telephone number. "Her real name is Montana Montez," said Brad. "Mexican." He winked.

Roy kept the number in his billfold for three days. *The BBC Handbook* was rather definite on this point: "Never phone radio celebrities at their homes," it said. "Radio is a strenuous life, and broadcasters require relaxation and rest. Unsolicited phone calls, well meaning as they may be, are a drain on their energies. If you should ever come into possession of a radio star's private phone number, destroy it immediately so that it can't fall into the wrong hands."

But Roy needed the company of an older and wiser woman. Royell was trying to hurry along the marriage by luring him into compromising situations. She lay in his arms on the Bradleys' basement couch and planted hot kisses on him, stroked the front of his pants, unbuttoned her blouse, placed his hand on her breast. Her breast felt small and damp. "Not yet," he said, "not yet."

"When?" she whispered.

"When I get into radio and get settled in a long-term position."

"Sometimes I wonder if you really love me, Roy Bradley," she said, putting her breast back into its hammock.

That evening, Roy slipped over to the Cape Hope Cafe and dialed Avis's number from the pay phone in the foyer.

Five rings, his heart pounding, and then a click, and a deep female voice said, "Yeah? Who's this? What you want?"

Roy let out his breath. He said, "My name is Roy Bradley and I'm calling from Piscacatawamaquoddy-moggin. You ask, who am I? and I suppose to you I'm only a fan, and yet I think I truly know you, Miss Montez. At least, I'd like you to give me that chance."

There was a long pause, and then she laughed. "Well, ain't you something!"

She laughed again and Roy heard the tinkle of ice in a glass. "I'm in no shape to meet anybody at the moment," she said. "I'm standing by the window in nothing but a dirty silk chemise, one strap falling loose over my shoulder, my lipstick smudged, a glass of Coke and bourbon in my hand, watching a green neon EAT sign flash on and off across a deserted street, and weeping like a teenage shopgirl because my lover, Leo Wynn, phoned about fifteen minutes ago and told me he forgot that this is his bowling night and he ain't coming. Do you believe that, Mr. Bradley?"

Roy had to admit that he didn't. It was Sunday and no bowling league in the world conducted scheduled matches on Sunday nights.

She took a drag on a cigarette. "I'm a *woman,* Roy. And women have needs too."

"I'd like to be there with you now. It would be entirely up to you, of course, but I would like to be."

"What would you like to do if you were here, Roy?"

His hand shook and he had to brace it against the wall, but his voice was calm. "I'd like to remove that dirty silk chemise, strap by strap, and hold you close to me. I'd like to take the glass and the cigarette and put them on the bedside table and kiss you. I'd like to do anything you'd want me to do."

Just then, there was a knock on her door. She excused herself and set down the phone. The door opened. Somebody came into the room. "Hi," she said softly, and then Roy could hear the unmistakable silence of a close embrace. The embrace went on and on, a long long kiss, and the glass fell to the floor and shattered and the ice skittered across the floor. Then there were footsteps, one pair, and the creaking of bedsprings. She moaned. Roy could hear the silk chemise lifted from her body. Whoever it was had a little trouble unfastening the strap. Then a jacket hit the floor, then shoes, then a belt and holster and a gun, then a pair of pants with change and keys in the pockets, then a pair of boxer shorts. The mystery lover did not remove his socks, Roy noted. Then the springs creaked again. "Oh," she said. "Oh yes. Oh darling." The bed began to rock and Avis moaned and finally Roy put the telephone receiver back on the hook and hiked home.

Avis was off the air the next day. In her place was

Karen Comfort, Front Line Nurse, sponsored by L'Amour Brand Nougat and Macaroons—"the story of a beautiful woman torn between the needs of others and . . . the hunger in her own heart"—had Avis been canceled?

He went to the Cape Hope Cafe and called her, and her number was busy. He sat at the counter and ordered a coffee. "You still at the puzzle plant?" asked Sandy Doodad, the waitress. "People say you're going to be leaving Piscacatawamaquoddymoggin, Roy." She was sweet on him, though she was married to Bobo.

"That's correct," said Roy. "I'll be leaving soon, perhaps next week." This astonished him, his saying it out loud before he had even thought it.

Poor Sandy. Married to a Doodad, living in a dumpy yellow bungalow with a yardful of trash and two nasty dogs who bit children and other dogs.

He dialed Avis's number again and she answered, her voice hollow with fatigue.

"What's wrong, Montana?" he asked.

"Oh, you don't have time to listen to my troubles, Roy, you're young, you have your whole life ahead of you," she said. "My life is over. I just can't see that there's any good in people. They all seem pretty rotten and low-down to me. I don't know why I'm still living."

"Don't talk like that," he said.

"Roy, I'm thirty-four. I'm too old to start over. I want a regular fellow. I'm sick of used furniture, Roy. This radio life is nothing but a cheat. My heart has been broke so many times it won't ever be normal again." She sobbed into the phone, and Roy began to feel weepy too.

"I'll come to you tonight," he said. "I'll come and I'll never leave you, Montana. I promise."

"It's too late, Roy," she said. And then she hung up. When he called back, her line was busy. Off the hook, he figured. He ran home, fished a twenty out of his cash jar, and caught the last bus to Bangor, arriving at two a.m., and dashed to the Dalemoor Apartments and rang her buzzer. No answer. He buzzed again and again. He knocked, and the door slowly swung in to reveal an empty room, dusty, and a day bed, coverless, and a hotplate and a kettle of cold beans with marshmallows in them, and a wall calendar with a photo of a Vermont winter scene, a cheap nightstand with a gooseneck lamp (no bulb) and a black ashtray containing four butts with lipstick smudges. Roy held one to his lips.

Royell was anxious as Christmas approached. "We could scoot up to New Hampshire and get hitched by a justice of the peace," she said. "No need for a big hullabaloo. I'll keep my babysitting job, and you can quit at the puzzle plant and look for a position in broadcasting."

"I'll think about it," said Roy.

"We've been thinking about it for years," she pointed out. "I don't think that thinking is what we need to do. Doing is what we need to do. That's what I think." She cried, "What more does a person need than someone to love them and a couple grand in the bank?" She was starting to notice her classmates' pictures in the Piscacatawamaquoddymoggin *Pilot*, slender and radiant brides on the arms of earnest and sincere young husbands. "Why should we wait until we're old to start living?" she told Roy.

"What's wrong with me that I can't get started in life?" Roy asked his dad one morning over breakfast, waffles with maple syrup oozing from the pores. "One day I want to be a broadcaster and the next day I don't."

"Radio is not your métier," Doc said. "You're a fisherman, and you don't realize it yet, that's all."

Roy shook his head. "I'm almost nineteen and I'm still living at home."

That day he consulted a local career counselor named Aadlund who also sold trailer hitches and motorized TV antennas. He gave Roy a test, which consisted of stirring water in a basin. "The patterns of stirring show a lot about you," he told Roy. He watched Roy stir for a while and suggested barbering.

Barbering, he explained, is like broadcasting, except that the announcer stands behind the listener and snips his hair. "There's an opening for a barber in Smallton, just up the pike. The one they had went berserk a week ago, and the shop is for sale cheap. My cousin is the real-estate agent. He's particular about who it goes to, but I'll put in a good word."

Roy had not been to Smallton since he was eleven and attended the Smallton Swine Exposition. He remembered the pigs screeching as their owners whacked them with canes, trying to steer them up chutes. Smallton was inland, populated by farmers, a torpid breed. On the other hand, the puzzle plant was not thriving—sales of puzzles of seascapes had declined with the advent of television—and it was rumored to be on the verge of shutting down. And Royell was breathing harder and harder down his neck. She called four times a day, she dropped in to talk, she wanted to go driving, she wanted to take her clothes off.

"I'm an old-fashioned guy. I don't take advantage of women," he told her when she hoisted her skirt to show him a small bruise on her thigh.

"It's not taking advantage if the woman offers," she said.

So he decided to buy the barbershop, using the two thousand dollars in bait shop profits as a down payment, and learn to cut hair. Royell offered to come along as a manicurist, but he said Smallton was not a manicure town. "We'll save up our money, get married, find a radio job, and settle down," he told her. "You see if it doesn't happen just that way."

She made him make love to her one night while her parents were at bingo. It was better than he thought it would be. "You're getting me all hot and bothered," he said, panting, groping around with his tongue. "You see?" she said. "It's better in bed with all your clothes off, isn't it." He groaned and moaned and slid around until his body was slick with sweat and he thought his heart would burst like a milkweed pod. He lost his mind for a moment and his voice went high and warbly.

"It's good, isn't it," she cried, as he lay back, trembling, his ammunition spent, his cannon crew exhausted. "You see what marriage could do for you? It could make you smile, Roy Bradley."

He went to Smallton and took over the barbershop the next day. It was a drafty one-room storefront with four chairs, green beadboard paneling, big prints of hunting dogs, and a plate-glass window that looked out on an empty street, a vacant lot, and Bud's Pamphlet & Magazine Rental, which seemed to be mainly in the porno business. There was a picture of a woman in the front window unzipping her leather bodice. She looked much as Roy had imagined Avis.

The barber, whose name was Poodles, sat in one of the shop's two chairs, crooning to himself, rocking, jiggling his right foot. He was pudgy and pink and nicely dressed for a lunatic. Mr. Aadlund's cousin the agent was with him. "Take it easy, honey," he told the barber. "You'll get your burger in a jiffy. And then we'll go home and watch *Sea Hunt.*"

"Here's the clipper," he said to Roy. "The combs are in the alcohol jar. The thing to remember about haircuts is, if it don't look good at first, keep trying and eventually it will come out right. And if it don't, then it'll grow back. So don't be afraid to cut. There's no permanent loss with a haircut."

The two of them helped the barber to his feet and out the door to the car, a late-model Eldorado. "Poodles here was a heck of a barber in his day, but he took the work too seriously," the agent said. "Don't you make that mistake. Enjoy!"

There were fourteen regular customers, Roy learned,

all of whom wanted a little off the top and not too short on the sides. It took weeks for their hair to grow out, and Roy passed the time reading some of Bud's rental pornographic materials so as to have interesting remarks to make on a range of topics, but it soon dawned on him that barbering was a long stretch of sameness: same haircuts, same talcum, same talk. Sometimes, a customer would carry on both sides of the conversation by himself. "So—how you been?" he'd say. "Well, can't complain," he'd reply. "Yourself? *I've been worse. Looks cloudy.* Yessir. Looks like we might get some rain. *Looks like it, all right.* Should be good for fishin'. *I heard someone say they were biting pretty good out around the sewage outlet.* Izzat right? *Yeah, I heard a couple guys got their limits.* Huh. Well, isn't that something. *You can say that again.*" Roy slept sixteen hours a day, and summer passed quickly, and the fall.

One day, noticing that his own hair was a mite long, Roy asked Bud for a trim, not too short, and Bud said, "Sure, no problem," and he took the scissors in hand and snip-snip-snipped while talking Roy's ear off about a favorite brochure of his in which fat girls wrestled in a vat of cream-of-celery soup, and ten minutes later, Roy's head looked like a used-carpet remnant. "How do you like it?" asked Bud. "I think *like* would be too strong a word," murmured Roy.

He locked the door, pulled the CLOSED shade, turned out the lights, and lay on the floor with his knees drawn up to his chin. He remained in seclusion for days, overwhelmed by waves of sadness. "You are no good," he thought. "No good to yourself or anyone else. Not worth the powder to blow you to hell." The haircut seemed to bear this out. "You will never amount to anything and certainly not in broadcasting."

He put on a knit cap and came home to Piscacatawamaquoddymoggin for Thanksgiving and found everyone in a grumpy mood. The puzzle factory had closed, and the demand for scallops was down due to traces of deadly aluminum found in a frozen dinner and the media had stressed the worst aspects of aluminum poisoning (dementia, drooling, lack of bladder control, facial collapse, etc.) and suddenly nobody in America would touch a scallop with a ten-foot pole. So the town was on the brink of disaster.

Royell told Roy, sobbing, that her job as a babysitter had come to an end. She had gotten so engrossed in a Stephen King book, the one in which a pet cat chews the throats of a family of six as they sleep and then drives away in the family car, that she hadn't noticed the children she was providing care for had shinnied up the cold-air vent and into a crawl space in the ceiling. The fire department came and cut a hole in the roof with a chainsaw and pried the kids loose with big pincers but then a cloud of asbestos fell out too, and now the kids were under observation in a Bangor hospital and Royell was getting registered letters from the law firm of Batter, Ravage, Pound & Payne.

Roy sympathized, but the bad haircut was on his mind. Big tufts of hair poked out from under the cap.

"I guess nobody notices that I'm wearing a knit cap on account of a hair problem," Roy grumbled.

"Let me have a look, darling," said Roy's mom. "Oh, it'll grow out," she said. "In six months or a year, you won't notice a thing wrong with it. Except maybe the back."

She told him to stop thinking about himself and start paying attention to his responsibilities. "You're going to have a family," she told Roy, "so wake up and smell the coffee."

"Family?" said Roy.

"Royell is three months pregnant," said Mom. "You didn't know?"

Royell came to Thanksgiving dinner, and she looked big in front. Roy embraced her, felt the hard knot in her belly, and her breasts poked him in the chest like accusing fingers. "We'll name him Roy Jr.," she cried. "And we'll roost right here in Piscacatawamaquoddymoggin! And to hell with radio. Who needs it."

Doc Bradley was late for dinner—he had been out fishing, and forgot—and the turkey was dry and mealy. They ate in silence. Roy went to the bathroom to put water on his hair, and when he returned to the table, he got both pants pockets caught on the arms of the chair and ripped them, his best corduroys. "That happened to me once too," said Doc glumly. Royell mentioned that the lawsuits from the crawl-space incident might total as much as eleven million dollars. "If it goes to a jury, they'll take one look at those little snots, and I'll spend the rest of my life on earth paying money into a fund.

My baby will have to work for a living, but those rotten brats will go through graduate school on my money."

They were almost finished with dinner when Mom's cat, Ernie, began choking to death under the table. Mom snatched him up in a flash though he was hefty, a thirty-pounder. He had swallowed a wad of dressing and lay limp in Mom's arms. Roy suggested opening up the cat's trachea with a steak knife, but Mom leaned down and sucked the dressing out of Ernie's throat. It made a sickening sound. The cat soon was resting comfortably, but Mom went upstairs and was ill for the next hour or so. Doc went to check on her and reported back that she wished everyone to leave quietly and she would be happy to see them for Christmas.

Roy walked Royell home through the thick fog that had rolled in from the sea. He told her that his life had been put on hold by his hair. "I can't get married looking like this."

"You're probably right," said Royell. He was surprised by her nonchalance. "You're not disappointed?" he said. "You know what's best," she told him.

Roy wasn't inside the Dobbs home ten minutes before Royell's dad asked, "Whatever happened to your dream of radio?" from deep in his BarcaLounger.

Roy said he was saving to attend broadcasting college, perhaps the LaRue School in West Bend, Indiana, which offered lessons by mail.

Dad Dobbs humphed. "Why not just call up my nephew Brad?" he said. "Brad left WBE and is president of Beale Broadcasting. Owns stations in Syracuse,

Scranton, Erie, Joliet, Racine, Duluth, and Sandpoint, Idaho. You want a job, he could give you one in a minute, I'll bet."

Royell saw Roy off on the bus to Smallton. It was confusing. She didn't hang on him like before. Roy explained that he might not return before the baby was born, and she said, "Oh, that's okay. No skin off my nose."

He said, "I'll do the right thing by you, don't worry about that."

"The right thing?" She laughed. "Who even knows what that is anymore?"

Back in Smallton, sitting in the barber chair waiting for a customer, Roy wrote a song on the back of his electric bill:

> You look into the bank of mirrors
> And realize your deepest fears:
> It's all gone, your charm and grace.
> There's nothing but this foolish face.
> This hair looks so dumb—disastrous!
> You'll have to move out to Nebraska,
> Live alone in some sod hut
> Recovering from your bad haircut
> While others garner fame and riches,
> The lucky sons of bitches.

It wasn't a bad song. Maybe he should have it recorded. Bud had a cousin in the song-publishing business who might open some doors.

That night, he had a dream in which he floated in a black abyss and then got on a bus. He rode for hours, with no purpose or destination. A luxurious bus with carpet so deep it almost sucked his shoes off. A woman sat across from him who hated him. "I am a disappointment to everyone I know," he told her. She pretended not to hear.

He felt blue for weeks. Christmas was coming, and some students from Smallton High came by to ask if they could paint a Nativity scene on the barbershop window for the Christmas-window contest. "Go to hell," Roy told them. "My life is a mess. You expect me to feel festive?" Once he told a customer to shut up and sit still. The man said he would find a new barber. "Good," said Roy. "I'm tired of looking at you."

And then, a week before Christmas, a big wild man with bloodshot eyes clomped in, grabbed Roy's shoulders, and growled, "Want my hair *wild,* mister. Want it to stick straight up in big clumps. Big hanks of hair with dirt 'n twigs in 'em. I want it matted down in back. And on the sides I want some *snarls.*"

Roy sat the wild man in a chair and did his best. He whirred the hair around with a hairbrush and globbed some syrup on it and tied snarls here and there.

"You from around these parts?" asked Roy.

The wild man snorted. "Am not, never was, and never will be. I'm from a little rat's-ass town called Parnassus, Mississippi. I sang gospel music every Sunday at the Children of Zion Sanctified Apostolic Holiness Four-square Gospel Precious Love of Jesus' Sweet Name

Church until I was fourteen and I got a-messin where I shouldna been a-messin and got a girl in a family way, and then I switched over to the devil's fornicatin music and got to rocking—*hoooo-ee*—playing in roadhouses for wads of money and driving a pink Cadillac full of loose women and living the wild-man life—how you comin with that hair, man?"

The hair looked like it had gone through a sausage grinder, and the wild man whooped and grinned and handed Roy a hundred-dollar bill. "Fifty years from now, mister, you can tell your grandkids you cut the hair of Jimmy Chuck Childs, Wild Man of the Delta," he said, and out he went, to a pink Cadillac. And then he stuck his head back in the barbershop. "Roy Bradley?" he said. "Ain't you a friend of Montana Montez?"

Roy nodded, thrilled to hear her name and his so close together.

"She told me she was looking for you. Went up to some little town near here, town called Piss-something, trying to find you."

Roy dashed out the door and up the street, and caught the noon bus to Piscacatawamaquoddymoggin, and off they went in a cloud of blue smoke.

—The hundred-dollar bill! He had left it lying in the open cash-register drawer! And the door to the barbershop stood wide open! And yet it didn't matter one bit when he thought of Montana.

The bus stopped with a squeal and a hiss. "Piscacatawamaquoddymoggin!" called the driver.

Roy tore up the road toward the motel, taking a shortcut through the Gun Club shooting range and over the ballpark fence and across the outfield and over the dugout and through the parking lot and around the Happy Clam Drive-In, its windows boarded, and up ahead the Cape Hope Cabins and in a window the silhouette of a woman unbuttoning her blouse. Roy came to the door as she reached behind for the clasp of her brassiere.

He opened the door and said, "Here, let me do that," but it wasn't Montana, it was Royell. And there was Bobo Doodad, his big eyes blinking, his bald head on the pillow, his big toes poking out from under the blanket.

"You're messing around with a *Doodad?*" Roy cried. Royell faced him, bare-breasted. "You had yourself a Bradley and you reached for a *Doodad?*"

He turned to the man in the bed. "This woman is practically my wife, for crying out loud! What will you people think of next?"

Royell said, "I tried for years to be your wife, Roy Bradley, and now you got no right to deny me a little pleasure."

Roy strode to the door. "This goes against every principle known to civilized man. This is disgusting. You will never see me in Piscacatawamaquoddymoggin ever again, either of you."

Back at his mom and dad's house, Ernie's dish was piled high with a month's supply of cat chow, and on the cupboard was a note to Sandy Doodad, Bobo's wife, asking her to please not water the plants so much as last time and to make sure the tank float was shut in the upstairs toilet. Sandy did odd jobs for the Bradleys. Roy wrote at the bottom: "P.s., Sandy, yr husband is in the sack with Royell Dobbs, in case he seems grumpy these days."

He picked up the phone and called Brad Beale and poured out his heart. The older man was sympathetic. "Bad hair and your affianced in bed with a Doodad—it's not how a guy imagines life will be, but heck, Roy, why not make the best of it? Bad hair can serve as a passport to places the well-groomed never know. Such as the Midwest, for example. I own a station in Duluth. You could be doing the midnight-to-five-a.m. shift Monday morning if you want. Maybe this is a blessing in disguise, getting you into broadcasting." He said, "If you don't do it now, Roy, you never will."

Roy arrived in Duluth on Sunday, took a room at the Duluth Hotel, and on Monday evening, hiked over to KDU, shook hands with the janitor, and at midnight, turned on the microphone and said, "Mornin, all you hoot owls, this is Big Daddy Bradley with the Blue Loon Ballroom, where the lonely come to forget their all-night blues—*a-wooooooooooooooooooo*—sponsored by Highball, the name to trust in women's undergarments and sleepwear." He played a Sinatra recording of "Bartender" and then Julie London ("Never Without You"), then Tony Bennett ("After You've Gone"), and the Ellington Orchestra playing "Solitude," and then he talked about sleepwear for a couple minutes. Highball made a satin nightgown that would keep you warm and yet make you feel as if you had no clothes on at all. Interesting. Then he played Sinatra's "One for the Road," and Elisabeth Welch singing "When You're Young," and then he talked about Golden Girl transmission fluid for trucks.

Roy had studied *The BBC Handbook*, the chapter on "Late Night" which said, "Speak in a low smooth voice. Don't talk too long. Imply as much as possible," and he did. He could talk about an approaching warm front in a way that made people feel they knew him intimately. They wrote to him, *I've been disappointed by people so often but never by you. You make me feel I could love someone again.*

He sat in the little nest of a studio, so comfy, the mess of news on yellow teletype paper, hundreds of tape cartridges on carousels an arm's length away, a script podium atop the control board, the big foam-covered microphone, the clock, the ring binder thick with commercials, the shelves of LPs close at hand, the three turntables, the stack of tape machines, and from this safe enclosure he spoke in a low voice, implied much, was loyal and punctual, and soon began to draw fan mail, on pale-lilac stationery in scented envelopes, in slanty handwriting with the *i*'s dotted with hearts. "I listen to you every night when I go to bed," they wrote. "It's like you're right there in the room with me. Send me an autographed picture of yourself. Or if you're physically repulsive, autograph a picture of someone good-looking and send me that. Are you married?"

No, he was not, and he never did get married, though

Royell wrote to him and suggested they get hitched. Bobo was out of the picture—he had gone to gargle one morning in the dark and grabbed a bottle of drain cleaner by mistake and the acid ate up his whole body except for the metal hasp on his pajamas. The baby, Roy Jr., was born in May, a big healthy boy. The million-dollar asbestos lawsuit had been thrown out by a jury of Piscacatawamaquoddymogginites who knew the Dobbs family and knew Royell would never harm a flea. "Could you forgive me too?" she asked Roy.

He was earning good money and had found his place in the world, which was the wee hours. *I am single on that show,* thought Roy. *Everyone else in radio talks with the voice of marriage and duty. I speak with the voice of one who eats his dinner at an odd time out of white cardboard containers while standing at the kitchen counter and reading the sports page. People sense this. They recognize it in my voice: a man who keeps his clean socks and shirts on the dining-room table and spreads newspapers on the floors to keep the dust off them.*

Year in, year out, Roy broadcast five nights a week, and it was exactly what people wanted, a familiar voice that didn't tell them too much, didn't hustle, didn't crowd them, that gave them the slack to make him whoever they wanted him to be, and a few years ago the show observed its twenty-fifth anniversary, and KDU presented Roy with a green Thunderbird.

The news from Piscacatawamaquoddymoggin over the years was nothing but dismal. Royell's mom went off in the bushes during a picnic and a swarm of black flies ate her, everything except her yellow anklets, and Royell's brother Ronnie was changing the oil in his Nash Rambler when, for no reason, the engine started and he was quickly sliced into small chunks by the fan. Royell's sister Rhonda was draining the bathtub after her bath and saw tiny people waving at her from inside the bubbles as they swept drainward and then suddenly *she was in a bubble* speeding swiftly toward the black hole of oblivion and then she was in the state asylum for the deranged in Bangor, restrained by canvas straps, wearing a ratty old hospital gown slit up the back so your hinder hung out. Royell's dad caught a pretty big lobster one day near the Cape Hope Spa and hauled it up on shore in a fireman's carry and had it almost to the spa's back door when suddenly it got loose and grabbed him and threw him into the hot tub and pushed him under and cooked him. The coffin at the service was small, the size of an eyeglass case.

"You are all I have left, Roy," wrote Royell. "Don't you think I've suffered enough for my indiscretion? Why not let's get married, what do you say?"

No way, he told her.

He almost got married once, to the Iron Rangerettes, a cowgirl singing group, who came in to do singing commercials for Golden Girl transmission fluid, four beauties who squeezed in close around Roy's microphone, pressing up tight against him with their young firm bodies and their slender thighs so lean and taut from years of farm work, and every night those thighs got tauter and tauter. And, being in show business, they were casual about nudity. A Rangerette'd walk into the studio with her underwear in her hands and her breasts dingle-dangling loose and free and say, cool as a cucumber, "Which bra do you think I should wear tonight, Roy? this one? or this one?" And then they'd be squeezed against him, singing, "Hey trucker, slow that big rig down, / What's your hurry to get to town? / We got all night, just you and me, / I like a man who drives deliberately," and then Roy said, "Golden Girl transmission fluid! Golden Girl is the fluid that really loosens up your truck's transmission, so if your clutch slips or you're losing your grip in the lower gears, try Golden Girl transmission fluid. Isn't that right, girls?"—and they sang, "O Mr. Trucker, you're so smooth and strong, / With Golden Girl fluid you can drive it all night long."

Roy wanted to marry all four of them, but radio was not ready for polygamy, he knew, and rather than ruin a good deal, he remained single. He is still broadcasting "The Blue Loon Ballroom," midnight–five a.m., and you can catch him as you're driving your load of potatoes east from Grand Forks to Duluth on Highway 2, a smooth voice in the night, and even though he doesn't say much, you know that this man has had some bad haircuts in his day and lost a true love or two. This man has come home to empty rooms and confronted Sunday mornings that stretched for weeks. He has wandered the trashy streets at 2 a.m. imagining that happiness might emerge from an alley and take him by the hand. He has known futility and grief in full measure. Heartbreak is what makes the broadcaster. Without it, there is no gravel in your voice, no weight, no twang, and nobody remembers you ten minutes later. Heartbreak is the key to broadcasting success.

GARY KEILLOR

When I was sixteen years old, I stood six feet two inches tall and weighed a hundred and forty pounds. I was intense and had the metabolism of a wolverine. I ate two or three lunches a day and three full dinners at night, as my family sat around the kitchen table and observed, and I cleaned off their plates too when they had poor appetites or were finicky. There was no food I disliked except muskmelon, which smelled rotten and loathsome. Everything else I ate. (It was Minnesota so we didn't have seafood, except fish sticks, of course.) I was a remarkable person. I was a junior in high school, Class of 1960. I was smart, so smart that poor grades didn't bother me in the slightest; I considered them no reflection on my intelligence. I read four books a week, and I sometimes walked home from school, all twelve miles, so I could relive favorite chapters out loud, stride along the shoulder of the highway past the potato farms, and say brilliant and outrageous things, and sing in a big throbbing voice great songs like "Til There Was You" and "Love Me Tender."

I had no wish to sing in front of an audience, songs were a private thing with me. I was an intense person, filled with powerful feelings, and I assumed that I would live alone for the rest of my life, perhaps in a monastery, silent, swishing around in a cassock, my heart broken by a tragic love affair with someone like Natalie Wood, my life dedicated to God.

I was a lucky boy. I had learned this two years before on a car trip to Colorado. My Uncle Earl and Aunt Myrna drove there that summer—he had been stationed in Colorado Springs during the war—along with my cousins Gordon and Mel, and I got to go too. I won that trip by dropping over to their house and being extremely nice. I'd say, "Here, let me wash those dishes." I'd say, "Boy, I'm sure in a mood to mow a lawn." And then she'd offer me a glass of nectar and a piece of angel food cake and I'd eat it and say, "Boy, I was looking at *National Geographic* the other night and they had a big article on Colorado. It was so interesting. Just the different rock formations and things. I don't see how people can look at those mountains and not know there's a God." And she'd smile at me, a good boy who mowed lawns and whose faith was pure, and I got to go. Of course my brothers and sisters were fit to be tied. "How come he gets to go? We never get to go. Oh no, we have to stay here all summer and work in the garden while he goes riding out to Colorado." They just didn't get it. Trips to Colorado don't fall in your lap. You've got to go out and earn Colorado.

We took off on the trip, and I was a very good passenger. I sat in the favored front seat between my aunt and uncle, looking at the scenery for hours, no stains on my clothes, my face clean, a good strong bladder, never got carsick, and had a subtle sideways technique for picking my nose—you'd never see it even if you looked straight at me. Far off, the mountains appeared, shining on the horizon for almost a whole day, and then we rose up into them—snowcapped peaks, like the last scene in a western in which justice and romance prevail, and when we reached Denver (*EL.5280*, the sign said, exactly a mile), we ate dinner at a Chinese restaurant and my fortune cookie said: "You are enterprising—take advantage of it." Well, there it was in a nutshell.

The mountains were startling in their whiteness and steepness, the valleys dark in the late afternoon, the peaks glittering in pure sunlight, beautiful stands of light gray-green aspen floating like fog, and my aunt took a picture of me with trees and mountains behind me. Just me, tall and intense. You would never guess I was from Minnesota. I thought, "This is my lucky picture. I'll keep it the rest of my life."

* * *

My family lived in the country, along the Mississippi River between Minneapolis and Tryon, and I attended New Tryon High School, which was bulging under a tidal wave of children from new subdivisions on the other side of the river, places with names like Riverview Estates and Woodlawn and Forest Hills. Our side, South Tryon Township, along the West River Road, was still rural, truck farms, and scattered houses on big rolling tracts, and we West River Roaders were the cream of the school. The editor of the school paper, *The Beacon,* Elaine Eggert, was one of us; so were the stars of the debate team and the speech team, three of the class officers, and the chairperson of the spring talent show, Dede Petersen, who rode on my bus.

I had been in love with Dede for two years, in an intense and secret way. She had bouncy blonde hair and wore soft sweaters, plaid skirts, penny loafers and knee socks. One winter day I wrote her a fourteen-page letter (single-spaced) saying that she was my ideal of womanhood, a person of pure taste, excellent judgment, stunning beauty, and natural intelligence, a woman to whom I could pledge myself in a spiritual friendship that would last forever no matter what. If the friendship should turn into physical love, good, and if not, fine. We would be friends for the rest of our lives, our souls communing over vast distances.

I did not, after long thought, give her the letter. I guessed that she might laugh at it and also that her boyfriend Bill Swenson might pound me into the ground. He was an intense person too.

One afternoon riding home on the bus, sitting behind her, I heard her complain to her pal Marcy about the miseries of planning the April talent show. Bill Swenson would be in it, lip-synching "All Shook Up," and he was terrific, but there wasn't much other talent around, nothing compared to last year, when all those guys sang "Bali Hai" with the coconuts on their chests, and the skit about school lunch when the kids pretended to vomit and out came green confetti, and of course last year there had been Barbara Lee. Barbara Lee was the most talented person ever to graduate from our school. She danced, she sang, she did the splits, she played the marimba. She was Broadway bound, no doubt about it.

I leaned forward and said, "Well, I think we have lots of talent." Oh? like who, for example? she said. I said, "Well, I could do something." *You?* she said. "Or I could get together with some other kids and we could do a skit." *Like what?* she said. I said, "Oh, I don't know. Something about the school burning down. It all depends."

"That doesn't sound funny to me," she said. Marcy didn't think it was funny either.

What burned my toast was her saying "*You?*" when I volunteered to be in her talent show. I was only being helpful, I was not claiming to be another Barbara Lee. I had no interest in the stage at all until I heard her incredulity and amusement—"*You?*"—and then I was interested in being interested. A spiritual friendship with Dede was out of the question, if she thought I was the sort of guy you could say "*You?*" to.

No one in our family sang or performed for entertainment, only for the glory of God and only in groups, never solo. We were Christian people; we did not go in for show. But I was an intense young man. Intensity was my guiding principle. And when I thought about joining that monastery after Natalie Wood rejected me and spending my life in the woodshop making sturdy chairs and tables, I thought that perhaps I ought to get in the talent show at New Tryon High first, get a whiff of show business before I gave my life to God.

It was one of those ugly and treacherous springs in the Midwest, when winter refuses to quit, like a big surly drunk who heads for home and then staggers back for another round and a few more songs that everyone has heard before. It was cold and wet, and we sat day after day in dim airless classrooms, the fluorescent lights turned on at midday, the murky sky and bare trees filling the big classroom windows, pools of oil-slicked rain in the parking lot, the grass in front dead, the Stars and Stripes hanging limp and wet like laundry. In plane geometry, I was lost in the wilderness, had been lost since Christmas, and in history, we were slogging through World War I, and in English class, we were memorizing poems. "These are treasures you will carry with you forever," said Miss Rasmussen, a big woman in a blue knit suit. In her wanderings around the classroom as she talked about poetry and metaphor, she often stopped in the aisle and stood looming above me, her voice over-head, her hand resting on my desk, her puffy white hand and red knuckles and short ringless fingers. Her stopping there indicated, I knew, her fondness for me. I was the only student of hers who wrote poems. She had even suggested that I memorize and recite one of my own poems. I declined. Part of the memorization assignment was reciting the poem in front of the class. My poems were far too intense and personal to be said out loud in front of people. I was memorizing Whitman's elegy on the death of Abraham Lincoln, "O Captain! My Captain!" I walked home through the rain one cold day crying out, "O Captain! my Captain! our fearful trip is done, / The ship has weather'd every rack, the prize we sought is won."

One day a fuel oil truck backed into our driveway and got stuck in the mud and the driver put it into forward gear and got dug in deeper. He gunned it in reverse and gunned it forward and rocked the truck loose and pulled forward and unwound his hose and started filling our fuel oil tank, but meanwhile he had left deep ruts in my mother's garden and the front yard. She was home alone, washing clothes. She heard the grinding and roaring from down in the laundry room and came outdoors to find her garden dug up and the tulips and irises de-stroyed, and the driver looked at her and said, "You ought to do something about your driveway." Not a word of apology, acted like it was the driveway's fault. My mother was the quietest, politest person ever, she felt that raising your voice indicated a flawed character, but she put her hands on her hips and said, "Mister, if you can't figure out how to drive a truck, then they oughta find you a job you'd be able to handle." And she told him to get out and she would be sending the company a bill for the flower garden. And he did. And she did. And the company sent us a check and an apology from the general manager, a Harold L. Bergstrom.

It was the first time in my memory that my mother had fought back and raised her voice to a stranger, a watershed moment for me. I heard the story from our neighbor, Mr. Couture, and I admired her so much for standing up to the jerk and defending our family's honor. Her principles had always told her to be quiet and polite and turn the other cheek and never make trouble, but there comes a time to let go of principle and do the right thing. To me, this seemed to open the door to show business.

And then, about a week before the talent show, suddenly I was in. The real power behind the show wasn't Dede, it was Miss Rasmussen, my teacher, the adviser to the talent show, and the day I stood before the class and recited "O Captain! My Captain!" she told Dede to put me in the show. The next day, Miss Rasmussen had me stand up in class and recite it again. It was one of the finest pieces of oral interpretation she had ever seen, she said. She sat in a back corner of the room, her head bowed, her eyes closed, as I stood in front and with dry mouth launched the Captain's ship again, and she did not see the kids smirking and gagging and retching and pulling long invisible skeins of snot from their nostrils and when my Captain died and I got to "O the bleeding drops of red, / Where on the deck my Captain lies, / Fallen cold and dead," they rolled their eyes and clutched at their hearts and died. Then, when she stood up, her eyes moist, and clapped, they all clapped too. "Wasn't that good!" she cried. "You really liked it, didn't you! Oh, I'm glad you did! He's going to recite it in the talent show, too! Won't that be nice!" A couple of boys in front clapped their hands over their mouths and pretended to lose their lunch. They seemed to speak for most of the class.

So I was in the talent show, which I wanted to be, but with an inferior piece of material. I suggested to Miss Rasmussen that "O Captain! My Captain!" might not be right for the talent show audience, that maybe I could find a humorous poem, and she said, "Oh, it'll be just fine," not realizing the gravity of the situation. "Never give up on beauty," she said. "Never compromise your standards out of fear that someone may not understand." Teachers were full of useless advice like that.

I tried not to think about "O Captain." I experimented with combing my hair a new way, with the part on the right. I was handsome at certain angles, I thought, and a right-hand part would emphasize a good angle. I stood at the bathroom mirror, a small mirror in my hand, and experimented holding my head cocked back and aimed up and to the right, a pose favored by seniors in their graduation pictures, which looked good from either side, and reciting "O Captain" with my head at that angle. I had good skin except when it flared up, which it did two days before the show, and it took a long time to repair the damage. There were six children in our family and only one bathroom, but I spent fifteen minutes behind a locked door doing surgery and applying alcohol and cold packs and skin-toned cream. The little kids stood banging on the door, pleading to use the toilet. I said, "Well, how bad do you have to go?" I was the one in show business, after all.

I worked on "O Captain" so that every line was set in my head. I recited it to myself in the mirror ("O Captain! O Captain! the fateful day is done, / Your blemishes have disappeared, the skin you sought is won") and for my mother, who said I was holding my head at an unnatural angle, and then, the Friday night before the show, I recited it at a party at Elaine Eggert's house, and there my interpretation of "O Captain! My Captain!" took a sharp turn toward the English stage.

Miss Rasmussen loved a recording of Sir John Gielgud reading "Favourites of English Poetry" and she played it once for our class, a whole hour of it, and from that day, all the boys in the class loved to do English accents. A little lisp, endless dramatic pauses, fruity inflections including shrill birdlike tones of wonderment, and instead of the vowel *o* that delicious English *aaoooww*, a bleating sound not found anywhere in American speech. In the cafeteria, when my friend Ralph Moody came to the table where all of us West River Road rats sat, he

stood holding his tray, peering down at us and the wel-
ter of milk cartons and comic books and ice cream wrap-
pers and uneaten macaroni-cheese lunches, and after a
long pause he cried "Aaaaooooowww," with a shudder, a
great man forced to sit among savages. So at the party,
surrounded by kids from the debate team and the newspaper, the cream of West River Road society, when
Elaine had said for the sixth time, "Do the poem you're
going to do on Monday," I reached back for Ralph's
Aaoooww and did "O Captain" as Sir John might have
done it:

Aoowww Cap-tin, myyyyy Cap-tin,
aower ———— feeah-fool twip eez done!
Th' sheep has wethah'd———— eviddy rack!
th' priiiiiiize we sot———— eez won!
But———— aaaoooooooowwwww
th' bleeeeeeeding drrrops———— of rrred————
wheahhhh ————
on th' deck————
myyyy Captin liiiiiiiies————
fallin————
caaaooooowwwld ————
and————————ded!

It was a good party poem. I recited it in the basement, and then everyone upstairs had to come down and
hear it, and then Elaine had to call up a friend of hers
in the city and I did it on the phone. It got better.
"Miss Rasmussen is going to burst a blood vessel," said

Elaine. She was a true rebel, despite the editorials she wrote extolling the value of team play and school spirit. I was starting to see some of the virtues in her that I had previously imagined in Dede Petersen.

Bill Swenson had worked for weeks on "All Shook Up," and he looked cool and capable backstage before the curtain went up. His hair was slicked down, he wore heavy eye makeup, and he was dressed in a white suit with gold trim, without a single wrinkle in it. He stood, holding his arms out to the sides, avoiding wrinkling, and practiced moving his lips to "A-wella bless my soul, what'sa wrong with me? I'm itching like a man on a fuzzy tree." Dede knelt, shining his black shoes.

He pretended to be surprised to see me. "What are you doing here? You running the p.a. or what?"

I told him I would be in the show, reciting a poem by Walt Whitman.

"Who? Twitman?" No. Whitman, I said.

"Well, I'm glad I don't have to follow that," he said, with heavy sarcasm. He glanced at my outfit, brown corduroy pants, a green plaid cotton shirt, a charcoal gray sweater vest, and said, "You better change into your stage clothes though."

"These are my stage clothes," I said.

"Oh," he said, his eyebrows raised. "Oh." He smiled. "Well, good luck." He did not know how much luck I had. I had my lucky picture in my pocket, the one of me in the mountains.

Dede brushed his forehead with face powder and poofed up his hair. She gave him a light kiss on the lips. "You're going to be great," she said. He smiled. He had no doubt about that. She had put him high on the program, right after "America the Beautiful," a dramatic choral reading from *Antigone*, a solo trumpet rendition of "Nobody Knows the Trouble I've Seen," and a medley of Rodgers and Hammerstein songs performed on the piano by Cheryl Ann Hansen. Then Bill would electrify the crowd with "All Shook Up," and then I would do "O Captain."

He was Mr. Cool. After Cheryl Ann Hansen's interminable medley, which kids clapped and cheered for only because they knew that her mother had recently died of cancer, Bill grinned at Dede and bounced out on stage and yelled, "Hellllll-ooo baby!" in a Big Bopper voice, and the audience clapped and yelled "Hellllooo baby!" and he yelled, "You knowwwwwwww what I like!" and he was a big hit in the first five seconds. He said it again, "Hellllllllllooo baby!" and the audience yelled back, "Hellllllllllooo baby!" And then Dede carefully set the phonograph needle on the record of "All Shook Up" and Elvis's hoody voice blasted out in the auditorium and Bill started shimmying across the stage and tossing his head like a dustmop. "My friends say I'm acting queer as a bug, I'm in love—huh! I'm all shook up," and on the *huh* he stuck both arms in the air and threw his hip to the left, *huh,* and the audience sang along on the "hmm hmm hmm—oh—yeah yeah"—he was the star of the show right there. Dede ran to look out through a hole in the curtain, leaving me standing by the record player. She was so thrilled, she hopped up and down and squealed.

I could see part of him out there, his white suit hanging loose, the red socks flashing, him pulling out the red satin hanky and tossing it into the audience, *hmmm hmmm hmmm oh yeah yeah,* and at the end the whole auditorium stood up and screamed. He came off stage bright with sweat, grinning, and went back out and made three deep bows, and threw his hip, *huh,* and came off and Dede wiped his face with a towel and kissed him, and the audience was still screaming and whistling and yelling, "More! More!" and right then Bill made his fateful decision. He went out and did his other number.

It was "Vaya con Dios" by the Conquistadores. Dede put the needle down and the guitars throbbed, and the audience clapped, but Bill hadn't worked as hard on "Vaya con Dios" as on "All Shook Up" and his lips didn't synch very well, but the main problem was that "Vaya con Dios" was "Vaya con Dios," and after "All Shook Up" it seemed like a joke, especially since the Conquistadores were a trio and Bill wasn't. Kids started to laugh, and Bill got mad—perhaps "Vaya con Dios" meant a lot to him personally—and his grim face and his clenched fists made "Vaya con Dios" seem even zanier. Dede ran to the hole in the curtain to see where the hooting and light booing were coming from, and there, standing by the record player, I thought I would help poor Bill out by lightly touching the record with my finger and making the music go flat and sour for a moment.

It was miraculous, the effect this had, like pressing a laugh button. I touched the black vinyl rim and the music warbled, and fifty feet away, people erupted in fits of happiness. I did it again. How wonderful to hear people laugh! and to be able to give them this precious gift of laughter so easily. Then I discovered a speed control that let me slow it down and speed it up. The singers sounded demented, in love one moment, carsick the next. The audience thought this was a stitch. But Bill sort of went to pieces. One prime qualification for a show business career, I would think, is the ability to improvise and go with the audience, but Bill Swenson did not have that ability. Here he was, rescued from his drippy encore, magically transformed into comedy, and he was too rigid to recognize what a hit he was. His lips stopped moving. He shook his fist at someone in the wings, perhaps me, and yelled a common vulgar expression at someone in the crowd, and wheeled around and walked off.

I didn't care to meet him, so I walked fast right past him onto the stage, and coming out of the bright light into the dark, he didn't see me until I was out of reach. There was still some heavy booing when I arrived at the microphone, and I made a deep English-actor type of bow, with princely flourishes and flutters, and they laughed, and then they were mine all the way. I held on to them for dear life for the next two minutes. I sailed into "O Captain," in my ripest and fruitiest accent, with roundhouse gestures, outflung arms, hand clapped to the forehead ———— I cried:

AOOWWW CAP-TIN, MYYYYY CAP-TIN,

AOWER ———— FEEAH-FOOL TWIP EEZ DONE!

TH' SHEEP HAS WETHAH'D———————— EVIDDY RACK!

TH' PRIIIIIIIZE WE SOT———————— EEZ WON!

BUT———— ————AAAAOOOOOOOWWWWW

TH' BLLEEEEEEEDING DRRROPS————————

OF RRRED————————

WHEAHH————

ON TH' DECK————————

BEEEL SWEN-SON LIIIIIIIIES————————

FALLIN————————————

CAAAOOOOWWWLD

————————AND————————

————DED!

It wasn't a kind or generous thing to do, but it was successful, especially the "AAAAAOOOOOOO-WWWWW" and also the part about Bill Swenson, and at the end there was shouting and whistling and pandemonium, and I left the stage with the audience wanting more, but I had witnessed the perils of success, and did not consider an encore. "Go out and take a bow," said Miss Rasmussen, and out I went, and came back off. Dede and Bill were gone. Dede was not feeling well, said Miss Rasmussen.

I watched the rest of the show standing at the back of the auditorium. The act after me was a girl from the wrong side of the river who did a humorous oral interpretation entitled "Granny on the Phone with Her Minister." The girl had painted big surprise eyebrows and a big red mouth on her so we would know it was comedy, and as the sketch went on, she shrieked to remind us that it was humorous. The joke was that Granny was hard-of-hearing and got the words wrong. Then came an accordionist, a plump young man named David Lee, Barbara's cousin, who was a little overambitious with "Lady of Spain" and should have left out two or three of the variations, and a tap dancer who tapped to a recording of "Nola" and who made the mistake of starting the number all over again after she had made a mistake. I enjoyed watching these dogs, strictly from a professional point of view. And then the choir returned to sing "Climb Every Mountain," and then Miss Rasmussen stood and spoke about the importance of encouraging those with talent and how lucky we should feel to have them in our midst to bring beauty and meaning to our lives. And then the lights came up, and my classmates piled into the aisles and headed for the door and saw me standing in back, modest me, looking off toward the stage. Almost every one of them said how good I was as they trooped past—clapped my shoulder, said, hey, you were great, you should've done more, that was funny— and I stood and patiently endured their attention until the auditorium was empty and then I went home.

"You changed the poem a little," Miss Rasmussen said the next day. "Did you forget the line?" "Yes," I said. "Your voice sounded funny," she said. I told her I was nervous. "Oh well," she said, "they seemed to like it anyway."

"Thank you," I said, "thank you very much."

OMOO THE WOLF BOY

I was born at Lost Land Lake in a pine paradise in northern Wisconsin that later became the Lucy W. Chequamagon Memorial Forest and I never intended to become a wolf but when I was eight my beloved mother died, and my dad married a nasty woman named Luverne, I took off, and the wolves took me in. It's as simple as that.

My mother, Lucy W. Chequamagon, for whom the Memorial Forest was named, was a famous beauty with long black hair, six feet tall and slim-hipped in her long leather skirt and lace-up boots, and she was devoted to me, teaching me the birds and trees and animals of the forest and also great show songs like "Oklahoma" and "Hey Look Me Over." She had been a Broadway chorus girl and had hoofed through 942 performances of *Let's Do a Show!* when she met my dad, Oscar, who was in New York visiting his brother Emil, a stagehand. All I can imagine, by way of explaining their romance, is that she must have been extremely fatigued. Dad wasn't much of a looker and even less of a talker. He was a woodcutter. Mother was an entertainer. She told stories of Broadway days. She sang. She made a wonderful lamb chowder with big chunks of meat and potatoes floating in the cream sauce. Our home was in the forest, a cozy one-room cabin with a green Oriental linoleum floor and pictures of castles and royalty on the walls. My dad cut wood and operated a string of vending machines in the forest that sold maps and candy bars to lost hunters, and then, when hunters who lacked correct change shot off the locks and black bears ate the candy, he became a fishing and hunting guide and was gone for weeks at a time. My mother and I didn't think about him when he wasn't there. We danced and sang:

> *Hey kid, whenever you're blue*
> *And you want to get happy—here's what to do:*
> *Put on your best clothes and pull back the rug*
> *And smile a smile that lights up your mug.*
> *Take a step to the left, a shuffle step to the right,*
> *Cry out "Yethir!" and reach for the spotlight,*
> *And step kick step kick all the way—*
> *You're in Show Business, U.S.A.!*

My mother was taken away from me one cold spring day after weeks of sleet and rain. She was wrapped in a tattered yellow quilt and carried out the door of our cabin, the fever burning in her soft hazel eyes that never left my face until the door clicked shut. She gazed at me long and sweet and whispered, "Remember me, my little Lyle," and then she was gone.

Dad's motto was "Don't look back, what's done is done, so live for today," and a few weeks later, he brought home Luverne, who had eyes like two brown stones and cheeks as cold as ice. "We were married in Hayward after lunch," he explained. She threw out Mother's pictures and put up her own, woodland scenes, though we had the woods there to look at. I hummed "Somewhere Over the Rainbow" quietly as I washed dishes and she said, "Hey, who stuck a nickel in *you?* Put a cork in it, wouldja? Who do you think you are, Luciano Poverty?"

The next morning, Dad sat on the step and got his pans soaped and his packs loaded for a long trip up the Namekagon. He leaned back and filled his pipe and lit up and smoked, and seemed about to say something, but then thought better of it. Dad could go for days without saying a word, so three hours was nothing. Finally, he said, "Don't forget, you're in charge of the woodpile."

He left to meet his party from Chicago, and Luverne lay in bed on her back and snored so the glasses rattled in the cupboard. I quietly poured corn flakes in a bowl and quietly ate them, letting them soak in my mouth to avoid crunching, but even a soft gumming sound awoke her. She yelled, "Wouldja kindly shuddup? Just put it back in the can and screw a lid on it!" and threw a shoe and went back to sleep, and I sat and read a book, turning the pages with utmost care, but even that slight rustling brought her charging up out of bed. She ordered me outdoors. "It's cold," I said, "and I'm only eight." She said it would be a good experience for me. "When can I come back in?" I asked. She said, "As soon as you're ready to be good."

I knew then that I was in for a long haul in the woods, given Luverne's standard of goodness, but as an avid reader, I had no fear of the woods. Bambi was there, and Thumper, Uncle Wiggily, Mrs. Tiggy-Winkle, Mr. Frog, Mowgli, Gub Gub, and the rabbits of *Rabbit Hill,* so I headed into the silent stately forest, keeping the tall pine over the cabin as a landmark, went deeper, keeping an eye on the tall pine, and then, much later, looked and realized that every pine in the forest was just that tall, and then I heard a whimper, and turned, and there was a big wolf standing on a fallen tree and staring at me with his big blue eyes.

He snuffled and tossed his head at me, as if to tell me to follow him, and turned and trotted along a path, looking back to make sure I was coming. We ran about a mile, and scrambled up a rocky slope and into a deep crevice and a dark den, and inside were five more wolves.

They gathered around, talking and laughing, sniffing me, discussing my clothing. And they lay down and I lay in the middle of them. And they licked my face and hands. They became my family and the den my home for the next ten years with my wolf dad and den mother, my two sisters, and my beloved grandfather Omoo.

They were deeply affectionate, always touching me gently, licking me, and I needed their comfort and support, because life was terribly hard sometimes. Wolf grammar is complicated: the vocabulary is only about a hundred "words" and each one has hundreds of possible meanings—*sneesha,* for example, can mean "the place where the deer come at night to browse" or "the way the sky looks when winter is approaching" or "Are we going to have squirrel for the fourth day in a row?" or "There were fresh droppings on the trail today—yours? No?"—and verb tense is indicated by the angle of your tail, and I didn't have one—so I was limited to the present. As for the diet, I just never developed a taste for very rare meat. On the other hand, I loved howling, which we did several times a week. I taught them to howl Rodgers and Hammerstein's "Oh, What a Beautiful Mornin' " even though it was night, and they did it right on key. They loved Broadway songs, especially my mom and Omoo. I put some pebbles between my toes and tap-danced on a stone ledge and sang a song for my mom:

> *Hey folks, step this way*
> *To see the greatest little lady in theater today.*
> *Get your tickets, grab your popcorn,*
> *Take your seats and a star is born!*

She's got the body and she's got the voice,
She amuses the women and amazes the boys!
So open the curtains and beat the drums
Cause, baby, here she comes!

And she beamed and Omoo barked, he loved it so much. I loved Omoo. He taught me to talk, he asked me many questions about music (he said he preferred Irving Berlin to Rodgers and Hammerstein, but Meredith Willson's *The Music Man* was his favorite), and when he died, the family and I removed his beautiful silver fur and I wore it for the next six years. And I took his name.

When I turned eighteen, my younger brother, who, due to wolves' shorter life expectancy, was now an old man, took me aside for a talk. "I love you," he said, "but it's time we face up to the fact that you're—well, you're different."

"You think I don't *know?*"

"You're a horseshit hunter, and on your own, you'd starve. You'd be forced to subsist on grubs and snakes, snack food. And worse, you have an accent, a pretty dumb one. Other wolves aren't going to help out anyone who pronounces words like you do. Nobody's going to invite you on the hunt, nobody's going to share his kill with you. You'll be a lone wolf. You'll die."

"I disagree. I'm smell-impaired, that's all. I'll be okay. Wolf society is changing. These things take time. But I'm going to devote my life to the cause of equality for us wolves who can't hunt. We have a right to a full, rich life, too."

"There's one other thing. You're a crappy singer too. You can't sing worth beans. And we're tired of *Oklahoma*. Grandpa only liked it because he was deaf. It's dumb."

And then he bit me. He bit my neck and he kept biting. He got me down and started chewing on my neck and it hurt so bad I smacked him across the snout and ran away and up a tree. He growled and barked for a while, called me a "pussy" and a "whiskerless wimp," called me a pantywaist and a cake-eater and a tenderpaws and a foreigner. And he turned and trotted home.

I walked in the other direction, wondering where I had come from, wondering what the future would bring, except I didn't have a tail to indicate future, and I walked for miles, then smelled a man, and heard a ding and a click. The man, who wore a red-plaid jacket and a fur cap, held a long gun. He stood with his back to me, putting a coin into what I now know was a vending machine, but at the time I thought it was the Mind of Death. He was humming a tune to himself that sounded to me, a wolf, as if he was saying, "There's a big hairy raccoon around here," which is a huge insult in our tongue. So as he took the map from the machine, I threw back my head and howled.

He jumped three feet, the gun went off, he tore into the underbrush, leaving fresh droppings in the grass, and I picked up the map and followed him. Eventually

I found a road. A sheriff found me. I was put in a hospital but nothing was wrong with me so they had to let me go. They sent me to a foster home in Wausau run by a Grandma DeLisle. At first, she had to feed me rats and chipmunks, it was what I was used to, and it was months before I could bear the feeling of underwear on my body. To wear trousers at all felt like my legs were caught in the jaws of a trap.

"Jell-O. Good," she said over and over, spooning green blobs into my mouth. "Napkin. Use it. And don't bite me. No. No bites. I'm a woman. That's me. Woman."

In wolf culture, we do a certain amount of playful biting, and I had to learn not to, and learn not to mark the door to my bedroom with urine, and for months, I greeted Grandma by poking my head up under her skirts and sniffing her hinder and making her whoop, and it was hard to remember not to. But love is tender in any language, and she'd pet me and murmur sweet things, and I recognized that she loved me and somehow she was able to see possibilities in me, even though I was so different.

She clipped my toenails, which *hurt,* but she was as gentle as she could be and sympathetic. It hurt her when I hurt—for example, when she bathed me and I screamed at the terrifying sensation of hot water and immersion, she hugged me, wet and naked as I was, and I clung to her, both of us dripping and bawling, Grandma and me. "Omoo, I know this hurts," she said, "but you must brush your teeth and use a mouthwash," and when it stung me and my gums bled, she hugged me again and again. She taught me to read and write again, and of course this brought back sweet and painful memories of my mother, Lucy W. Chequamagon. I lay in bed and wept and moaned for days and days, and when I crawled out of bed, I had decided to wear a dress. In memory of my darling mother and in tribute to Grandma. Trousers were too painful. Trousers reminded me of my dad and he was a jerk.

Grandma accepted this, and so did her grandniece Doreen, through it took her awhile. She was eighteen. She came and visited us in our cottage every weekend. Doreen was beautiful, though not so much as she imagined, and she was bossy. "Why such big skirts?" she said. "It's too loose. You have a very lithe, trim, erotic body, why not show it off more? And I don't like your hair at all, but that's up to you."

In honor of Grandma, I had bleached my hair white and then used a blue rinse. She and I had blue hair in the same powder-blue shade. I wore voluminous white skirts with petticoats, a T-shirt, and tennis shoes, and had blue hair, and I sang "Oh, What a Beautiful Mornin'" and "Till There Was You" with dramatic howls interspersed.

One day, Doreen was helping me fit a skirt and she reached up between my legs and touched my rooney, as we wolves call it. "Well, maybe you *should* stick with loose clothes," she said, smiling. "You got quite a member there."

A few weeks later, she went into heat, and I took her

clothes off. She didn't seem to know that she was in heat, or what effect this had on me, and she yelled at me to stop. I tried to mount her and she hit me, but this sort of foreplay is common in the wolf world, and I persevered and coupled with her, and she accepted it. She even cried my name and kissed me. She bitched to Grandma about it afterward, though, and made a holy fuss to her brothers, who came with guns and drove me out into the woods. No problem. I enjoyed it. I found a rocky den near the house, spent my nights watching, guarding, and brought fresh meat every week, and in the spring Doreen had a litter of three babies. I was allowed to move back in.

We married and we live with Grandma in her house and we get along fine. Doreen watches too much television, but then I enjoy looking at the river flow, and it's all the same. Everything's goin' my way, as it says in the song, and all I need to do is sit and watch it go and keep an eye on the kids. They are only a year old but they lope around and get their noses into everything, a regular floorshow. We're bringing them up bilingual.

THE COUNTRY MOUSE AND
THE CITY MOUSE

Annie was a Minneapolitan and Mesa Bob was from northern Minnesota on the Mesabi Range, north of Duluth. They met in Minneapolis. Her play, *Nothing but Zero*, had opened in a 1958 Oldsmobile at a junkyard, and he was "with the post office," as he told her, though he didn't mention that his job was chewing mail and that he was a volunteer. They met at a reception. She invited him to her play the next night, and although he considered her slightly overdressed (rhinestone whisker clips?) and she was put off by the acorns on his breath— when their whiskers touched and their dark eyes met, they fell instantly in love. Her play was eighty words long, and he couldn't follow it. Nonetheless, he punched out a mouse in the back seat who sneered in Annie's direction.

"I am infatuated," she said. "Come to Kenwood. I live with a family in a huge house there, you'll love it."

"Oh, I'm too plain for the city," he said. "I came down here in a trucker's lunchbox by mistake, and I can't wait to get back to the woods."

"I love you!" she cried. "Let's breed!" They crouched together, breathing hard on each other. He mounted her in blind happiness and they made love and squeaked for pleasure.

"You will love it here!" she said. "I can't wait to show you around."

"I like the country," he said. "I have a burrow in the granary, with a warm bed of corn husks and all the oats I can eat! You should come and see it."

"Sure. For the weekend sometime."

"The silage is especially good this year," he said.

"May I be frank?" she said. "Mice aren't supposed to live in the dirt, eating leaves. The city is the place. Great food, shows—you can wallow in luxury to your heart's content. Why live like moles?"

They headed down into a Hennepin Avenue sewer and found the uptown pipe and grabbed an empty milk carton and rode a wave up to Kenwood, bumping and swaying in the flow of muck, and hopped out and squeezed through a crack and climbed up a crevice and soon were in the wall of a large old house, looking into the dining room, where the remains of a major dinner party littered the table. Platters of cheese, grapes as big as their heads, rolls, wine, brandy, scraps from a rack of lamb—they scampered up the table and dug in—

"Try the lamb," she said. "Fabulous with Dijon."

But before he reached the lamb platter, there was a deafening screech and a clatter of dishes and a cat with flaming yellow eyes was right on top of them! Mesa Bob and Annie leaped screaming from the table and hit the floor running, the cat's breath at their backs, and they tore into the hole just as the cat skidded into the wall. They lay on their backs, panting, trembling, weeping, having escaped death by a tenth of an inch.

Finally the country mouse whispered, "How can you live like this? Traveling in sewers, eating dinner with death hovering nearby—at least in the country, we're safe."

"It's not the city you hate, it's me, isn't it!" she cried bitterly. "You're dissatisfied with me. Well, to hell with you. I'll raise the children myself."

"No. You're great, I love you," he said. "But Minneapolis is such a dark place."

"*Life* is a dark place. I'm sorry. Cats are a menace. But let's live. Time for dessert," she said. "Smell the cheese? It must be nearby. Stilton, if I'm not mistaken." She crept into the dark and around the corner. "It's near here," she said. "I can smell it. Beautiful."

"Be careful, darling," he whispered, and then he heard the sharp *snap* of the trap and the thud of metal on flesh.

"Annie?" he called. "*Annie.*"

There was no reply, of course. His lady love was dead, her neck broken, her glassy eyes aimed at a chunk of cheese she would never eat.

Mesa Bob returned to the north woods in a sack of mail and resumed his life in a peaceful burrow, his heart filled with black grief. He had loved her, and she had been all wrong for him, and now she was gone, and there would never be anyone else. Silage, acorns— nothing tasted good anymore.

The local mice lacked Annie's glamour, her dash, her sense of the moment. He missed her every day. Life is short for a mouse, and he needed to breed, and yet he never could forget his lost love.

He took to drinking and running around late at night, and whooping and yelling, and of course it was only a matter of time until he went too far.

He was raising hell and tearing around, and felt a whoosh of wings overhead as the owl took him in her talons and flapped and up he went. It hurt for one split second and then he felt as numb as a piece of wood. The ground fell away beneath Mesa Bob, his burrow and his silage and his warm bed soon were far behind, and he was too stunned to feel even the slightest bit of loss or regret.

CASEY AT THE BAT
(ROAD GAME)

It was looking rather hopeful for our
    Dustburg team that day:
We were leading Mudville four to
    two with an inning left to play.
We got Cooney on a grounder and
    Muldoon on the same,
Two down, none on, top of the
    ninth—we thought we'd won the
    game.
Mudville was despairing, and we
    grinned and cheered and clapped.
It looked like after all these years our
losing string had snapped.
And we only wished that Casey, the big fat ugly lout,
Could be the patsy who would make the final, shame-
    ful out.

Oh how we hated Casey, he was a blot upon the game.

Every dog in Dustburg barked at the mention of his
name.

A bully and a braggart, a cretin and a swine—

If Casey came to bat, we'd stick it where the moon don't
shine!

Two out and up came Flynn to bat, with Jimmy Blake
on deck,

And the former was a loser and the latter was a wreck;

Though the game was in the bag, the Dustburg fans
were hurt

To think that Casey would not come and get his just
desert.

But Flynn he got a single, a most unlikely sight,

And Blake swung like a lady but he parked it deep to
right,

And when the dust had lifted, and fickle fate had beck-
oned,

There was Flynn on third base and Jimmy safe at second.

Then from every Dustburg throat, there rose a lusty cry:

"Bring up the slimy greaseball and let him stand and
die.

Throw the mighty slider and let him hear it whiz

And let him hit a pop-up like the pansy that he is."

There was pride in Casey's visage as he strode onto the
grass,

There was scorn in his demeanor as he calmly scratched
his ass.

Ten thousand people booed him when he stepped into
the box,
And they made the sound of farting when he bent to fix
his socks.
And now the fabled slider came spinning toward the mitt,
And Casey watched it sliding and he did not go for it.
And the umpire jerked his arm like he was hauling
down the sun,
And his cry rang from the box seats to the bleachers:
Stee-rike One!
Ten thousand Dustburg partisans raised such a mighty
cheer,
The pigeons in the rafters crapped and ruined all the
beer.
"You filthy ignorant rotten bastard slimy son of a
bitch,"
We screamed at mighty Casey, and then came the sec-
ond pitch.
It was our hero's fastball, it came across the plate,
And according to the radar, it was going ninety-eight.
And according to the umpire, it came in straight and
true,
And the cry rang from the toilets to the bullpen:
Stee-rike Two.
Ten thousand Dustburg fans arose in joyful loud derision
To question Casey's salary, his manhood, and his vision.
Then while the Dustburg pitcher put the resin on the
ball,
Ten thousand people hooted to think of Casey's fall.

Oh the fury in his visage as he spat tobacco juice
And heard the little children screaming violent abuse.
He knocked the dirt from off his spikes, reached down
and eased his pants—
"What's the matter? Did ya lose 'em?" cried a lady in
the stands.
And then the Dustburg pitcher stood majestic on the
hill,
And leaned in toward the plate, and then the crowd was
still,
And he went into his windup, and he kicked, and let it
go,
And then the air was shattered by the force of Casey's
blow.
He swung so hard his hair fell off and he toppled in dis-
grace
And the Dustburg catcher held the ball and the crowd
tore up the place,
With Casey prostrate in the dirt amid the screams and
jeers
We threw wieners down at him and other souvenirs.
We pounded on the dugout roof as they helped him to
the bench,
Then we ran out to the parking lot and got a monkey
wrench
And found the Mudville bus and took the lug nuts off
the tires,
And attached some firecrackers to the alternator wires.
We rubbed the doors and windows with a special kind
of cheese

That smells like something died from an intestinal disease.

Old Casey took his sweet time, but we were glad to wait

And we showered him with garbage as the team came out the gate.

So happy were the Dustburg fans that grand and glorious day,

It took a dozen cops to help poor Casey get away,

But we grabbed hold of the bumpers and we rocked him to and fro

And he cursed us from inside the bus, and gosh, we loved it so!

Oh sometimes in America the sun is shining bright,

Life is joyful sometimes, and all the world seems right,

But there is no joy in Dustburg, no joy so pure and sweet

As when the mighty Casey fell, demolished, at our feet.

HERB JOHNSON,
THE GOD OF CANTON

Talent is a kind of wealth, and if you find it under your pillow one morning, you are as surprised as anybody else. One fall day when I was twelve, I picked up a football and ran with it, crazy-legs style, across the backyards of Canton, Indiana, jumping bushes, running circles around my older brothers, and when I was sixteen and started getting my growth, I eluded everyone. I was 165 pounds and big across the shoulders. I became the star halfback and captain of the Trojans. I was All-State. I was, I think it safe to say, regarded as a god, Young Herb the Boy Wonder and Bringer of Good Things, the Hero Who Vanquished Our Deadly Enemy Forest Park, and as a sign of the town's devotion was given my choice of young women and selected Elayne, a beautiful blonde with the prettiest breasts in a hundred miles. I got to hold Elayne's breasts every Friday night after the game. They were perfect to a high degree, small and pointed and lively, and she was charmed by them herself. "Nice, aren't they," she said, looking down. Elayne became an economist and today those breasts live in Washington, D.C., and go to work at the General Accounting Office.

Football was like a long sunny afternoon for the most part. My body did the work, my head sat on top and looked down in amazement, the maroon-and-gray silk uniform with the numeral 27 and my feet finding the hole before it opened, other guys grunting and cursing and crying out in pain and horror and happy me waltzing toward daylight, the linebackers lunging a moment too late, then freedom, the wide-open expanse of grass to gallop over and the secondary defenders backpedaling, panic in their eyes. I scored more touchdowns than anybody in the history of education. I was a healthy young horse, and everybody in Canton did me favors; people I hardly met were very good to me, such as my physics teacher, Mr. Foresman. He gave me a B even though I didn't understand physics at all. "Herby," he said, "you know more about physics than anybody, you just don't know that you know it. You *are* physics, Herb."

We lost to Gridley my senior year, a terrible shock to my system. Gridley was the best homosexual football team in Indiana, or so we kept telling them across the scrimmage line. They beat us 19–14. They had a little fairy field-goal kicker from Mexico, a tiny greaseball with long black hair and big lips and a thin mustache. "Hey, Pedro sweetheart, kiss me," we called to him and made smacking sounds, and he kicked four field goals from way out around the thirty-five-yard line, four big boomers that sank our ship. We slunk away astonished to the locker room and hid in there for two hours.

I attended Indiana State on a scholarship, and Myra Jordan was the coach there. She was twenty-seven, tall, blonde, tough as nails. I'd drop a pass in practice and she'd look at me in disgust and shake her ponytail and say, "Johnson, get your fat ass down on the ground and do me a hundred push-ups while I think of what else I can do TO GET YOUR ATTENTION, BUTTHEAD."

I loved that woman. I would've done anything for her. My freshman season, I was All-Conference, and my sophomore year, I set a season-scoring record—206 points in twelve games. First game of junior year, I was tackled from behind by a 200-lb. buffalo and tore ligaments in my right knee and sat out two games and then, against our archrival, Kentucky, she asked me to go in for the last play of the game.

We had the ball on their fourteen-yard line, fourth down, two seconds left, Kentucky leading 20–14.

"Herby," she said, her arm around my shoulders as forty-eight thousand Indiana fans sat praying to their God in the big stadium, the afternoon shadows lengthening across the field, "I want you to go out there and take the ball over right tackle and into the end zone. Think you can do it?"

I told her I could do it.

"If you do it, I'll marry you," she said.

I told her I was going to do it.

"I'll marry you and have your babies," she said. "I'm a wonderful lover, Herby, and I believe I can make you very, very happy. And I bake."

I told her I was going to do it.

"Think you can do it, angel?" she asked. "Think of me taking off all my clothes and lying on top of you and kissing your chest. Think you can do it?"

I told her that I knew I could do it.

I took the ball over right tackle and cut left and cut right and on the second cut my right knee came half out of its socket and then I cut left and felt a wave of pure pain wash through me and as I ran for the end-zone corner each stride sounded like a man chewing peanuts. In those fourteen yards, the cartilage and ligaments were shredded into tiny chips that surgeons are still finding today, and I flung myself across the line just as two tacklers hit me in that knee. They almost tore it from my body, and in some respects life would have been easier for me if they had.

It's been thirty years of bum knee, five operations, physical therapy accomplishing nothing, painful sessions with a chiropractor, and after all these years, my leg throbs with pain when I get out of bed in the morning, pain when I walk, pain if I swing a golf club too hard.

I have not run since that October afternoon in Kentucky thirty years ago. It's been all I can do sometimes to place one foot in front of the other, especially as I put on the weight. You quit football, you tend to bulk up.

Myra and I had four girls, and she was right, she *is* a wonderful lover. But with my knee, even that was painful sometimes. But I love her as I did when she was the coach and made me do push-ups. I would crawl through a minefield for that woman.

Three years ago I received the Icarus Award from the Disabled American Football Foundation banquet at the Canton Regency Hotel, an award that goes to "a man who heroically exceeded the limits of his ability and fell, wounded, to the earth, a hero who can never fly again." I was introduced by the local TV weatherman, Tommy ("Twenty Percent") Patterson, who said, "I'm going to say just two words to you people right now, and those two words are: *Herb Johnson.*" They stood and clapped, maybe hoping to see me shed a tear of overwhelmment, but I refused to. I told the banquet: "I don't regret it one bit. I ran fourteen yards with a broken leg and the pain is still vivid to me but at the end of those fourteen yards I found my wife, my love, the mother of my babies. Life's greatest treasure is love, gentlemen. Some guys suffer all their lives and never find it. I suffered for fourteen yards and found love that lasted thirty years. So don't feel sorry for me, boys. I AM THE LUCKIEST MAN ALIVE."

They stood and clapped for three minutes. "Love it! Love the humility!" cried Twenty Percent. "Don't you?

That's humility talking! Humility is what that is! All the great ones have it. Humility. And you know something? I love it!" They clapped again. They would have carried me away on their shoulders, except that I then weighed 490 pounds.

My doctor says my knee problem is worse because of my weight, and I'm sure he's right, yet food is a comfort to a man in pain and Myra is a good cook. Recovering from my operations, I lay in bed and ate her gorgeous omelets for breakfast, the kind that conceal six eggs and a quarter-pound of cheese, and then half a chicken for lunch with the crispy skin I love so much, and a sixteen-ounce flank steak and baked potato and banana-cream pie for dinner, and a few weeks later, when I hauled myself out of bed, Myra would let out my trousers.

"I like a big man," she would whisper in my ear at night, and when the lights went out, I felt like I was 165 again. We'd sport around and get excited, and she'd be moaning and groaning and scratching and squeezing, and I was suddenly, briefly, a god again. *Oh you darling Myra. My light and my treasure.*

Then in the morning, I'd drop my pajamas and see myself in the mirror and be horrified to see how far things had gone and think, *Here I stand, I can eat no more.* I would poke a finger in my face in the mirror: "Weight must be lost, Herb. No more ribs, no more burgers. Total burgerlessness. Carrots and celery. Miso soup, bok choy. Asian-lady food. Dry toast. Tea. Fruit. You let this continue and you will soon be wearing XXXL shirts,

shirts like tents, and not tucking them in, going around in that shirttails-out look that says, *Here come de fat man.*"

But the fat man kept coming. He could not be stopped. From 490 three years ago, I gorged myself to new levels of obesity, a man with a butt like a Percheron and a garbage-bag gut and three chins that go wibble-wibble-wibble when the fat man chuckles, which I always do—fat guys aren't allowed to be sad, it depresses people, we have to go *hohohohoho* all the time or folks don't care to be with us.

People would come to our house for dinner and I rose from the couch, a whale in a vast blue satin shirt and pants with an eighty-inch waist, I laughed heartily and hugged my beautiful slender daughters and rolled my eyes and chuckled and hooted and cackled, I'd sit down and whack away the calories, put down three plate-loads and toss back a dozen rolls, chomp a couple desserts, and the guests said good-night with a big grin and a glance at my gut and said, "Herb, I don't know what your secret is, but you're the happiest man I know. God bless you, Herb." And I would haul myself upstairs and sit in the can and lock the door and cry.

When a fat man cries, his big body shakes so hard it feels as if his bags will fall off him. Last summer, the last time I left the house on my own steam, I squeezed into the car and drove to a truck stop thirty miles from home and drove onto the truck scale, and found out that, deducting the weight of the car, I was 911 pounds.

I went to a surgeon who said, "I could pump out four

hundred of that with liposuction, but first, you'd have to lose two hundred on your own before I could do surgery. You're too fat to open up."

I went to a nutritionist who said, "You could become slender again if you would skip the butter and the dessert. Try dessert substitutes, such as erasers. A plate of erasers served on a slice of sponge contains less than two calories. You could also eat less by provoking fierce arguments at the dinner table. Insult your wife, get her to scream at you, scream back. It helps."

"I love my wife," I said. "I could never be angry at her."

"Then try disgust. It's a helpful tool in weight loss. Imagine your food was dropped on the floor and scraped up and served to you with hair on it and parakeet poop. Imagine that the caramel rolls were used as toilet paper by old veterans. Imagine the roast beef is the flesh of your beloved grandmother. Think of the eggs as the eyeballs of horses. Imagine the cheese as having been scraped from between the toes of elderly patients in the hospitals. Imagine that the butter is solidified pus collected from diseased cattle."

I went straight from the nutritionist's to a restaurant, sat in a dark corner, and ordered dessert.

"Hi, my name is Tina," said the tiny waitress. "Our dessert special today is the Chocolate Slab with Ice Cream, Whipped Cream, Chocolate Sauce, Pecans, Chunks of Toffee, and Hot Buttered Brandy Batter, and it comes in five sizes: the Ballerina, the Allegro, the

Diva, the Extra Diva, or the Wild Swine Loose in the Corncrib."

"Give me three of those big oinkers," I said. "I'll look at the dinner menu afterward."

Thus did I become a star of the traveling Nelson & Barney carnival, spending three hundred days a year spread out on a king-size bed in a mobile home parked next to the Ferris wheel on a shopping-mall parking lot somewhere in the Midwest, with an electric fan blowing on me and people paying seventy-five cents to come and gaze down at my vast bulk and to read the sign above my head:

PLEASE DO NOT FEED THE FAT MAN

DO NOT POKE HIM OR MAKE RUDE REMARKS—HOW WOULD YOU LIKE IT IF YOU WERE TOO LARGE TO MOVE AND PEOPLE TORMENTED YOU?

HE WAS ONCE A 165-POUND HALFBACK, FLEET OF FOOT, DARTING LIGHTLY AND AVOIDING TACKLES.

DO YOU BELIEVE IT?

NO PHOTOGRAPHS, PLEASE—PHOTOS ARE ON SALE AT THE CARD TABLE. PHOTO REVENUE IS HOW FAT MAN HOPES TO PAY FOR SURGICAL REMOVAL OF PAIN-FUL SORES ON HIS HINDER. YOU MAY VIEW THE SORES FOR AN ADDITIONAL PAYMENT OF $15.00. NOT REC-OMMENDED FOR THE SQUEAMISH

COMMONLY ASKED QUESTIONS

1. HOW DOES HE TAKE A CRAP? HE IS DRAINED WITH A PUMP.

2. HOW DOES HE WATCH TV? THROUGH A SPECIAL MIRROR MOUNTED ON THE CEILING.

3. HOW MUCH DOES HE WEIGH? CURRENTLY, HIS WEIGHT IS STABILIZED AT EIGHTEEN HUNDRED POUNDS.

4. HOW DOES HE MOVE? HE MUST BE LIFTED WITH A SPECIAL FORK LIFT OR ON A SLING RAISED BY A CRANE. HE IS LIFTED TWICE DAILY AND TURNED. HE IS LIFTED THREE TIMES A WEEK TO BE JIGGLED, TO PREVENT CONSTIPATION. AND HE IS LIFTED EVERY MORNING SO HE CAN BE HOSED DOWN.

5. HOW DOES HE MAKE LOVE? DON'T BE SILLY.

Myra wrote the sign by hand. She also drives the truck that tows the mobile home and operates the fork-lift, and she remains ever loyal and true, my constant friend, my beloved wife. When the crowds leave, she sits and holds my hand and we watch our favorite shows. I am guaranteed a hundred thousand dollars a year, and earn that much again in photos, an all-time record for earnings by a fat man. I have put my girls through college and graduate school. Margaret is a resident in obstetrics in San Diego, Matty is at Yale Divinity School and hopes to become an Episcopal priest, Molly went to Bryn Mawr and is now studying film at Columbia, and Johanna is in women's studies at Northwestern. They are all beautiful and smart, and I am proud of them. Mostly, we talk by phone, what with my busy schedule.

I often doze off on my bed, catch a nap in the morning, cut some Zs after lunch, snooze through the late afternoon, and in my dreams I smell the grass and sweat and mud and leather. I feel how it felt to fly and to float and turn and race for the goal, and the crowd is standing and their mouths are open and I hear a rush of wind and then I awaken, my beloved wife standing above me.

I used to think that when a hero falls, he becomes tragic, but I'm not tragic, only *former,* an object of curiosity. People drive a hundred miles to see me who wouldn't go see any ordinary fat man, because I once was a star halfback. I understand that it's quite a sight. Some come back again and again. One lady named Janis has hundreds of photographs of my body, 8 × 20s. "Would you like one?" she said. "They're quite professional."

"No, thank you," I said. "I would rather remember me as I was."

"Do you ever think," she asked, "that you'd be able to lose weight and be slim and quick again?"

"Yes. Anyone can. It's a matter of eating less fat, substituting carbohydrates, and getting more exercise."

She told me that I am an inspiration.

I said, "Well, there's always hope. Where would we be without hope?"

EARL GREY

Earl Grey flew to San Francisco to speak to the Tea Congress and stayed overnight at the Fairmont so he could drive to Berkeley in the morning and speak to a toast symposium there. He was awakened at five a.m. by some jerk singing Gershwin and took a shower and mistakenly turned the Hot and Cold handles so that scalding water struck him in the chest, and as he recoiled, he slipped and banged his head, stunning himself, and suffered bright-red burns, and spent six days in the hospital, in a room with a boy who had swallowed an orange, a bad week for the fifty-one-year-old Grey, the only living American to have a popular beverage named after him, Dr. Dave Pepper having passed away a few years before. Though his worldly air and good haircut bespoke travel, books, wealth, he was badly burned and his head throbbed like an agitating washer. He felt like warmed-over death on rice.

The hospital tea was gruesome, of course. They had teabag tea, which tasted like hot rinse water from a mop bucket, and they had obscenities like powdered iced tea, carbonated tea, and various "natural" concoctions such as Apple Mint and Raspberry Jasmine, all useful if a person needed to vomit, but nowhere in that institution of healing was one person who cared to make a proper pot of tea, using boiling water and decent tea leaves. So he drank juice for a week. His chest hurt, and his head ached, and he became so despondent, he turned on the TV set and watched for hours. Then he switched to martinis. When he was a complete wreck, they released him.

Earl Grey was a middle child, the third in a family of five, so he was accustomed to suffering. When he was small, his family often forgot to call him to the table for meals. He was a chubby boy with size-12 shoes, a hard one to overlook, but they did, all the time. Sometimes they called him "Vern" by mistake, and when he corrected them, they said, "Oh well. Whatever."

Pardon a digression here, but as a middle child himself, the author is moved to elaborate: In other cultures, middleness is not a losing position, perhaps because those cultures are less linear, more circular, than ours.

For example, in Sumatra a middle child is cherished as the bright jewel of the family, and is referred to as "our central child" (*olanda rimi mapindi*) and is carried around on a litter, or *pajandra,* but in America the middle child is the invisible one. The firstborn child is usually dutiful, earnest, the First Child, the Living Miracle, and the younger kids are disturbed, with tiny haunted eyes, they grind their teeth, they wet the beds, they strangle cats. The middle child is the normal, friendly one. In between their grievous mistakes, the parents have done something right and produced a keeper. So the middle child is ignored: because he or she is so nice and *requires no special attention*. Parents devote themselves to the troubled children and become close to them. The middle child, the healthy child, is a stranger to his parents. Earl Grey liked to bring a fresh pot of tea to his mom and dad as they sat in the Walnut Room of their spacious mansion in Chevy Chase and rested from the day's labors. "Oh, thanks, Vern," they said. "Here's a quarter."

TEA NOTE. INTERESTINGLY ENOUGH, EARL GREY'S TEA TODAY IS AMONG THE WORLD'S MOST POPULAR, AND YET HARDLY ANYONE REQUESTS IT BY NAME. THE CUSTOMER SAYS, "I'D LIKE TEA," AND THE WAITER SAYS, "EARL GREY? IS THAT OKAY?" AND THE CUSTOMER SAYS, "OH, SURE."

Earl Grey's dad was the Minority Whip in Congress, and Earl grew up in Washington, a city of broad streets and wide steps ascending to immense granite porches, a good place for a boy with a bike, and it was full of curiosities, such as the National Cold Beverage Museum and the Museum of Coasters & Napkins and the national headquarters of the American Association of Holes in the Ground. But the Grey family lived under a cloud, dreading the next election, afraid that each term would be their last. Daddy was a conservative Republican from Georgia, and his seat should have been safe, but he was careless, something of a bon vivant, and didn't bother to keep his political fences mended.

Daddy loved Washington. He enjoyed the lunches at Le Louis, the parties at the embassies where black servants circulated with silver trays of buns with pork in them. He loved the little restaurants, loved to sit in them and drink tea and read the gossip and arts sections of the Washington *Post*. He belonged to a madrigal ensemble and a sonnet circle. He read Proust. He was a civilized man and it was hard to get him ginned up for elections. Every even-numbered year, in the spring, his wife and children begged him to please do whatever he needed to do to get re-elected, but he hated the thought. "Oh pooh," he said.

He kept putting off rehearsing his campaign speech, in which he said, "Mah fray-ins, this is a tahm of gret pay-ril foah owuh blovid cuntrah." He hated that speech. He got terribly depressed when Mrs. Grey *made* him practice it—"Why can't I go down there and talk about federal support of the arts, Margaret? Why do I have to talk like a pig farmer?"

And then in the fall, the Greys trooped south to fight for their lives.

"Daddy's got to say some mean things, children," said Mrs. Grey, "otherwise we'll have to live here in

Georgia and learn to eat lime Jell-O again and attend square dances and have clunky furniture and linoleum floors."

For the campaign, they rode around on hay bales in the back of a pickup truck, waving bandannas, dressed in Sears outfits, Daddy and Mom, the dull plodding Vance, the troubled Vivian, Earl, and the ill-tempered twins, Vince and Vera. The twins were spoiled rotten and stuck out their tongues at the voters and gagged. "Oh pew! Gross! Smell those big honkers out there! Bleauggghhh!" But Earl stood and smiled faithfully and looked up at Daddy with moist rapturous eyes, as a Republican child is trained to do.

Don't slump, children, whispered Mrs. Grey, her face grim, her undies all bunched up. *Don't be glum. Glitter, sweet pea. Smile. Big white one*—as a country singer in a blue velour suit sang "Ain't it Grand to be an American" and "God Bless the Good Ole U.S.A." and other songs of the common man and then Daddy rose and spoke out for the American flag, the American family, the American family dog and cat, the American lawn, and railed against the State Department for selling out our country's vital interests abroad. "Ah tell yew, mah fray-ins, if we c'd git thim pin-strahped ayghaids down heah t' meet yew good folks, waall, mebbe they'd have thim a bitter idee whut a gret cuntrah we got heah— the Yew-nighted Stets of Uhmurka," he'd cry, mopping his brow with a red bandanna, sipping from a Dixie cup. "B'lieve yew me, I look for'ard to the day whin th' bur-den of public ser-vice is lifted from muhsilf and muh dear fam'ly and we kin leave the hip-ocrisy and false valyews of Washinton and git back heah and scootch down amongst the fawnest pee-pull in the en-tar worruld."

And then in November, Daddy got re-elected and the Greys made a final appearance at the victory rally at the Ramada Inn, grinning, hugging, their brown eyes glistening with tears of gratitude, and Daddy got choked up and called them "the grettest famly in the worruld, Vance and Vivian and Vince and Vera and that little skeeter there in the middle, doggone him," and Daddy looked at Earl vaguely—and Earl mouthed his name—*Earl, my name is Earl, Daddy*—but when you mouth the word Earl, it looks like you're puckering up for a kiss, so Daddy puckered back—and then they took off the dumpy clothes and packed them in a cardboard suitcase they stored in Daddy's sister Earlene's basement and made a beeline back to Washington, glad to be done with the dirty business for another two years. They put on their nice clothes, and talked normally, and Daddy resumed his lovely life of receptions and dinners.

At the Grey home, dinner was served promptly at seven o'clock, and once his mom looked Earl straight in the eye and said, "It's suppertime, Timmy. Time for you to get home. Your mother is probably worried sick, wondering where you are," and Earl had to tell her, "You are my mother, Mom, and you're not worried about me at all. You don't even know I exist."

"Oh, don't exaggerate," she said. "I just didn't recognize you in this dim light." But poor lighting had nothing to do with it, of course. Earl was a middle child.

INTERESTING FACT. TODAY EARL GREY TRAVELS MORE THAN TWO HUNDRED THOUSAND MILES A YEAR, SEEING TO HIS FAR-FLUNG TEA BUSINESS, APPEARING AT CHARITABLE FUNCTIONS, AND WHEREVER HE GOES, PEOPLE SAY, "EARL GREY! ARE YOU THE EARL GREY WHO INVENTED THE TEA?" AND HE SAYS, "YES, I AM HE." AND THEY SAY, "OH, GOOD," AND TURN AND TALK TO SOMEBODY ELSE. ONCE A MIDDLE CHILD, ALWAYS A MIDDLE CHILD.

In 1956, Daddy had a real stinker of an opponent, a bullet-headed, red-necked, carpet-chewing radio preacher named Gerald K. Wills who accused Daddy of losing touch with the district and being a secret liberal who intended to tax the hide off people and spend the money subsidizing pornographic pictures of men with their whangers hanging out. He crisscrossed the state in a cheap wrinkly suit waving dirty pictures and yelling, "Where's Grey, the big phony? Why's he afraid to show his face in Georgia? Is it because he knows what I know about him and his ladida pals and the high life they live in Washington, D.C.?"

Mrs. Grey read about him and told Daddy to get down on the floor of Congress and yell and pound the desk and light into the State Department.

"I have friends in the Foreign Service," he said. "They're among the finest people I know. They'd think I was a creep if I engaged in demagoguery like that."

May went by, and June and July, and in August

Daddy had a tennis tournament to play in, and early September was when his madrigal group gave its big recital at the Folger Library, so it wasn't until September 22 that he and Mrs. Grey and most of the kids trooped down to Georgia to do their business.

They forgot to bring Earl. He was standing by the car, about to climb in, and his mother said to him, "You be sure and mow the lawn every week, Hector, that's what we pay you for." Earl's eyes filled with tears, he turned to blow his nose, and away they went without him.

So he spent the next six weeks with the housekeeper Anna Tin, a nice Sumatran lady who took excellent care of him. She was dark and slender and spoke in whispers like a breeze in the banyan trees and she adored Earl for all she was worth. Being Sumatran, she saw Earl's middle-child status as blessed, a divine calling—he was a living keystone, a bridge, a bond, a fulcrum, a vital link. Every evening they sat together on the terrace and sipped tea and listened to the crickets, and she wrote poems to him in an exquisite hand: *O divine child, our threeness, completing the triangle of life, we regard you with unsullied joy and thanksgiving.* That sort of thing.

Meanwhile, down in Georgia, the rest of the Greys traipsed around Daddy's district trying to be wholesome and perky, bravely ignoring the polls, while Gerald K. ran circles around Daddy on the stump. Gerald K.'s slogan was "Honor America and Send a Real Man to Washington" and he flew hundreds of flags at every appearance, outflagging Daddy by a ten-to-one margin.

Daddy used small tasteful flags and Gerald K. had flags as big as barns. He spread rumors that Daddy had only one testicle, smaller than a dried lentil, and he accused Daddy of having a secret plan to strip seniors of their pensions, and before Daddy got his drawl back, Gerald K. found photos of Daddy singing in his madrigal group, wearing a foofy shirt with chin ruffles, his hair curling out around his ears, a garland of daisies on his head, his mouth open in a prim oval for a *falalalala* that—well, the picture did Daddy no good. But what really killed him was tea.

One hot night, in Marietta, at a debate on a flag-draped platform in the courthouse square, when Congressman Grey was waxing hot and heavy about the pinheads in the State Department and how, if elected, he'd clean them out of there and replace them with God-fearing folks with a farm background, suddenly Gerald K. jumped up and strode to the podium and hollered, "What you got in that Dixie cup theah?" And he snatched it from Daddy and sniffed it and yelled, "Tea."

"Tea?" the crowd murmured.

"Tea!" yelled Gerald K. "This peckerwood is standing up here peckin at a cup of tea. Well, ladida. Ain't we fine?"

Everyone laughed, and Daddy was dead.

It was the tea that did it. Conservative men didn't drink tea, except if they were down with the flu. Tea was for wimmen, fruitcakes, pantywaists, college perfessers, hermaphrodites, and elderly Episcopalians. Gerald K. held up the picture of Congressman Grey *falala*ing and said, "You folks intendin to vote for a poof and a priss and a pansy? I smelled that man's Dixie cup and it smelled of *tea,* people. And I say ole Oolong has been in Congress Toolong!" and that was that, everyone laughed, and the election was over. Daddy yelled and he hollered and he got a flattop haircut and he drank gallons of Coca-Cola laced with bourbon whiskey and offered to have his urine tested for tea and he cursed the State Department, bureaucrats, unions, communists, porno pushers, welfare cheats, the media, rapists, and flag burners, but he was swamped on Election Day by a lavish margin, and the family slunk back to Chevy Chase, heartsick and bitter.

There was Earl, dazed with pleasure, having been adored all the long summer. "What's wrong?" he asked.

"We got our butt kicked," said his mom. "We've got to put the house up for sale and go be powerless. And it's your fault. Why weren't you there?"

BELIEVE IT OR NOT. EARL GREY TEA IS NOW THE MOST POPULAR TEA IN GEORGIA. IT OUTRANKS BOURBON AMONG MALES BETWEEN TWENTY-FIVE AND SIXTY AND IS STEADILY GAINING ON COFFEE, COKE, BEER, AND ORANGE JUICE. IT IS THE FASTEST-GROWING BEVERAGE IN THE ATLANTA AREA.

The Greys did not return to Georgia. They spent a last Christmas in Washington—Earl's mom gave him a rod and reel, a Bob-Bet Bait Box full of Sassy Shiners and Can-Do Lures and a Bang-O-B bait and two Lazy Ikes and a Worm Hotel, though Earl had never fished in his life and had no desire to. In January, Daddy took his remaining hundred thousand in campaign funds and

they motored west to California, where Daddy would
have a job at the Hoover Institution, thinking about
great issues. They stopped in Minneapolis, where he de-
livered a speech on campaign reform at the Stassen Institute, and the following afternoon they stopped at the
Lucky Spud restaurant in Platt, North Dakota, for
lunch, and half an hour later they went off and left Earl
there.

The Spud specialized in mashed potatoes: there were
twenty-four varieties on the menu, including Big
Cheesie, White Cloud, Land O'Gravy, Tuna Whip, and
the Elvis Parsley. Earl, a slow eater, ordered a Big
Cheesie *and* a White Cloud and sat and savored every
bite, while Daddy paid the check and went to the car
with Vance and Vince, and Mom, who had been in a
sour mood for months, said, "We're going, Earl, and
we're not going to wait for you, and I mean it," and
then she disappeared with Vivian and Vera. Earl finished
up the last four bites in a big hurry, but when he ran
out the door, the car was gone.

The waitress tried to comfort him. "They'll be back
in a jiffy, snuggums, just you wait and see. Here. Have
some more spuds." But the family never returned. Never
called, never wrote, never filed a missing-child report.
They cruised on to Palo Alto, enjoying the scenery,
without a peep out of his brothers and sisters as to the
empty place in the back seat. But he had taken up so
little room in their lives, why should they notice his
absence?

Does this story strike you as far-fetched, dear reader?

Then you are not a middle child. Middle children have similar experiences all the time. You go to your family's for dinner and your mom is put out with you for some reason, won't look at you, just talks to your brothers and sisters and their spouses, not to you, so you take her aside after you've washed and dried all the dishes and ask her, "Mom, what's wrong?" and she bursts into tears and says, "Why didn't you come to our fortieth-anniversary party last summer? I can't understand it. Everyone was there except you and you never called or wrote or sent a present or anything!" So you explain to her: "Mom, I *organized* that party. The party was my idea. I put up the decorations, I bought the chocolate cake and ice cream, I hired the polka band, and I cleaned up afterward. I was there for sixteen hours, Mom." And she says, "But then how come you're not in any of the photographs?" Because middle children are invisible. And because we're the ones who *take* the photographs. (That's why there are coin-operated self-portrait booths in bus depots—for us, so we can be in pictures.)

None of the Greys ever said, "Hey, where's Earl? Gotta get Earl in this picture!" Never. And if they had reported him missing to the police and the police had asked, "What does the boy look like?" the Greys would've looked at each other and said, "Now, what *did* he look like? He was medium height, wasn't he? Didn't he have brown hair? I seem to remember that it was brown."

TEA FACTS. EARL GREY TEA HAS BEEN USED AS A WASH

BY NUMEROUS PROMINENT ARTISTS TO LEND A RICH BUT
SUBTLE BROWN TONE TO WATERCOLORS AND DRAWINGS.
BUT EARL'S HAIR IS, AND ALWAYS HAS BEEN, BLONDE.

So Earl grew up in Platt from the age of fifteen. He
was raised by the owner of the Lucky Spud, Jack, and
his sister Paula, the waitress. They lived in the apartment over the Spud and Earl bussed tables and washed
dishes. The Spud was two rooms, a back dining room
with brown plastic-top tables and a green carpet, and
the front room with the counter and stools and vinyl
flooring with a pattern of large maroon chunks. The
Spud was full of patrons all morning and afternoon, old
guys grousing about the government, the weather, fishing, farming, and their wives who sat and chain-
smoked, eyes straight ahead, saying nothing.

Paula believed that by smiling and brushing her teeth
and keeping her underarms dry and her home as neat as
a pin, she could stay on God's good side and avoid disease. Every day, she brushed every hair on her head into
place and then sprayed it shut and put a net on it. Jack
was big and clunky and lay on the couch with his cat
Kathy on his chest and drank Old Crow with raspberry
Kool-Aid and chortled at the dumb things said by celebrities on television: "Ho, ho, ho, get a load of that.
Look, it's Myron Gumball, the big dummy. What is he
supposed to be, funny? Look. C'mere! He's got a big
booger in his nose. You call that comedy? I heard better
jokes from a Swede. And look, his barn doors're open."

Paula didn't like to hear bad things said about people. "What goes around, comes around," she said. Paula

was a tea drinker at heart, though sometimes she back-slid when coffee was offered. "Oh, all right," she'd say, not wanting to make a fuss. But tea was her preference.

"We don't get good tea in North Dakota," she con-fided to Earl. "That's the main reason for our meanness. Coffee makes people ornery and they go out and kick the dog and throw trash in the creek. Tea brings out the best in people." North Dakotans, she said, prefer their coffee bitter with a rainbow of oil slick on top.

It wasn't only tealessness that cursed the prairie, Earl thought. The land was bleak and windswept, the people were like Canadians, vague, boring, not clearly delin-eated. Canadian migrant workers, or "frostbacks," flocked over the border to pick broccoli and soybeans, bringing their boring culture with them. It offered no possibility of self-esteem, no sense of irony, not even many good crossword puzzles. And for spiritual comfort, the church offered even less. The very sight of the Platt Lutheran Church made Earl's skin clammy. Christianity taught that humanity is worthless and vile but that if we agree to hate ourselves God will forgive us. Earl longed to leave; he dreamed that a silvery spaceship de-scended from the sky, a ship shaped like a fish, and it smiled and he entered its mouth, stepping over the sharp teeth, and was carried to California.

Earl wrote numerous letters to his dad at the Hoover Institution, which were answered by an assistant who thanked him for his interest and passed along the Con-gressman's best wishes. Earl didn't fare much better at the Platt Public School, where he was regarded with disgust and amusement, perhaps because he brought a teapot to school with him. For that, he was nicknamed Potty, and boys drew pictures of him wearing a dress, with snot pouring from his nose, and a petunia sticking out of his butt.

But Earl couldn't survive a day without tea. To him, tea represented civilization and the spirit of caring.

He found a book in the Platt Free Lending Library, *Wild Teas of North America,* and from it learned to make dandelion tea, sassafras, rhubarb tea—each one delicious and comforting. Paula thrived on the teas he made, became lovelier and more self-assured. "They are even better than a high colonic," she said. Her color improved. She let her hair hang loose and told her boyfriend, Butch, to get lost.

Butch was a grizzled old trucker with weak kidneys who came through town once a month or so and got a ten-dollar room at the Bronco Motel and drank six beers and called her up and said, "Paula? Come on over. Let's party. We'll order a pizza, and watch a video. Come on over, have a Coke! See if you don't have a good time—if you do, great! and if you don't, that's okay, I'll bring you right home. I promise. All you have to do is say, Butch, take me home, and I'll take you home. No questions asked. It's a deal." By the time he reached Platt, he was desperate for company.

So Paula would put on her best dress and doll herself up and go to the Bronco, expecting a social occasion, and there was no party, no pizza, the video was one of trucks at truck pulls, and there was Butch, alone, groping toward her in the dark, drunk.

This time when Butch called, Paula told him to stick his head in the toilet and flush it.

Butch hung around the Spud for two days, groveling in a purposeful way, and Paula wouldn't give him the time of day. She slapped his mashed potatoes down on the counter in front of him without a word and didn't say thanks when he left her humongous tips. Once he left her a twenty on a bill of $2.12. No smile did he get.

Butch told Earl, who was washing dishes at the Spud after school, "You don't get what you want in this world. Keep that in mind and you'll be a wiser man than me, boy. People are no damn good for the most part." He said it so Paula could hear, and she still said nothing.

Earl said, "Butch, that's a coffee philosophy. I could make you a cup of tea that would change your way of thinking. This tea could turn on the porch light in your eyes. If you drank tea, Paula would love you to pieces."

Paula, her back to them, snorted.

"Truck drivers do not drink tea," said Butch. "It does not happen. Only thing that could put a light in these eyes would be if Paula pulled up her dress and gave me the green light. And that's not going to happen either."

"You're right," she said softly.

TEA BULLETIN. TRUCK DRIVERS NOW DRINK TEA BY THE THOUSANDS, AND NOT ONLY THE ONES HAULING LOADS OF

FROZEN QUICHE OR LACE CURTAINS EITHER. GUYS HAULING
STEEL BEAMS, CARS, EVEN HOGS AND STEERS——MORE AND
MORE, THEY REQUEST TEA AT TRUCK STOPS AND TELL THE
WAITRESS HOW TO MAKE IT CORRECTLY. *NEVER* BRING A
TRUCKER A CUP OF HOT WATER AND A FRESH TEABAG LYING
NEXT TO IT ON THE SAUCER. *NEVER*. THE TEA MUST *ALWAYS*
BE PUT *IMMEDIATELY* INTO THE BUBBLING BOILING WATER.
AND A TEABAG IS VASTLY INFERIOR TO FRESH *LOOSE* TEA
WRAPPED IN A TINY *CLOTH* TEABAG THAT CAN BE TIGHT-
ENED WITH DRAWSTRINGS.

For a few years, Earl kept checking the Personals section in the Platt *Pilot,* hoping to see: *"Lost: our beloved
son Earl Grey, at a restaurant. Call home, honey, and we'll
come and fetch you. We love you so much. Mom and Dad."*
But no such ad ever appeared, only ads from men seeking younger women *(Married Guy, 57, seeks single woman
18–19, must be a real looker; pert and perky, and have a
thing about bulky fellas who don't say too much. Send photos.)*

"Your folks're sure missing a good thing, not watching you grow up, honey," Paula told Earl six years later,
when he was twenty-one. It was January and the arctic
winds swept the frozen tundra and moaned in the
weatherstripping around the front door of the Lucky
Spud and whistled in the chimney. It was cold and dark
and a heavy pallor hung in the air, the aroma of burnt
coffee.

And then a beautiful thought occurred to him: *I don't
have to stay. I can go.*

(Middle children often suffer from stationariness as a
result of being crunched in the middle with siblings on

either side, and many of them take years to realize that choice is an option—that a person can, if he wishes, have a will of his own, decide things, and act.)

Earl withdrew his savings from the Platt State Bank, $420, and arranged a ride with Butch, who was hauling a load of soybeans to San Francisco.

"God bless you, Earl Grey, for making my life a lot less dingy," said Paula, and they had a last pot of tea together. It was delicious. So calm and good. While Earl was rinsing the cups, the phone rang. Paula answered. It was Butch.

"Just come and spend twenty minutes with me, Paula honey," he said. "That's all I ask. Twenty minutes. If you don't like it, I'll bring you right back. Just say, Take Me Home, and back you come. I promise. Twenty minutes. Find out what kind of a guy I am. When I'm relaxed. When I'm being myself. Try it out. What do you have to lose? After twenty minutes, if you want to stay half an hour, great, I couldn't be happier. Otherwise it's *hasta la vista,* and you never have to see me again. All I'm asking is a chance to make you happy. Twenty minutes. If you don't do it, you'll spend the rest of your life wondering, what if? So give me a try. Not asking for a night or even an hour. Just twenty minutes. What do you say?"

"I say go put your head farther down the toilet," she said.

"A man can't get what he wants in this world," Butch told Earl as they cruised west in the big rig. "Don't you forget that." Earl dropped off to sleep, and when he awoke, the truck was in Palo Alto, parked in front of the Hoover Institution, a Spanish-mission edifice like a California bank.

"Well, this is as far as you go, I guess. Hope you enjoy your family. See you around," said Butch, anxious to get going.

"Goodbye, Butch," said Earl, knowing he probably would never see him again. He climbed down from the cab and a moment later the big rig pulled away and disappeared over the hill.

TEA LORE. TEA IS A PART OF FAREWELL CEREMONIES IN MANY CULTURES MORE ADVANCED THAN OUR OWN. AMERICANS, ESPECIALLY AMERICAN MEN, DON'T GO IN FOR EMOTIONAL GOODBYES AND LIKE TO PRETEND IT ISN'T FINAL, EVEN IF IT OBVIOUSLY IS. BREAKING UP WITH A WIFE, FOR EXAMPLE, THEY ARE LIABLE TO STROLL AWAY AS IF GOING TO THE CORNER STORE FOR A PACK OF SMOKES. IN OTHER CULTURES, PEOPLE SAY GOODBYE BY SITTING AROUND A TABLE AND ENJOYING A LAST POT OF TEA TOGETHER. THEY BELIEVE THAT TEA GIVES THEIR TEARS A BITTERSWEET FLAVOR. THEY WAIT AS THE TEA STEEPS, RECALLING LOVELY INCIDENTS FROM THEIR YEARS OF ACQUAINTANCE, RELISHING THEIR COMMON HISTORY, FEELING THE TUG OF TIME'S PASSAGE, AND THEN THE TEA IS POURED INTO EACH CUP AND DOCTORED WITH SUGAR OR MILK OR LEMON AND SLOWLY SAVORED, FOLLOWED BY A SECOND CUP, AND THEN:

1. STANDING
2. BOWING
3. EMBRACING AND WEEPING

4. EXCHANGING SORROW AND REMORSE
5. CLOSING THE DOOR AND BURSTING INTO SOBS
6. KEENING AND RENDING GARMENTS
7. FACING THE FUTURE BRAVELY

The Hoover Institution was locked. He pushed the buzzer and a voice came over the intercom: "State your name, your business, and whom you wish to see."

"My name is Earl Grey, and I am here to be reunited with my father, Congressman Grey," said Earl, looking into the intercom speaker as if it had eyes he could appeal to.

"The Congressman is gone," said the voice. Earl asked, Where? The voice said it did not know, nor did it know when he would return. Furthermore, it said, he had never mentioned a missing child.

Earl asked if he could leave a message for his dad. "Go ahead," said the voice.

"Tell him," said Earl, "to go and get stuffed."

Once he found out once and for all that he was abandoned, Earl Grey was free to go and make his own life. And he did, with one stroke of rare good fortune after another. He met Malene Monroe, who was then singing with the Tommy D'Orsay Orchestra, and he made her a pot of Earl Grey tea that cured her croup and enabled her to go on and record "Tea for Two." His royalties from that paid for three years in Sumatra, where he perfected his tea blend and also had two children by Anna Tin. He set up shop in London, promoted his tea, and developed a nice accent, and when he arrived back in

America in 1970, people assumed he was English nobil-
ity, and his tea took off.

But success didn't affect him. He knew that
middleness is an inner quality and you carry it all your
life, in all circumstances. A middle child can become a
star, stand on a stage in a gold lamé suit with six spotlights trained on him and his beautiful pectorals, and
sing his heart out and people in the audience will be
looking at the band, the third saxophonist from the
right, and thinking, "He reminds me of somebody, but
who? A guy who was at my wedding . . . But which
marriage? The third, I think. Was he one of the cater-
ers? Was he Barb's brother? Or was he in the orchestra?
Of course. He was in the orchestra! And he played saxophone, didn't he? Yes! He did. It was him! That man
played saxophone at my wedding!"—meanwhile, the
middle child has just wound up a version of "My Way"
that traversed six octaves of vocal dexterity and is now
about to sing the Sextet from *Lucia,* all six parts, but the
audience is unable to focus on that golden figure—his
essential middleness deflects their attention to the decor,
the candle in the lamp on the table, the waiter—doesn't
he remind you of someone who was in a movie once?

Once Earl thought he had found a sacred Shoshone
tea leaf that gives one the power to transcend
middleness, but it was only parsley, and Shoshone Indians did not make parsley tea. They put parsley on their
fish and they made tea from tea leaves wrapped in very
thin paper that the white men gave them in exchange
for Idaho.

Earl and his folks were reunited on a cable-TV show called *Bringing It Home* in 1987. His mom and dad grinned, and the host of the show, a smiley man named Brant whose hair was as big as a breadbox, said, "I think all the folks out there are ready to see a good hug right now, aren't we?" and the studio audience clapped, and Earl joined in the hug, but without pleasure. He didn't hug hard or long.

Oddly, Brant participated in the hug too, though he had met the Greys only fifteen minutes before. His eyes glittered with tears, he whooped, and he grinned like a house afire. "Earl Grey," he cried, "today your tea business has made you a multimillionaire, your name known around the world. Wouldn't you have to agree that maybe, *just maybe,* your being left behind in North Dakota may have been the best thing that ever happened to you?"

Earl looked at him in disbelief. "No," he said, "of course it wasn't. Don't be ridiculous. Children should never be abandoned by their parents."

Brant was not perturbed. He looked at Mrs. Grey and said, "He's quite a boy. You must be proud of him." And Earl realized that his answer was going to be edited out of the program and that they would edit in a "Yes, you're probably right" he had uttered earlier. But Earl was a middle child and there was nothing he could do about it.

WINTHROP THORPE TORTUGA

In early June, in the seventh inning of the broadcast of a Twins day game, the team behind 2–0, Winthrop's mailman, Kevin, knocked on the porch door and said, "If I'm not mistaken, your stockbroker has sent you a rather hefty check." And there it was: $126,830, a heck of a profit on an investment of $450 three years before in that little gene-splicing outfit, and the Twins won 8–2, and the next Monday Winthrop took a leave of absence from his job at Wheaties the Breakfast of Champions to devote himself to his family.

By mid-July, he had cleaned out the garage, rebuilt the engine of an old Dodge Dart for his son Dylan, paneled the basement, and installed a Ping-Pong table, and the Twins were in first place in the western division of the American League, three games ahead of Oakland. They swept a Saturday doubleheader from the A's, Kirby going six for nine, and what a rich Sunday morning it made—the planets in Winthrop's favor, his ducks all in a row, a sunny day, his windfall tucked away in an excellent mutual fund that was paying fourteen percent, the onions and green peppers diced for the breakfast omelets, the electric dicer working like a gem (those crafty Krauts), the Costa Rican coffee freshly dripped—"O Costa Rica!" he thought, standing in his blue pajamas. "Your dark beans are what drive Minneapolis to work in the morning! Without you we would all be in nursing homes, on respirators! Thank you, José!" He drank the coffee and dressed for church—a light-tan suit, a blue shirt, dark-blue tie with red dots. He would return home after church, awaken the sleeping household, make the omelets, and be a good father.

The grass in the backyard was tramped flat from his daughter Janis's birthday party Saturday night, a few long strands of red crepe paper wound through the hydrangea bushes. A lone beer bottle sat in the birdbath, left there perhaps by the same boy who, too shy to ask to come in and use the toilet, had vomited in the garage. Janis was sixteen. She was asleep upstairs with her boyfriend, Freddy—not his real name, which was Trent or Brent—*a good boy*, thought Winthrop. Freddy was quiet and polite to adults and he was crazy about Janis and made her cry out in pleasure late at night. The juggler who Winthrop hired for the party had arrived six hours late, ten p.m., full of apologies, upset that he had misread his calendar, and it took Winthrop fifteen minutes to quiet the kid down until, finally, he could do his act, standing on the back steps under the backyard light, the party guests strewn on the dark lawn. He did balls, clubs, and for his finale, he juggled a banana, a baseball, a banty rooster, and a brassiere, and Winthrop glanced over and saw Freddy's hand deep into Janis's shirt and thought, "How nice for her, to be with a boy as spirited as her daddy."

Winthrop and Dodie Tortuga had three children, Janis, and Dylan, nineteen, and Liz, who was twenty-three and in the Los Angeles area, and all of the family was going through a difficult period right now, everyone but the dad, he was a Twins fan on a roll. Janis was flunking her courses in school except for English, where her journals of sex with Freddy earned her B+'s, and Dylan went around in a black T-shirt with DEATH silk-screened on it and bit your head off if you spoke to him. Liz was unemployed and experiencing car accidents late at night. Dodie was struggling through an affair with her chiropractor, Dr. Haynes. Only Winthrop was taking care of business. What a good father. Who else in south Minneapolis would welcome Freddy under his roof and not say a word to Janis except to make sure she was protected against pregnancy—*who else but him?* His son cursed him and wandered lost through his days, shut up in a Walkman, but Winthrop was patient, he sympathized, he paid the bills. He sent Liz six hundred dollars every month and talked to her on the phone when she called at three or four a.m. oblivious to the time difference. Two or three mornings a week, he arose to find notes in his shaving kit, *Hi love, I'm at Haynes's tonight. Home in the morning.* And when Dodie came home, Winthrop fixed her breakfast, a terrific omelet. She was always exhausted. "You're my prince and he's my slave," she groaned—was that how a mother of three and a lifelong Congregationalist should talk? But Winthrop was kind and understanding. After all, he cared for her, she was his wife, and when your wife has an affair, don't you want it to be a good one, a great experience for her?

"Is Haynes still upset about what you told him about his feelings for you not being deep enough?" he asked her.

"No, he faced up to it very well, and last night he was so emotional, so intimate in a way I've never seen him be before. He was crying and laughing."

"That's good. Must have been very gratifying for you. I'd love to meet him, by the way."

It *had* bothered Winthrop for a while that Dodie's nightgown was under Haynes's pillow, but he learned how to protect his anger and now he was okay with it, and as he ambled out the front door this sunny morning and headed to church, he felt that his anger was well in hand. Nothing that his minister, Curtis Jon Ekerholm, had ever said about love and forgiveness was the slightest use to him. He went to church because it was a place to be alone and think. The peace that other people claimed to find through prayer, Winthrop found in random acts of cruelty to strangers. He was able to be a loving father and husband because he channeled all his anger into bigotry and meanness. That was how he kept his balance. He pushed into revolving doors ahead of spastics and when they stepped into the chamber behind him, he gave the glass a shove and whooshed through and heard their pitiful cries. He wrote hate letters. He let air out of the tires of cars with Sierra Club or Greenpeace bumper stickers—let the ecology jerks walk, he thought. He threw dog turds onto the lawns of upstanding people. He honked at senior citizens as they hobbled across the street at a red light and the geezers practically had heart attacks. He scratched swastikas on the lavatory wall at church, which so upset Pastor Ekerholm that he called a meeting of the congregation and stood up in anguish and cried, "This to me represents the utter failure of ten years of ministry here!" The good man wept and had to be hugged repeatedly, and out of this crisis came a big Holocaust Day observance, and a performance of *The Diary of Anne Frank.* The next day, Winthrop phoned in a bomb threat to a home for indigent actors. It was how he kept afloat.

On this morning, the church parking lot was almost empty. Summer doldrums. Fifteen worshippers in the pews, scattered, like a connect-the-dots picture, and Curtis J. in the pulpit, speaking on "The Need to Be Needed," one of his more murmury sermons, and Winthrop took out a pen and wrote in the hymnal, "Your Fly's Open, Dick Head." He resolved that when he got home he would ask Dylan to play tennis with him. He would patiently draw the boy out in conversation. The boy could not bear levity or criticism, he would mutter, "There you go again," or screech, "Stop putting me down!" It was like talking to a terrorist, Winthrop thought, his son was like a man crouched in a stairwell, holding a bomb. But Winthrop would try again. A very fine father.

Liberals like Curt were kind and loving to strangers, at least theoretically, and full of warm feeling for abstract entities such as The Poor and The Oppressed and The Minority, but liberals are hard as nails on their loved ones, preaching at them and holding them to impossible standards, perpetually shocked and disappointed by the flawed humanity of their flesh and blood. Liberals love a crowd, from a distance, and they treat their families like shit. Look at Curtis Jon, murmuring now about the needy and the needed, the necessity of need—what a cold fish he was to his wife, Martha, never acknowledging her physical presence with even a slight glance or a touch. A sad fate, to be attached to a Good Man. A good man in the worst sense of the term.

"Winthrop," said the pastor at the door after the service. "We've got to get you on the Christian outreach committee. It needs new blood."

"I don't have much blood left over," he said.

He slipped a note into the pastor's Ford Bronco, "We comin for *you*, mothuh," and walked home, feeling top of the world. A championship breakfast, a couple sets of tennis, a heart-to-heart with the boy, and he'd be back on the porch for the Twins vs. Oakland, one-ten p.m. on

WCCO with a cold Grain Belt and a plate of chicken wings. On his way to tennis, he should be sure to mail the letter he'd written to Dr. Jomo, a consultant to the Minneapolis School Board on the teaching of African-American culture: "Hey woolhead, you are about as African as I am but if you want to be ridiculous, go, be my guest, put a disc in your lip, put big wooden discs in *both* your lips, but go shake your spear on your own time, okay? Don't ask us taxpayers to foot the bill."

Bigotry acted as a stimulant to minorities, Winthrop knew. It got them roused up, all righteous and happy. He once wrote a letter to the National Organization for Women that was printed in a fund-raising letter:

"Dear ladies, I see you've got your tits in a wringer about so-called sexual harassment in the workplace—well, if it's too hot in the office, why not try the kitchen? This country took a wrong turn when American women decided to farm out their babies to day care and go to work so they could live the yuppie life. Result: millions of workers we don't need who file a lawsuit if you lay a hand on their shoulder, plus a generation of children with no moms, and society paying the price for years to come. Somebody ought to slap some sense into you broads."

He came home to find Janis slouched in the breakfast nook in her ragged pink bathrobe, her dirty feet propped up on the yellow wallpaper, puffing a cigarette and chatting away on the phone with someone who seemed to be in Sydney, Australia. He opened the back door to let air in. Freddy was upstairs taking a long shower. It continued as Winthrop broke the eggs and shaved the provolone and put a fire under the skillet and got the omelet going. Elapsed time on Freddy's shower was now forty-three minutes.

"You know what I feel like doing today?" he said when Janis got off the line from Australia.

"How in the world would *I* know?" she said bitterly. "I hate it when people say, 'Do you know what I feel like.' " She exhaled a torrent of smoke and scratched her legs. She looked pained. "I think there's something wrong with my uterus," she said.

Winthrop said, "What I feel like doing today is going to the Mega Death Mall and doing a major job of shopping, get us some clothes, look at CDs, load up on *stuff,* take our mighty credit cards and shop till we drop. What do you say?"

Her voice softened. "Okay. But I gotta get this IUD checked. I think it's stuck in my tubes or something."

"I'm sorry to hear it, darling. We will find you the best gynecologist in town."

And then Dodie wandered down. She wore gray sweatpants and a yellow tank top. Winthrop was smooshing the eggs around, buttering the toast, dripping a fresh pot of coffee, setting the table. Freddy's shower was now to the point where Winthrop wondered if the boy had collapsed from steam inhalation. Dodie kissed him on the ear and fixed herself a cup of tea. "No eggs for me, sweetie," she said. "I've got to run out and buy a swimsuit. If Haynes calls, tell him our flight's at four o'clock and he ought to be here by two-thirty."

It was none of Winthrop's business, of course, where she went with Haynes, but he wondered about it through his solitary breakfast—Janis and Freddy had to meet someone at McDonald's, Dylan was asleep—and to make himself feel better, he sat down and wrote some letters. He wrote to the gay coalition ("How exactly is society to blame for you boys giving each other an incurable disease? Am I missing something? Did you really expect us to run into the bedroom and pull your wieners out of your butts?") and he wrote to a neighbor woman, an animal-rights activist ("I guess I can understand why a dog-faced bitch like you has a thing for animals—you can bribe them to like you and they never get bored—but when you start terrorizing scientists, trying to save the lives of bunnies so that people can die of cancer, then it's time for someone to put strychnine in your tofu, Bubbles"), and he wrote to his congressman ("About the Disabled Act you voted for that requires the taxpayer to make the world flat for the handicapped—why not make public transit bed-accessible while we're at it? Why should the bedridden be denied the right to public transportation? Why don't buses have four-foot seats for lard butts like yourself?").

At two-forty-five, a shiny red Triumph pulled in alongside the Tortuga garage, *fast,* with a squeal of rubber, and a man in a seersucker suit jumped out, removed his driving gloves and mirror shades, saw Winthrop on the porch listening to the Twins, came up, and stuck out his hand—it was Haynes.

"I'm Dodie's chiropractor, been treating her for three years, trying to alleviate those terrible neck pains—"

Winthrop said, "I know that you're lovers and it's okay. Relax. Have a beer."

Haynes took a seat on a wicker bench, his back to the sun. He was wiry and hairy. Chest hair, thick. Hairy hands, and hair on the back of his neck. "We didn't get involved—you know, sexually involved—until just about two months ago. It was a sudden thing, surprising to both of us, and we went to my place in Aspen for the weekend—"

Dodie had gone to Aspen? For a whole weekend? He hadn't noticed.

"—and I suppose we thought it was only the sexual fascination, and a weekend would satisfy that and we'd go back to our families, but then she walked into my place and saw my art standing around and we realized that we were both welders, art welders—"

Dodie? Welding?

"—so we're thinking about getting divorces, and going to Mexico. We might open a workshop and gallery in Oaxahuacapocapetl and live there, in an adobe hut, in the village with the Pocapetl Indians."

The Twins were getting pummeled in the top of the third, Jack Morris was throwing high fastballs and the A's were distributing them to various corners of the outfield and bleachers. "Dodie has told me so much about you," Haynes said. "She said that you are the most wonderful husband she can imagine."

"Well, she's only had one, so what would she know?"

The bases were loaded, there were no outs, the score was 3–zip. Maybe this was the turning point of the season for the Twinkies. They had faded in July before.

And then Dodie came downstairs, out of breath, naked, dripping wet from her shower, a towel tossed over her shoulder. "You're late," she told Haynes. "I clearly told you to be here at two-thirty."

"I got lost." He shrugged.

"I had no idea you welded, Dodie," Winthrop said softly.

She threw her head back and snorted. "You didn't hear me? at night? the sparks flying up?"

"I guess I thought you were—I don't know—*basting*. Browning the meat. But you're really thinking about moving to Mexico?"

"Never mind that, I'm looking for my Tampax," she said.

"Maybe Janis borrowed it," said Winthrop. "Want me to run out and get some?" He noticed she had a tattoo on her left hip that said *All Night Long*. He didn't want to ask how long it had been there.

"We can stop on the way to the airport," she said, and ran up to get dressed.

"Pardon me if this sounds dumb, but what is the way to the airport?" Haynes asked. Winthrop couldn't believe that a grown man didn't know where the airport was, but he got out an envelope and a pencil and drew a map. "I can barely find my way to the office," said Haynes. "I can't tell you how often I've wound up in St. Paul."

Winthrop drew in a route: Lake Street west to Hiawatha, south on Hiawatha past the VA Hospital and right at the light and look for the signs. "You wouldn't take 35W?" asked Haynes. No, said Winthrop, 35W gets backed up at the Crosstown and you can sit there for fifteen or twenty minutes. "Hiawatha is your best bet," he said.

Dodie came down and gave him a big hug. "You're a heckuva guy, Winny, that's all I can say. This has got nothing to do with you, believe me. This is all about me. I was never cut out to be a south Minneapolis mom. I tried. I went to church, I went to Twins games, I was active in the Democratic-Farmer-Labor party, but it doesn't work for me. Too smug, babes, too earnest, too bor-ing. It's all forehand, no backhand. I keep running into pathetic people trying to look hip by wearing French T-shirts and leaving *New York* magazine on their coffee table. I hate this life. I despise winter. I don't much care for my kids. But you're good with them, Winny. Take care, now. See you soon. Thank you for all your wonderful love." And she gave him a peck on the lips and out the door they went and the Triumph roared away. Water dripped in the sink, and a cat meowed in the peonies, the neighbors' cat, Timmy, who had diarrhea from all the spicy food they fed him.

The Twins jumped into the lead on a Kirby Puckett triple in the sixth inning with two men aboard, then Kirb came home as the A's bobbled an easy grounder to second. A three-run lead, and then in the seventh, the A's got a two-out pinch-hit grand slam by a reserve second baseman batting .137. A lucky poke by a guy who'd be back in Paducah driving a bread truck next summer. A bummer.

She shouldn't be with that weasel, Winthrop thought. She should be here with her husband.

He had met Dodie at the University. They were juniors. She was a poet. Her poems appeared in little magazines with names like *Opus, Still Water, Whisker Cafe,* and *Portugal.* She was so fair: fair-skinned with shining brown eyes and a long thin nose, and slightly bow-legged. After they made love for the first time, she wrote a poem—"Under a brown canvas tarp, / taking turns being on top so that each could see the stars, / we went as high as we could, like children / on the swings at night, Andromeda / between their bare feet. / And suddenly I saw the tiny house / where I have been living for years, my love, / and, my love, I don't want to go back." He considered it an honor to be immortalized as a lover, though they had not made love under the stars but in the Gopher Motor Lodge near campus, in a bed, not outdoors. The poem appeared in the next issue of *Portugal,* and he married her, and she never wrote another poem, which was a disappointment to him. He was in business administration and liked the idea of marrying a poet.

Haynes was her attempt to resume her lost writing career. She said so herself. "Adultery is just another branch of fiction," she told Winthrop.

The Twins had two on in the eighth with none out and Hrbek at bat when the Triumph roared up in back, and an angry voice cut through the still afternoon. It was Dodie, telling Haynes to go screw himself.

Winthrop stepped out on the back porch in time to see Haynes slam the door of the Triumph so hard the side mirror fell off. He put it back on, and Dodie opened the trunk and grabbed her duffelbag and yelled, "All you had to do was to stop at a gas station and ask for directions! We had time! But would you stop and ask for directions? *No, you wouldn't,* ya dummy!"

And Winthrop thought: Did I tell him to turn right at the light after the VA Hospital, instead of turning left?

Haynes yelled, "I'm glad this happened now, so I didn't have to go all the way to Mexico to find out what a miserable bitch you are!"

Winthrop called out, "Did you miss the plane?" She stormed into the house and, a moment later, was in the shower. Like a losing pitcher.

Haynes advanced across the grass, ducking under the clotheslines, and stood, hands on hips, and said, "I hope you're getting a big kick out of this now, because believe me, in two weeks, you'll be sorry she ever came back." And he turned, not remembering how close the clothesline was, and it caught him across the neck, where a guillotine would, and dumped him on his back. He limped to his car, rubbing his neck, and drove away forever.

AL DENNY

So much dead wood and garbage in our lives, phoniness, grandstanding, humbuggery: how to rid ourselves of it and move on to richer, deeper things? how to shuck these lures and snares and give the beauty within us space in which to grow and bloom? how to be more the good person we set out to be when we were nineteen instead of this dull greedy old weasel snarfing all the food on the plate who we turned into instead?

These questions began to bear down on me a few years ago, when I was in San Francisco to participate in a conference on Birthing Our Self-Affirmation of Wellness and I enjoyed a beautiful massage from a holist named Sha-tsi that completely emptied my being of all havingness (just as she said it would) and afterward my billfold was gone. It wasn't in my briefcase or in my overcoat.

And there was no name tag on my garment bag or my carry-on.

A great massage, but I could not recall my home telephone number or even remember where I lived.

Suddenly I recalled Thoreau's advice, "Simplify, simplify." So I called my agent, Larry. "Where am I from?" I asked. He wasn't sure either. Ohio, he thought. I looked at a map of Ohio. Nothing rang a bell. I had been on the road for three years since I wrote *Being the Person You Are*, and gradually Mona and I had lost touch.

"How many children do I have, Larry?" I asked. He thought three. Three sounded right. Mona had been the primary care-giver in the family, so I wasn't sure. Three daughters, he thought, but I thought I remembered a boy.

Arnie?

I never thought this would ever happen to me. *Being the Person You Are* was short, thirty thousand words, and nobody at Chester White Publishing thought the book would cut much lumber in the self-esteem field up against giants like Wayne Dyer and Leo Buscaglia, but it went out and it sold five million copies or so in more than eleven languages and seventeen dialects.

Not bad for a Methodist minister who, in fifteen years of Sunday sermons, never had anyone come up to afterward and requested a copy.

So many people have told me that *Being the Person You Are* completely changed their lives, and others have had their lives changed partially.

Well, it changed mine too. The book was about taking charge of your life and tapping into your deep inner power sources, but the success of the book was like a flash flood, and I floated away like a loose canoe. I ballooned from 180 to 238 pounds and chewed my fingernails and my hair got thin and three months later there I was, a big lumbering galoot with bleeding cuticles climbing in and out of limos and adjusting his toupee, and though I could afford a good one, not nylon, still I felt stressed, jumpy, owly, and the baldness affected my balance so I was liable at any time to topple over into a heap.

I fell on a woman in the lobby of the Four Seasons Clift hotel in San Francisco. She was small and delicate, Japanese, visiting our country perhaps for the first time, garnering impressions, and suddenly a big load of blubber lands in her lap.

I fell across the head table on the dais at the Bobist Institute in Santa Fe, tumbled into the tofu salad. People applauded, thinking that I had made a bold point that would be clearer to them later.

Doctors puzzled over my dizziness. An acupuncturist put needles in my knuckles, an herbalist made a saffron sachet to hang around my neck. One morning, I woke up in Dayton, Ohio, fully dressed, sprawled across a hotel bed, my pants moist from creamy desserts stuffed in my pockets. I was registered there under the name Dr.

Santana Mens, and a pink name tag with the Mens name on it was gummed to my breast pocket. It was a name tag from a large bookstore in a nearby mall, and I assumed I was supposed to go and autograph books, but when I called, they said that I had been there a week ago.

Was Dayton, Ohio, my home? Had some homing instinct brought me there, some unconscious imprint of flight schedules? There was no Al Denny in the phone book. Had Mona gone back to being a Thompson?

"You've got to get your life on track, Al," I thought, and Larry had provided a week's break on the lecture tour, so I hunkered down in the Mayfair Hotel in Chicago and wrote *Rebirthing the Me You Used to Be*, and that sucker sold fourteen million copies—in fact, it's still selling—in thirty languages, including a New Guinea tribal dialect in which my book was the first written literature. Through an interpreter, the chief, a man named Wallace Boogada, invited me to come and be their deity. They had been Christianized by Army chaplains during World War II, but God had disappointed them and they wanted to try me.

Evidently, *Rebirthing* rang the wind chimes of a lot of folks, and it certainly dinged my doorbell too. I thought, "Al, you have got to simplify your life now."

One day, I met Larry for lunch and noticed his tie, deep blue with a majestic stag elk standing on high rocks as ducks wing across an autumn sky and an Indian paddles a canoe across a broad pine-rimmed lake— "Larry," I said, "I'm taking the loot and buying a mountain and building a log lodge on top of it and moving up there with nothing but dry clothes and a notepad and some coffee beans and warm bedding and a Scout knife. Doggone it. And I want an elk. And a canoe."

"Great," he said. "I'll take care of that, while you finish up the lecture tour."

I told him I desperately needed to get out into nature and put my priorities in order, but he had put together a great package, "An Evening with Dr. Al Denny," thirty lectures in twelve cities, at ninety thousand dollars per crack, and it was too late to back out, so I went—BIG SUCCESS, standing room only, hockey arenas packed with quiet people in meaningful T-shirts, people with interesting hair, there were press conferences and blizzards of questions about polarity and rebirthing and chrysalis-awareness and re-aging and the ancient Inca secrets channeled through a Cleveland man now known as El Hugo, and three-hour autographing sessions and people fawning over my every word—I'd say, "Hi, how are you?" and they would say, "Yes! Of course! *How* are you! It's not the whereness or the whyness or the whoness of the You, it's how! How!"

A month later, the tour ended in Tallahassee, and Larry sent a Learjet to take me to the mountain. Except it wasn't a mountain, it was more like a plateau, and it was in Iowa. A vast complex of buildings he had bought from the Maharishi for two hundred million dollars. He drove me around fast in the dark on a golf cart, pointing out a dormitory here and a dormitory there, a gymna-

sium that would be our TV studio, a barn where the llamas would be housed.

"Llamas?"

"A very peaceful creature. You'll love them. They'll
be in the petting park, with the deer," he said. "People
will come, live here at the resort, go to the spa, take
your courses at the study center, be rebirthed, pet the
llamas, visit you in your home, and have a tremendous
two weeks. We have more than two thousand reserva-
tions for June already. You're hot, Al. People want to be
near you."

All the buildings looked the same to me, three-story
light-brown brick things with narrow windows and flat
roofs, like nursing homes or an office park. The gymnasium had a thirty-foot satellite dish in back of it.

"For your cable show," he explained, parking the cart,
and we opened the big steel doors and there was the studio, three hundred feet long, bleachers for two thousand,
six cameras on dollies, a set with a long white couch and
fake windows and plants. "State of the art," he said,
proudly.

So I had to write another book to pay the overhead.
Coexisting with Your Other Self did not do as well as *Rebirthing* but it sold five million and had a blue cover
with primitive masks on it. It was about using your inner potential to create an outer protective self to guard
the secret beautiful you.

Meanwhile, I moved into my home on the grounds of
the Dr. Al Denny Study Center, fully furnished, tooth-
paste and night-light and wine carafe, throw rugs, ac-

cent pieces, all there and ready. Larry took care of it. I seldom left the home due to the disciples lurking in the trees and because I was a little down since losing track of Mona and the children. Mona and I had been married for twenty-four years, and I loved her, but I was never clear on exactly what she did—some sort of teaching, I believe, or investment services—so it was hard to trace her through professional associations. I believed she used to attend meetings now and then in Chicago, but forgot why. I laid low for awhile. I watched old movies and slept, and every day Larry drove a van into the garage (attached) and closed the door, I climbed in and lay on the floor, he zoomed out past the disciples and took me to the studio.

On *The Circle of Life with Dr. Al Denny*, a half-hour program carried everywhere in America, I sat on the couch in front of the audience and chatted with persons of wisdom such as quilt-makers, for example, and wood-carvers and southern people and farmers and old blues singers and old ballplayers and old shepherds and Io-wans and people over eighty and country doctors and guys named Walt, people you seldom see on TV. Their simple philosophies were deeply moving to me though also confusing.

They all said that the best things in life are spiritual, and I myself was in a very acquisitive stage of life at that point.

I owned four Bentleys. I owned paintings. I owned two fine horses, who terrified me. I owned 164 cases of a 1952 Bordeaux that I loved to drink with a particular kind of lobster that was flown in live from the Mindanao archipelago. I kept buying sweaters and loafers and those baggy pants with the fronts that pooch out. I purchased expensive dogs, one after the other, because I kept losing track of them. I'd leave them in stores and places. One was a Dalmatian, and another was a Weimaraner, I think. Somebody said it was, and then it was gone too.

Once on my show there was a heavyset gal from Mobile named Vernelle Tomahasset who devoted her life to creating art from bread bags and said the most important thing in life is to keep busy—she gave me a little horse made out of nine hundred bread bags—and a one-armed accordion man said he felt lucky because he had his health, and the very same day I paid seven thousand dollars for a German-made CD player. Only a hundred like it in the world, and I have one, and Prince Charles has another. It was like that a lot of the time.

A shepherd came on and said, "Waste not, want not, that's my motto. Also: there's such a thing as too much of a good thing."

Meanwhile, I owned three separate houses within ten miles of each other, two on the Study Center grounds, and one in Mason City that I never saw, the remodeling went on and on.

An old rug-hooker from Omaha said, "Dr. Al, you know it's true: there's no summer without winter."

I had just purchased a $3.5-million home on a private island off Antigua where I planned to spend December, January, February, March, and the first part of April.

But before I got to fly down there, a child Autoharp-player named Little Ginny came on the show. She was terminally ill, and Larry had read somewhere that dying children possess preternatural wisdom. She died a few days afterward of a mysterious raging fever. She was an assertive little tyke and she spoke right up in her sickly voice and told you what she thought. She wasn't whiny or grumpy. When I asked her what her name was, she said, "God gives us new names in heaven, and I want to be a Theresa but right now I'm Ginny."

I'll never forget the hush in the studio when that tiny pale child staggered to the couch in her pure-white dress, lugging the harp, and climbed up, and sat there with an oxygen tube in her nose, her chin on her chest, listing to one side, and strummed "O Dem Golden Slippers" and faintly sang, "I'se goin up de ribbah wheah de golden rainbow shine," as her relatives collapsed sobbing in the wings. She was white and had learned the song from an old book of spirituals.

The audience clapped and clapped until our production people had to tell them to hush.

At this point, she was supposed to tell me a folktale about a mother hen and her chicks, but instead she climbed up on my lap and draped her skinny arm around my neck and put her little cheek next to mine.

My gosh, she was hot, burning up with fever, and sweat poured off her. An extremely hot damp child. A bead of her sweat fell on the back of my hand and—this sounds insensitive, I know, but nobody had informed me if her fatal illness was contagious or not—I thought to myself: "Al, you need a fatal disease right now like you need a hole in the head."

I tried to pry her loose but her bony fingers were clamped onto my wrist and my lapel, and when I tried to bend her fingers back, she flopped around like a dying fish and her eyes rolled back up in her head.

I tried to signal the staff with my eyebrows to come and take this hot potato off my hands, but they were overcome with emotion, I guess. When I tried to stand up, she clung to me like a bat and tore the rug off my head, and then Little Ginny pressed her burning face to mine and whispered in her hoarse little voice, "God says to cut out this shit. He says, stop it and shape up."

I knew right then that my career had peaked and that the long grim slide had begun, but of course I couldn't know how far it was to the bottom.

I smiled and said, "Friends and neighbors, I know this show is one I'll remember as long as I live. What do you say we invite Little Ginny to come back next week?" Everybody clapped again, but Little Ginny looked at me with pure disgust. She said, "Don't be stupid. You know I'll be in my grave next week."

And she turned to the camera and whispered, "Every word he says is a big fat lie."

She died a few days later.

I sat at home and thought, "What shit am I supposed to cut out?"

Am I supposed to give away money? Fine. But where do you draw the line? There's the heart fund and the bladder fund and the Save the Snakes foundation and the Center for the Dull and there's a cabdriver whose mom is waiting to come over from Zagreb and a waitress with a slight limp and who do you say no to? Once you start giving away dough, if you say no they'll write long accusatory letters and lurk around your home and attack you with coat hangers. No, a rich man can't buy peace of mind.

I began to discuss these issues in *Empowering Others by Enabling Yourself*, and the next thing I knew, there was a knock on the door and it was the FBI.

An unfriendly agent in a shiny gray suit talked to me for four hours. He asked me about some Life Savings Certificates that had been sold across the country by mail, certificates issued by the Al Denny Savings Institute—I hadn't heard about that at all!

Evidently, fifteen thousand people had mailed in sixty thousand dollars apiece on the promise that they could live at the Study Center through their declining years and be rebirthed.

Some of them now wished to obtain their money back.

"Talk to Larry," I told the FBI, but they said that Larry was gone. He had flown to the private island off Antigua, and he was not answering the phone.

The FBI drove me to Mason City and led me through a gauntlet of TV cameras and flashbulbs and put me in a small, cinder-block cell.

Then they located Mona. She was in *Akron,* Ohio, not Dayton. Akron. And we had two daughters and a son named Aaron.

"Al, you big wombat, how the heck are you?" she

cried, throwing her arms around me. "I always said you oughta be locked up. Gosh, I love you, you big lug."

She wasn't a teacher or an investment person, it turned out—she was a *lawyer,* and a darned good one. She got me out of the clinker and back to Akron in a jiffy.

The kids all have her red hair and big beak and melting brown eyes. My son looked up as I walked in and said, "Did you remember the butter brickle?"

"No, I forgot," I said.

"Oh." He wasn't surprised. Evidently, forgetting had been a habit with me.

It's good to be a regular daddy again instead of a big cheese, and I have promised the kiddoes not to write a book again. I started one called *Starting Over*, which was about men finding new roles as daddies and homemakers, but then I got too busy to write. You make breakfast for Mona, pack her a healthy bag lunch, send her off, wake up the kids, and shepherd them through the cleansing-dressing process, answer all their questions, feed them, get the kids out the door with their lunches and homework in hand, wash the breakfast dishes, and go from room to room with a vacuum and a feather duster, and change the beds and scrub the bathrooms, and after five hours your urge to sit and write and regale the reader with insights has mostly dissipated, you would rather go dig in the garden and put in the crocus bulbs. Life is good. More than good. You have a clean house and feel like a clean man! You have not told a single lie and it is almost lunchtime! Praise God for His goodness! Now you must plan the supper.

GEORGE BUSH

The day the barbarians came, George Bush was out in a boat on the Potomac River with Willie Horton, fishing, and Willie said, "Mister Butch, how come you always be jigglin and tappin yo foot? Man, those fish ain't goin to come within a *mile* of us if you makin this racket. Let your foot be, man. Sit still."

"Willie," said the President, "you know the—we're going to clean up here, get some fish, have a heck of a time. Not a vague hope. Talkin promise now. Serious fishing. Got you out of prison for the afternoon. Little favor. Don't mention it. Didn't bring you out here to get a tan, Willie. Came to do a little *fishin.*"

"Mister Butch, I'm grateful for the afternoon off, but you keep tappin away with that foot of yours, you drive away the fish, man. What is it with you? You always drummin yo fingers, you always gettin up and shiftin around and takin yo hat off and puttin yo hat back on yo haid, you always changin yo bait, changin yo sinker, you takes yo line up, you put it back down, up, down, up, down, you pop open yoself a cold Budweiser and then you let it set there in the hot sun, you open the cheese curls and you pick at 'em awhile but you don't eat 'em—what's eatin at you, Mister Butch?"

The President looked away off up the Potomac to the Jefferson Memorial, the perfect dome of glimmering white in the sunshine, a temple to intellect and art and democratic civility, and he crunched on a cheese curl and pulled the brim of his L. L. Bean fishing hat down and took a long pull on a Budweiser. The fact was, he had been tired of fishing two minutes after they started, and he was tired of Willie. Despite all he owed to the man, he didn't much care for hanging around with the guy. Too pushy, too talkative by half, like so many cons—lots of time on their hands, years, so they read book after book, law books, all the classics, Great Book stuff—fine, great, but *don't tell me about it, okay, pal?* No sense of humor, some of these guys.

And Willie was right, something was eating at him, and it was the barbarians. Vast hordes of barbaric Huns had invaded Chicago that morning, and a reporter had nabbed him as he headed for the car to come fishing— told Marlon, "No press, no press, no press," and out the door he goes and there's this beaky guy with a cassette recorder shoved in the President's *face* and he yells, "The Huns are wreaking carnage in Chicago, Mr. President! Any comment?"

What could he say? He had only seen a brief clip of the invasion on the *Today* show, twenty seconds, bunch of ugly people waving burning sticks—what the hell? he thought, but he turned to the reporter and gave him the maximum *presidente* look, the George Bush in Crisis Mode look, and said, "Bob, we're following that whole *Hun situation* up there very, very closely, and right now, I must say, despite the loss of life which, as you know, is *always regrettable*—a President sits up late nights thinking about things of that nature—and yet, I have to say, by willikers it looks encouraging, better than anybody ever hoped, so I'm just going to go way out on a limb here and describe myself as concerned, yes, but relaxed and definitely chins-up and in charge. The President is in charge, Bob. That's part of the job. I think that people who think the President is not in charge are going to have a very big surprise coming. I don't want to say what that is."

The President reeled in his line and checked his hook—no worm, just as he suspected. "You think there's no fish, think again," he said to Willie. "Who ate that bait? Snapping turtles?"

The President put a fresh worm on his hook and lowered it into the water. How ironic, he thought. Beautiful day. Perfect day. And yet all the suffering in the world. The beauty-suffering irony.

At that moment, the good citizens of Chicago were fortifying the Loop, building barricades across Michigan Avenue and pulling up the drawbridges over the Chicago River, jamming taxicabs ten deep along Lakeshore Drive, and organizing scalding-oil brigades along the canyon of the Illinois Central tracks that ran between the city and the shore of Lake Michigan, but their cauldrons never got hot enough, and the hordes broke through. The barbarian boats landed in Lincoln Park near the bird sanctuary, and thousands of them poured through the North Side—wave after wave of squat, flat-nosed horsemen in leather skirts riding their ugly stump-legged steeds came galumphing down State and LaSalle, trotting past the bookstores and coffee stores and the Benettons and Gaps and Banana Republics, waving their hairy fists, rolling their little red eyes under the long black hairy eyebrow, grunting and blatting and howling, *Haroooooo, Haroooooooooo,* and bellowing at women in a coarse, unintelligible tongue like irate geese.

For three days, hordes of Ostrogoths, Visigoths, Hloths, Wendells, and Vandals came down from Wisconsin, swept through Evanston and Morton Grove and Skokie, swarmed into the Windy City with relentless, locustlike ferocity, and put the torch to hundreds of churches, performing-arts centers, and historic restorations, and dragged away monks, virgins, associate professors, and postal employees to be sold into slavery, and seized great stores of treasures, heirlooms, and sacred vessels, and tore down libraries, devastated excellent restaurants, and traded away the Cubs and Bears.

Mr. Bush, back from fishing, rested, capable, conferred with John Sununu, met with the Cabinet, weighed his options, was on the verge of taking some kind of dramatic action. To those close to him he appeared burdened but still strong, upbeat but not glib. Then he made his move.

The President ordered the armed forces to enforce a complete blackout on all news of the invasion. "We will deny the enemy what he most desperately wants, and that is our attention and that of the American people." All journalists were to be kept at a holding area in Peoria, 128 miles southwest of the action.

Thirty minutes later, in came the President's pollster, Robert Teeter, with a poll showing that seventy percent of the American people thought the President was doing an excellent job with the barbarians. Mr. Bush was seen as confident and in charge but not beleaguered or vulnerable or damp under the arms the way Jimmy Carter had been during the Iran-hostage situation. Most Americans admired the way George Bush played down the story and wasn't weakened or distracted by it. They felt that he was doing exactly the right thing, that sticking the press in Peoria was just what they would've done, and they viewed Chicago as a place where pretty rough stuff goes on most of the time anyway.

So the President didn't have to address the nation on television after all, a huge relief to him. He walked through the West Wing, calling out, "Strike the set. Speech is off. Kill the lights. No speech." He hated giving speeches, especially those long drony serious ones from the Oval Office. *Hey, it's just not me, okay? Give me a break, pal.* The White House issued a statement saying that barbarianism is a long-term problem, no quick solutions, the answer is education, everything that can be done is being done and will continue to be done. It called for bipartisanship. It said the President would decide soon whether to name a barbarian czar to coordinate the federal effort. That evening, a White House dinner went on as planned, honoring Arnold Schwarzenegger for his work on behalf of fitness. "Anyone who says George Bush is a girly man is dead meat," said Arnold, grinning. The President appeared calm but interested.

The barbarians made their squalid camps in the parks and on the boulevards and took over the savings-and-loan offices. "Savings and loan" sounds similar to the Hun word *chfnxnln,* which means "hen-house." They broke out all the plate-glass windows and covered them with sheepskins, they squatted in the offices around campfires of teak and mahogany desks and armoires, eating half-cooked collie haunches and platters of cat brains and drinking gallons of aftershave. Their leader, Mogul the Vile, son of Generic, squatted down beside a speakerphone on the thirty-eighth floor of American National, called the White House, and babbled and screeched for more than twenty minutes. His English was horrendous. He seemed to be demanding a ransom of three chests of gold and silver, six thousand silk garments, miscellaneous mirrors and skins and beads, three thousand pounds of oregano, and $166 billion in cash.

The President, who did not speak to him personally, pondered the outrageous demand as he did his low-impact exercises in the White House gym. He appeared quiet but wakeful, thoughtful but not grumpy. On the one hand, a major American city was in the hands of rapacious brutes, but, on the other hand, exit polling at shopping malls showed that people thought he was handling it okay. So he flew to Kennebunkport for a week of tennis and buzzing around in his boat. He appeared relaxed but hearty, animated but restrained.

A few days later, the Hun sacking of Chicago was old news. It had already happened. Mr. Bush, in striking a note of determination right at the beginning and then refusing to be stampeded into action, had outflanked the story and avoided any loss of public support. He spoke to Willie by phone and Willie said, "You sure cool, Mister Butch, you the coolest dude I ever hung with, man, you be like the brother who these mean mothuhs, they point the gun at him, they say, Man, give us that there car of yours—the brother looks at the mothuhs, he says, Man, I don't *want* that car, he says, Man, I *never* wanted that car. You cool like that brother, Mister Butch."

"I must say, there's a whole air of I don't know what you'd call it frankly, a kind of unreality that's operating here, it's like a guy is lucky to—I mean, if you can come to the end of the day with both nuts intact, you're ahead of the game," said the President. "So I guess I must be doing okay. I got both of 'em. Right here."

There were stories in the press, of course, about the pillaging up north, but most of the press was in Washington, not Chicago, and what could you say about Huns that everybody didn't already know? Huns perspire heavily; they make terrible farmers and lousy husbands, they don't eat vegetables, only meat and gravy and desserts, and they drink bad sweet wine; their clothes are ill-fitting and covered with lint; they smell rancid and their hair is limp and dull, and they're ugly as a mud fence—short, flat-faced, thick-lipped, illiterate, grunty people with heavy brows, hairy backs, and no necks, that's your basic Hun horde. And their relationship with the press is very, very poor. Huns do not take well to criticism. They are not easy to talk to. They've never seen movies, never read books, never done anything interesting except rape and pillage. And how long can you talk about rape and pillage?

On the other hand, the country was tired of hearing Huns bad-mouthed by the same old liberal doom-and-gloom writers. *Give me a break.* The country was curious about Huns and Hun lifestyle. *Vanity Fair* did a Hun cover, showing Bruce Willis eating half-cooked collie haunches with a naked virgin tied to a chair next to him, her head back, fainting—it was a big topic of conversation: *Did you see the Hun on the cover of* Vanity Fair?

Some ministers protested that it was tasteless, but that was the whole point, of course, and the owners of collies protested, but the fact was, collie haunches can be drop-dead delicious if you braise them with plenty of garlic over a trash fire, and the *Vanity Fair* writer who cooked collie concluded that the barbarians were barbaric, hell yes, but unmistakably thrilling and possessed of a true visceral authenticity—"Call it vicious, ruthless, brutal, degenerate, call it what you will, but barbarism is here to stay, and we may as well learn to enjoy what it has to offer, a directness and a frankness, a you-have-it-I-want-it-I-take-it sensibility that is frankly refreshing after all these years of boring boring boring humanism."

The President, a devoted dog man, wasn't interested in trying collie haunches or wearing Hun outfits, but he decided not to interfere with the takeover attempts in the savings-and-loan industry—sure, there were these pesky yammering voices in the press about how he ought to step in, etc., etc., as if it were that *simple.* Easy for the press to point the finger, much harder to be the pointee who, darn it, is just trying to do a day's work and get home in time for a hot shower and a highball before you got to go to the damn banquet, sit up there, and pick at your damn chicken surrounded by a bunch of Bible fanatics and right-wing creeps with their tiny narrow ties and their squinty eyes, and you grinning and backslapping like mad, but you *know* they never liked you and they *know* you know that and it sure does not make for a nice evening out for the Bushman. Boy oh boy.

He told the Secretary of the Treasury to pay the $166 billion, not as a ransom of any type—no, absolutely not, there was no element of ransom involved nor was it ever discussed for a moment by anyone in this Administration—but as ordinary government support, plain and simple, absolutely nothing irregular about it, and the next day, the Huns and the Vandals rode away, carrying their treasure with them, and the Goths sailed away up Lake Michigan. Gothic boats are hard to handle, though, being built of stone, with great high arches that make them tippy, and they all sank in Lake Michigan in a light breeze, carrying half the loot to the bottom, but not before the President's chopper landed in Grant Park. He had flown to O'Hare aboard Air Force One, then boarded a Marine Corps helicopter for the five-minute hop to the Loop.

Willie watched it on CNN from his prison cell. How cool the man was, he thought. The twitchiest, jumpiest foot-tapping, finger-drumming, facial-ticking nervous mothuh you ever saw, but capable of such cool moves the man coulda held up liquor stores with nothing but a potato in his hand, he was that cool.

It was a serious-faced George Bush who stood at the water's edge, hair blowing from the rotor backwash, and announced that the barbarians had been removed. He said that the savings-and-loan industry was sounder than at any time in the nation's history. He announced that he was deeply moved by the heroism of the people of Chicago and reiterated his lifelong opposition to human suffering of any kind whatsoever.

CHRISTMAS IN VERMONT

It was Christmas Eve in Vermont, and through the howling blizzard struggled the runaway nearsighted boy Jim, his red-plaid shirt frozen to his back, his skinny arms limp from hauling his big golden retriever Tony, who was wet and therefore much heavier than if the weather had been warm and sunny. Jim had left home that morning, because his folks were talking about going contra-dancing on New Year's Eve and leaving him with the servants, and now big wet flakes were falling so thickly he couldn't see the nose on his own face—and Jim did have a good-sized beezer. "I'm done for, Tony," whimpered the myopic child wearily. Death was near. If only he had worn a sheepskin coat or asked Basil to drive him in the limo! And suddenly, with a loud *whump* and an *oof,* he walked into a small statue or something and fell down with Tony on top of him. It was an antique carved wooden figure of a fisherman! He was back at his mom and dad's house! He had wandered through the blizzard in a full circle back to Hickey Avenue in Redford and the palatial colonial home of his wealthy and irrepressible parents. He pounded weakly on the door with his small plump hands.

Before the door opens, let me say that this story is made possible in part with the financial help of the folks at Bert & Willy's Ice Cream and their forty-four thousand business associates in the Bert & Willy work experience. Bert and Willy were two dope-crazed hippies who drove to Vermont in 1968 in a stolen car loaded with dynamite, intending to blow up draft-board offices, but instead bought a couple of used ice-cream freezers and made a hundred quarts of vanilla crunch and sold it for three dollars a quart to tourists, which is the effect Vermont can have on people. Bert & Willy became multimillionaires, but guilty ones, and they both made it a point to live in small ugly homes like ordinary people and to use their money in good ways, such as subsidizing stories. A story can be very expensive to develop. This one, for example, was conceptualized in 1983 by a couple in Plainfield, then sold to a fiction company in

Montpelier, then bought by Vermont Power & Light, which spun it off into a fiction/ski-resort/leather-goods/homemade-preserves subsidiary in 1987. At that point, the story was a bare outline—Rich Boy Finds True Meaning of Christmas and Dies in Blizzard with Dog—but it had an assessed value of six hundred thousand dollars. Bert & Willy's bought the option for seventy-five thousand and turned it over to me for development. Thanks, guys!

❄

The big redwood door with a carved face of John Muir on it opened, and there was Sarah, Jim's size-8 mom, in a homespun calico dress from Italy or somewhere. "Jim! What?" she said. "You're outdoors! Sharon said you were in the solarium, working out on the ski machine."

(Sharon! Why would she believe his sister Sharon, who was a singer/songwriter and was abusing mulled wine?)

"I ran away from home eleven hours ago, Mom!"

"Oh. Who's this?"

"It's my old dog, Tony. I've had him since he was a pup."

"Oh—I thought you had a pony."

Jim's mom was a busy woman, involved in quilt-making, shape-note singing, storytelling, Shaker dancing, the restoration of an old Shaker movie theater, and Shaker baking, so she did not always stay current with her two children. She was not a hands-on mom, preferring to help them set their own priorities and then leave plenty of room for personal growth.

"I never had a pony in my life, Mom," said Jim in disgust.

The immense traditional-style home twinkled with handmade Christmas lights she had purchased from native Vermont craftspeople, and the quarter-acre log-paneled family room was gaily festooned with pine boughs that she had gathered with a traditional bough-gathering group, singing solstice songs in Gaelic and drinking maple punch. How rich with traditions Vermont is!—the red Navajo Christmas streamers, the little angels with heads made of dried apples and cornsilk hair, the French-Canadian wreath hung over the vast Shaker fireplace, where the imported English Yule log blazed away and the free-range chicken stock bubbled in the antique pot. In the dining room, the table was decked with green Irish linen, Swedish candlesticks, beautiful earthenware made by a blind lesbians' collective, and crystal goblets from Mexico. So much ethnicity! So many values! Such diversity! And through the great arch he could see, standing thirty feet high in the Amish rotunda, the Christmas tree, the most beautiful one anywhere in the world! It was a Shaker Christmas tree, lean and angular and tasteful, strung with lights, each string blinking at a different tempo, a contrapuntal tree, and it cost four thousand dollars.

"It looks nice. Jervis did a good job. I like it traditional," said Jim, though he was so nearsighted the tree looked like an upturned skiff. His mom always had the house professionally decorated at Christmas. Last year, Jervis had gone for a Georgia O'Keeffe look, with sand, cactuses, stones, bleached bones, and Christmas bulbs inside cow skulls, and the year before it was Finnish. Then Jim noticed the table was set for fifteen persons. But there are only four of us, he thought to himself.

As I mentioned, Bert & Willy's Ice Cream is picking up most of the tab for the writing of "Christmas in Vermont," but corporate underwriting can't hope to cover all of the writer's costs. E.g. rewriting to make the story phenomenally good—that first paragraph, with the boy struggling through the blizzard with the dog in his arms, took almost *three months.* It was hard work, and in the midst of it, I had to run off to Sumatra and rescue a threatened species in the big rain forest they have there, and that's why I'm coming directly to you, my readers, and asking for your support. Only your generous gifts will insure that many more stories of this quality will keep coming your way and insure that I don't have to let those animals perish. It only takes a minute to do this.

$10 (Contributor) _____

$25 (Patron) _____

$50 (Sustainer) _____

$100 (Good Neighbor) _____

$500 (Real Pal) _____

$1,000 (Racquetball Partner) _____
$5,000 (Best Friend, limited to six) _____
Visa __ Master __ Am Ex __ Other __
_____
Exp. Date _____
Signature _____

THANKS FOR YOUR SUPPORT!

❄

"Why fifteen? Who's coming for dinner besides us?" asked Jim. His mom shrugged. "Some people we met. I don't know. Vermonters. Storytellers. People from public television. They seemed nice. Some fund-raisers for nonprofits, our coffee dealer and his lover Bert, and Dr. Will, the holist. He was on our whale-watching cruise last fall."

"Tony's cough is pretty raspy," Jim said. "You don't suppose Dr. Will could give him a shot or something, do you?"

"Holists don't give shots, Tony. They work with nutrition and relaxation."

"Well, Tony's sick. Please help him. I'm all pooped out. I gotta grab some shut-eye." He hauled the poor old pooch up the grand staircase and into Sharon's vast bedroom, adorned with giant Matisse prints and furnished eclectically with white Scandinavian bookshelves, antique Victorian chairs and tables, and an elegant

Shaker fireplace and hearth. He boosted the dog up into her canopied bed. Tony groaned. How ironic that the dog might die on Christmas, here in this ornate colonial bedroom the size of a gymnasium!

A moment later the door opened, and there was Sharon, Jim's tall, willowy songwriter sister, in the arms of Vince, her boyfriend the ceramicist, who was tugging on the shoulder strap of her blue jumper, trying to access her bosom. "Beat it, Jim," he snarled, and raised his fist to pound on the child. Vince shaped pots and plates all day and his right arm was as powerful as a trip-hammer.

"Grrrrrrr," growled Tony, trying to leap up from under the covers, though he was too weak.

Just as Jim was about to be pummeled by Vince, Jim's dad, Jack, waltzed in. "Hi, kids," he said. "Hi, Tony. How's tricks?" He smelled of a cilantro after-shave, and he looked youthful and tanned and taut and extremely fit. In fact, he appeared to be several years younger than either of his children. He smiled effortlessly. "Look what just came from my kiln!" he cried.

"What is that?" asked Sharon.

Jack grinned at her. "It's a trivet," he said.

❄

With literary costs rising each year, it becomes more and more difficult for writers to offer their stories to readers at a reasonable price. The Vermont Christmas Catalogue is one way you can help me keep from having to raise my rates. When you purchase one of these gifts, a portion of the price is earmarked for fiction:

COLORFUL TILE TRIVETS. These handcrafted earth-tone tiles from Vermont are fascinating additions to any kitchen counter. 6 × 6: $40 each.

OLD-TIME HOLLY WREATHS. A traditional Christmas is yours with a supply of fragrant holly wreaths, sprays, and garlands from northern Vermont, harvested by traditional Morris dancers whose mountain lodge has been a center of tradition since 1981. One large crate: $164.

JUICY APPLES. A selection of Vermont's finest. One doz.: $15.

SHAKER LOVE SEAT. Handsomely fashioned from white birch. The classic simplicity of this heirloom piece will add distinctive charm to your home or office. $1,900.

❊

"Tony's dying, I think, of pneumonia," said Jim.

"That's too bad. We'll get the best medical care available, regardless of cost," said Jack. "I think Dr. Will is coming for dinner. Maybe he can save him. We met him at the Woffats'. He seemed nice. He does a program of Renaissance music and storytelling on public radio on Sunday afternoons from one-thirty to three. I'll ask him to have a look."

Downstairs, the bell rang—*bongggg, bongggg*. The door

opened, and there were murmurs, and Sarah yelled up the stairs, "Never mind. It's only the wine man."

Tony's eyes were dilated and red, his nose was dry and scaly. His tongue was whitish. Jim stayed near the bed, wondering if even the vast, ill-gotten fortune of his parents could make the dog well. Tears ran down his cheeks. "Why did we come to Vermont?" he sobbed. "Why didn't we stay in New York, where there are great veterinarians?"

Jack sat on the edge of the bed. He'd attended a workshop on male intimacy, and knew how to handle the situation. He touched Jim, to validate him, and instead of telling Jim to shut up and quit bawling, he asked if he wanted to talk about it.

"Yes, of course I want to talk about it! Why else would I bring it up?" yelled Jim.

"I sympathize with your anger completely and I am grateful to you for sharing it with me," said Jack.

Jim poured out his hatred of Vermont. All the white frame houses with dark-green shutters, picket fence, and maple trees, and the perfectly stacked woodpile, the white spire of the Congregational church, the cemetery full of Jareds and Obadiahs and Samuels, snow falling, candles in the windows, and the ghosts of Emerson, Thoreau, John Adams, Robert Frost, wandering around with their strong cheekbones and lantern jaws and flinty blue eyes and big white incisors. So much rectitude! "I hate the constant drumming of ethics! It makes me wish I were in the arms of a fat sweaty woman," cried Jim.

"I didn't realize that you knew about fat sweaty women," said his father.

"I read pornography all the time. Scratch 'n Sniff books with naked girls in them. It's my main pleasure in life," cried the child. And he reached down into his pocket and pulled out a copy of *Shake It, Shaker Babes*, with a picture of angular women, their black homespun dresses around their ankles, simple tasteful Shaker breasts perched proudly on the lean rib cage, hands joined, singing:

> *The gift to be simple is the gift to be free,*
> *The gift to take our panties down and pee.*
> *And when we pee in the place just right,*
> *We'll take off our blouses and dance all night.*
> *We'll make a mess of garlic shrimp,*
> *And drink till we're silly and laugh till we're limp,*
> *And grab hold of strangers and dance the Wahoo,*
> *And I'll sleep on the floor with my arms around you.*

"I want to howl. I want to party. I want to get down," said Jim. "There's too many values up here, too much woodsmoke, too much cinnamon. It's like Iowa with scenery, relentless good taste, one after the other. Fresh-ground coffee and baguettes and sunsets and colonial structures—Dad, I miss rock 'n roll. I miss grease."

"But we have a McDonald's here," said his dad.

"It looks like a Quaker meetinghouse. The golden arches are carved on an antiqued wood sign beside the door, and the gold is dull and cracked, it's pre-aged. The

Big Mac is served on an oak cutting board, and people eat it with a knife and fork, with a wine. And there's a ski-up window. It's not a real McDonald's. It's Vermont."

Their dialogue was interrupted by the sudden arrival of Dr. Will, a pleasant open-faced man in a blue running suit who looked truly healthy through and through. "Jim, Jack—what a pleasure," he said. "Sarah asked me to check on Tony. How is he doing?"

"Near death."

"Here. We'll just have a look. Hmmmm. Let me just check his eyeballs. Nnnhnnn. Sort of red. Corneal infection, I'm afraid. But no prob, Bob. We'll just do a corneal acupuncture. Don't worry." He took out a fistful of needles and a hankie. "All we do is place needles in the energy junctions on the corneas and he'll be feeling great in a jiffy."

"No, please. No," Jim said. He looked away in pain.

"It'll hurt a little, but don't worry. As long as he doesn't blink, it won't bleed much."

You're lying, just trying to reassure me, thought Jim, and then he heard two little ticks as his dog's eyeballs were pierced with long needles. Tony moaned.

"That's him, Jim," said Dr. Will. "Now we'll just rub some of this alfalfa balm on him. And then I'll stick in twenty more."

❄

Have you ever thought you'd like to go on a winter cruise but not with thousands of owly senior citizens grumping around the tropics? Join us for a cruise on the S.S. *Burlington.* Ten days sailing through the sparkling blue, sun-drenched Caribbean with people just like yourself: young, physically fit, thoughtful people. Vermonters. Readers. Not John Jakes's readers or Danielle Steel's or Stephen King's. My readers. Such as you, for example. My kind of people. I am hoping to be there, and maybe we can stay up late talking and talking, just talk, me and you.

Starts at $4,500, double occupancy.

❋

"We'll have Tony put in a special place for blind dogs. There's a beautiful one in Middlebury, a farm. It was donated by one of the Peabodys," Mom said. "He'll be happier there than with you, hard as that is to accept. He'll run free through the meadows and the forests, and you'll go away to Yale soon, honey, and life will be good for both of you."

"You're lying. You're going to have him killed in a gas chamber!"

"I promise you that Tony will be sent to a training center for seeing-impaired dogs, where he will learn to work with a seeing-eye bird and lead a life that is almost normal. They use canaries that sit on the dog's shoulder and hold in their beak long reins attached to the dewlaps."

Jim looked down at his poor old pal; a bandage covered Tony's head except for his dry, brown nose and big, floppy ears and slobbery lips. A bandage very poorly wrapped, he couldn't help but notice. Tape slapped on, the way a post-office clerk would do it. Downstairs. Dr. Will was hobnobbing with the other guests over steaming mugs of hot cider. The house rang with the careless melodious laughter of the well-to-do. "Dinner is free-range swine. It's delicious. Why don't you join us?" his mom said. But Jim couldn't leave Tony.

Or could he? Dinner sure sounded good to him, and maybe Mom was right; you can't live a dog's life for him, can you. A blindy like this one, he'd have to learn how to depend on himself and not expect favors. Lots of blind dogs nowadays just lie around getting fat and lazy probably. That's a rather poor attitude. Maybe he ought to leave Tony and go downstairs and talk to Dr. Will and the other influential guests, in hopes of garnering recommendations for future employment, graduate school, etc. Maybe he ought to ignore Tony completely, so as to make him less emotionally dependent.

❋

VERMONT WOODSMAN'S SWEATER. Woven by authentic elderly rural women from 100% rough-cut wool with natural oils intact, in the centuries-old "herring net" style, this handsome garment, with traditional shawl neck, is guaranteed to be absolutely distinctive, unlike anything your friends have seen. Specify size. Black or navy blue: $215.

ANTIQUE COPPER BATHTUB. This finely crafted copy of a nineteenth-century Vermont tub, with filigreed edging, turtle-claw feet, and inscription on base, can be used for bathing, or to store firewood, or simply as a work of art. 52 × 28 × 36: $2,800.

PINE BRIEFCASE. Handcrafted with brass handles, quilted lining, and carved folk figures all over, this beauty is patterned after those used by lawyers in rural Vermont, and its investment value is well proven: $18,500.

❊

I'd just like to close with a big thank-you to Bert & Willy's and wish a Merry Christmas to their happy employees and express my sincere thanks to those who gave so generously to support my writing program and wish bon voyage to the folks on our cruise (I can't get away to join you, sorry!) and thank the customers of the Christmas Catalogue. Allow eight weeks for delivery. Tony, by the way, went to the blind-dog farm, and Jim's family was pulled together by the crisis and learned the true meaning of Christmas, which is not *how much* but *how well.* It's a time for quality of life. Jim is headed for college, aiming for a career in theology, and Sharon split up with Vince, who was a brute even if he was instrumental in the revival of New England ceramics, and—how can I say this?—she is marrying me on Wednesday morning. It was a whirlwind romance, and after a honeymoon on St. Bart's we'll be home in Plainfield in our eighteen-room redwood cabin on the edge of a ten-thousand-acre wildlife preserve. A person could retire there and never be seen again.

NORMAN CONQUEST

He filled the electric teakettle, ground the beans, boiled the water, set the filter in the cone in the carafe, poured the water through the coffee, and all the time he was reading a scary article in the *Register* that said sleeping near an electric socket may cause depression, among other things. It quoted a Dr. Denton, who described four people who'd been miserable for years and years and then went on long camping trips, felt better, and finally figured out what sleeping near sockets had done to them.

The doctor said that some people recommended sleeping ten feet away from sockets, some said fifty, and others felt that a quarter-mile would not be too far.

Norman's bed was within four feet of three sockets. Evidently, the person who designed this little bungalow was someone who needed appliances in the bedroom. *Is this socket business silly?* he wondered, and yet he *had been* a little depressed. He was depressed right now.

The article jumped to page 24, talking about Garth M., a cancer counselor who moved from his heavily socketed apartment into a teepee outside of Pittsburgh and hasn't had a smidge of depression for almost three years—and in the adjoining column was a tiny obituary for a man of forty-four, six years younger than Norman, who conked out at a tennis club. Heart attack. A passerby attempted to revive him mouth-to-mouth but no soap. No wife listed, only the dead guy's kids, Amber, Trevor, Kimberley, and Josh. A divorced guy. Norman had been divorced from his late wife Judy, and their daughter's name is Kimberley, her boyfriend's name is Trevor. The dead guy had been scheduled to fly to Maui the next day, the story said, for a vacation. Norman guessed the dead guy probably had a girlfriend—who would go to Maui alone?—probably a thirty-one-year-old teacher, trim, tan, a terrific tennis player, a woman who made the dead guy forget all his troubles. How nice for him. Norman had nobody. He was as celibate as the Pope. He wondered if electric sockets kill your sex drive too.

Suspicion of sockets seemed like a big price to pay for reading a newspaper, but the paper had been there on the doorstep and he didn't want it to blow away down the block, forty pages flapping across the snowy yards of East Des Moines, and now he'd opened it and out came a barrel of trash to fill up his mind. A story about a boy named Jojo in Baraboo who dropped a yoyo down his tuba. A story about a boy who killed his father with a mallet and put him through a food processor. A story about America in the year 2010, a land of ashes and dead trees, cities boarded up, Americans with hair on their palms, illiterate, cancerous, gloomy as bears, breathing the acrid fumes of strange chemicals.

The house feels tired, even the furniture exhausted from old marital battles, the old green sofa looks like it has been awake sobbing all night. Norman's cleaning lady Carmelita quit in November and returned to Guatemala and now it is January. He is economizing. He is living on rice and beans, seeing no movies, hiring no cleaning ladies, buying no clothes or books, no alcohol. Norman, a lover of Laphroaig whiskey and old port and Armagnac, is being a good soldier, staying off the sauce while he finishes his novel.

It's entitled *The Big Box*. A man is afraid to leave his house and he establishes a relationship with his refrigerator. So far there are four hundred pages in Norman's computer and every day he deletes whole slabs and yet it keeps growing.

Norman was a freelance humorist for twenty years until starting this book. Judy supported him, working as a veterinarian's assistant, as Norman found a market for his humor among the thousands of specialty magazines such as *American Power Tool Quarterly* and *The National Geographic Collectors' Magazine* and *Plastic Purse Collector* and *Walleye Fisherman* and *Rolodex Owner* and *Decaffeinated Coffee* and *Heating, Ventilating, Air-Conditioning Contractors' Digest*. And gradually he prospered, through hard work and plagiarism and the judicious use of boogers, hairballs, gerbils, chickens, and farts, the surefire laugh-getters. He prospered to where he was earning upwards of thirty-five thousand dollars a year.

Judy thought that his booger writing was trashy and sophomoric, but then she thought that about all his writing, whether it employed mucus or not. He had written a piece for *Videocam* about a man at his daughter's wedding who fishes around in his left nostril as the video camera scans the reception line and he hooks onto a major vein of snot, about a quart's worth, as the groom's grandma approaches him, and of course the quart of snot is sitting in his right hand—it was a passage so funny, people practically crapped in their pants, they banged their heads on the breakfast table and fell over wheezing, but to Judy, it was another in the string of strange embarrassments that was their marriage. Judy had, while Norman wrote about boogers, put herself through veterinary college and graduate school and become the leading bovine periodontist in the country, which was to say the top cow-gum doctor in the world, flying off to bovine conferences in Bombay and Copenhagen and Buenos Aires and Cairo. A cow is a chewing machine, and good gums are crucial, and Judy earned

$180,000 in 1992. "People ask me what you do," she told Norman, "and I say you're a writer, but I don't say what. I wish you'd write a novel."

"You wish I'd write awful?" said Norman, ever the kidder.

"You heard me."

"But I'm a humorist, not a novelist."

"Suit yourself," she said. "Fine. Don't write a novel. Do whatever you want to. Be the Bard of Snot. I don't care what you do. I'm sorry I ever brought it up. Don't give it another thought."

So he thought about it for days. How *hard* it is to write funny, especially if you're French to start with, which he was, born in Lyon, the son of an apache dancer named Monique who had no interest in being a mom. *"Si jeunesse savait, si vieillesse pouvait,"* she used to say, sitting on the balcony in her pink underwear and eating breakfast at three in the afternoon, Grand Marnier on cornflakes. It was a lousy life. The lonely boy sat in the filthy apartment all day watching Cary Grant movies on television. Cary was the father Norman never had, it was good to see him. And one day, Norman said, *"Au revoir, ma maman,"* came to America, rid himself of his maître d' accent, and became a humorist. He met Judy in a malt shop, an American dream girl, and they merged into marriage. He hung around bingo parlors and flea markets and watched Donahue in barrooms, trying to soak up American life. Gradually he got the hang of being American and learned to tell jokes. A triumph for an immigrant, to make people laugh in another language.

Him and Victor Borge and Ludwig Bemelmans and who else? He would have preferred to be humorous in an elegant way, like Cary Grant, but in America, people laughed at boogers and farts—who knew why? it wasn't for him to explain, he was French, he only wanted to fit in. It took him four years to write his first collection, *Sew Buttons on Your Underwear*, which earned slightly more than eighty-five thousand dollars. Not bad for a bucket of boogers. Judy refused to read it. She didn't read any of his other books either—*It Must Be Time for Lunch, Sidney, Somebody Cut the Cheese* or *Is That a Bird in Your Nose, Baby? No, It's Snot* or *I Don't Care for TWA Coffee but I Do Love TWA Tea*—and if any of their friends mentioned Norman's writing, Judy got up and left the room.

One summer, the same summer Kimberley started work as a go-go dancer, Judy met a man named Michael Fredericks at a bovine conference in Edinburgh. Michael was a veterinarian from Yorkshire, married, with two little daughters, but he canceled everything and moved to Des Moines to become Judy's lover and lab assistant. Judy moved out and Norman hardly noticed—it was as if she'd simply taken a vacation. Norman was busy anyway, trying to rescue his daughter. "Grandma dances topless," she said. "Yes, but she is French," he replied. Norman met Michael at a supermarket once—the man was slightly obese and practically bald on top. Like most Englishmen, he looked sour and pasty-faced.

"We're two mature men and we can handle this," said Norman. "This town's too small for us not to get along.

I'm genuinely glad for both of you and I wish you the best of luck." But two months later, Judy and Michael were driving to Ames for a bovine conference and struck a bridge abutment at sixty m.p.h. and were instantly killed in a flaming explosion.

Losing Judy awakened Norman's love for her, a deeper, finer love than he had known in marriage. "I will live for you, my darling," he whispered at her grave, his arm around his sobbing daughter. "You will be proud." He set out on his novel, a big novel. For her. Some days he wrote two thousand words. It flowed out of him like froth off a boiling pot.

This morning, he starts in again to rewrite chapter seven. *The Big Box* is the story of a man known only as He, who has not seen another living human being except the pizza delivery person, Herb, in six years and whose life has come to be focused on his refrigerator, Fred. The action takes place entirely in flashbacks and also in Dallas. He keeps asking himself, Where did my life jump the tracks? and He keeps thinking back to a family softball game six years ago where He took a called third strike. His father was pitching, and He couldn't swing the bat. The pitch was in the dirt, and his mother, who was umpiring, called it a strike. In the third, fourth, and fifth chapters, there's a lot more about this game, the sisters jeering at him in the outfield, etc. In chapter six, we discover that He has an answering machine, on which He has saved all his calls for six years, fifteen phone calls, eight of them from a Toro sales representative named Bernardine who wants to sell him a snow blower. Her persistence inspires him. He's never offered her a bit of encouragement, never even spoken to her, and yet she keeps calling. She talks and talks about herself and her boyfriends who used to shovel her walk but they're gone, the unfaithful bastards, and she has a snow blower and she'll never go back to sex as a tool for getting your snow shoveled, snow blowing is it for her. He looks into the refrigerator and He sees himself and Bernardine in there, in the snow of the freezer compartment, and He throws his arms around the refrigerator and it falls on him and kills him. In chapter seven, we find out that the whole story is written by a spore on a dill pickle in the refrigerator. And that not all of it is true. But we don't know how much. This is the chapter he needs to fix today, so it segues nicely into the second half of the novel, set in a dump, where the refrigerator becomes a home for a runaway boy named Bob.

The telephone rings. It is Kimberley. "Hi, Daddy," she says. She is crying and nobody can cry like her, she weeps buckets. After her mother's death, she quit dancing and devoted herself to geriatrics. She went to work in a nursing home. "Daddy," she told him once, "do you realize that in thirty years, sixty percent of the population will be over sixty-five?" Now, weeping, she says, "I'm twenty-four and my life is a mess. I can't bear it another day. It's too painful, Daddy." She and Trevor are breaking up. That's exactly what Norman tried to tell her to do when she met Trevor. Trevor is a weasel who lies to everyone, steals money off countertops, listens to gruesome music, and drinks himself into a stupor. She stuck with him, the jerk, right up until last night, when he threw all her clothes out of the window. "I don't want a big comment from you on this, okay?" she says. She is all broken up over it, poor child.

"I love you, baby. Hang in there. I'll come and get you. Where are you?"

"I'm at work. I'm off in an hour. My stuff is at the reception desk. In the main building. Can you pick it up first and then get me? I'm in Building D."

"What about your cats, honey? They coming with you?"

"Of course. Is that all right?"

Norman sighs. "How many are there now?"

"Six. Daddy, if you don't want me there, it's okay, I'll go to a motel. It's just that I thought of you first, that's all."

"Okay," he says. "Fine. I'll pick up the cats."

The Oak Ridge Nursing Home was a dreadful dreary place. Geezer Camp. "It's all in how you look at it," Kimmy has told him, but it's also a matter of what's there to see. Old green indoor-outdoor carpeting with pee stains on it, the smell of disinfectant everywhere, eight or ten residents parked in their wheelchairs, collapsed against the straps, the light in their eyes gone out. What a powerful argument against growing old. He picks up six cartons of stuff and a bag of cats from the reception desk, then drives to Building D. A cell-block for old farts imprisoned in themselves.

Kimmy is cheerful with these cadaverous folks, squeezes their withered hands, lavishes jokes and one-sided repartee on them, and then out in the parking lot, she bursts into tears. "I can't live without him, the big creep!" she cries.

All the way to Norman's house, she cries. Her life is a wreck. "What do I *do?*" she says. They pull up in the driveway, the phone rings in the house, she tears inside while Norman lugs the boxes in and the cats. She is smiling. It was Trevor, and she has agreed to meet him at ten-thirty and so, a few hours later, she whizzes off in Norman's car and Norman sinks exhausted into the sorrowful green sofa—the complicated lives of the young!

Two of the cats appeared to be unwell. Listless, rheumy-eyed, with snarls in their fur. Their meows were raspy and faint. "That's Little Boy and Tigger," she said as she unpacked. "I found them in the alley last weekend, somebody'd stuck them in a garbage can. Can you believe it? People are so cruel."

"They sure are," said Norman, thinking of Trevor. When she had met Trevor three years ago, she told Norman, "You won't like him, Daddy. I'm just going to have to live with that, okay? He doesn't read books and he doesn't have much sense of humor. He listens to a lot of heavy-metal rock. I don't think you'd consider him exactly smart. But I love him."

Now Trevor, having thrown her away like a used shopping bag, was beckoning her back into his life. Norman had offered to go beat the crap out of him. She laughed and she left in the car.

That night all the cats were unaccountably drawn toward Norman. Kimmy stayed out until midnight, came home—Norman was sleeping on the couch so he could get up early and work on his novel and not disturb her—he heard her tiptoe in, and the herd of cats stirred around him, four at his feet and two by his head. He tossed them on the floor but in the morning they were nestled close to him.

Kimmy went off to the nursing home at six a.m. She seemed cheerfuler. Norman worked on his novel. The cats gathered around the computer, their eyes fixed on him and his fingers on the keys, watching the screen when he rolled the text up. He was trying to make the dill pickle into a blood clot in his main character's brain, so that in chapter fourteen we finally see the truth—this entire novel is a single neuron of pain in the mind of a dying man, and there are billions of such neurons. The phone rang five or six times—twice, someone hung up when Norman answered, probably Trevor, and once it was the editor of *Ding Dong* wondering if Norman could do seven hundred words about tits by six o'clock that evening—"I'm working on a novel," Norman told him—and once it was a lady from next door. "I know it's none of my business, Mr. Conquest, but don't you think she's a little young for you?" Norman explained that Kimberley was his daughter. "Right," said the woman, "your daughter." Then it was his mother, calling from Lyon to find out how Judy was.

"She's dead, *maman*. I've told you ten times. She and her lover died in a car crash," he said. Norman told her that he was writing a novel.

"For a humorist, you're such a grim person," she said.

"A novel! What does the world need with more novels? People haven't even read *Anna Karenina* yet."

"It's all right, *maman*. I don't need your support. I'm an artist now. We are used to derision."

She said something he didn't understand—his French was rusty, he had lost a lot of vocabulary over the years—and then she said, "So—are you with anyone yet?"

No, Norman said, he wasn't.

"My darling boy, this is not good," she said. "You need someone or you go cuckoo. A lover, a roommate, a mama, somebody. When an elephant goes by in the street with a red parasol in its trunk, you need somebody to say to, 'Look, an elephant, and that parasol is similar to one my mama used in her nightclub act.' Otherwise you become a sad little man who eats meat pies alone in cafeterias and has pee stains on his trousers."

Norman said he was busy to live with anyone. "I'm almost done with my novel. Parts of it are pretty good, actually. Judy suggested that I write one. I never would've thought of it myself."

"You never desire to have sex?" she asked. "Are you sick? Are you loping your camel?"

He said that he did not wish to discuss his sex life with her, because there was none to discuss.

"Let me come and take care of you," she said. "I'll be good for you. We'll talk, laugh, hug, do all those things we missed when you were a little boy. I wasn't ready then. Now I want to be a real mama to you, Norman. I'm old, my boy. I have been an eighteen-year-old dancer for fifty years, same blonde hair and baby-doll outfit and the lacy pants, but now everything is droopy and my tits are like prunes, and I perform by candlelight, wrapped in gauze, and, Norman, I want to be your mother!"

He said he was sorry she was unhappy.

"Make me happy, Norman," she said. "Send me an airplane ticket. Forgive. Open your heart. We will be for each other."

He promised that he would give it serious consideration.

He had thought that Mom liked living alone. She used to say she preferred that her lover come to her once a week—"I rejoice to see him and I rejoice to see him go," she had said. "A man is like a fish, only good for a couple days and then it starts to smell." Mom lived for her audience at the club, the old boulevardiers who sat at the front tables lusting and longing for a glimpse of her breasts. For lovers, she preferred intellectuals, writers, men who needed loneliness and were grateful for an hour of love now and then. "We are each and every one of us alone, and all else is a lie," Mom had said to him once. She was nobody's fool, and her astringent view of life had somehow prepared him to love Americans, their goofy manners and vast sentimentality, their wonderful dumb booger jokes. To think of her pining for him, longing to relate to him and renew the family bond— had she lost her mind? Was she sleeping in doorways, wrapped in garbage bags?—he could see her, his mama, fishing through trash cans for returnable bottles and crusts of pizza and weeping for her lost boy—how could he refuse her? *Easy,* he thought. *Just say no.*

The next night, Norman accompanied his daughter to a Guns n' Roses concert at the Iowa State Fairgrounds. She said, "I have this extra ticket, but you don't need to go, okay?" So he went. Of the fifty-some thousand people there, most were young men with their shirts off, well-molded pectorals, earrings, upper-arm tattoos, and cans of beer in their hands. Norman was the only one in slacks, a pressed white shirt, and a houndstooth sport coat. The stage at the end of the field was high and draped in black; long runways extended to either side, where the bare-chested guitarists pranced back and forth like cannibals in an old B movie, leering, glowering, their fists thrust in the air. All of it blown up on monster TV screens, with twenty spotlights, strobe lights, billowing clouds of fog, flash pots blowing fifty-foot columns of flame into the air, bombs bursting onstage, beach balls bouncing in the crowd, people swinging their long hair round and round and back and forth in time to the music, girls in front of the stage reaching up toward the savages, articles of underwear thrown onstage and snatched away by roadies scooting in from the wings, slam-dancing at the other end of the field, and the crowd standing throughout the music, nobody sitting down. "Are we still in Iowa?" Norman wondered. In front, the guitarists danced and hopped around and strutted, and there, at the prow of the stage, was a powerful spotlight aimed straight skyward with a grille over the lamp where the lead savage stood, a bare-chested man on a spotlight, fist thrust in the air. The music made a great racket that twanged your small intestines—it felt good—does a person's interest in being twanged ever completely disappear? He turned to Kimberley to yell, "I like it!" but she was gone. Vanished into the maw of the crowd. And two minutes later he saw her on a TV screen, her face fifty feet high, she was perched on a guy's shoulders, her arms in the air, her shirt off, her young breasts wobbling, as fifty thousand young men emitted a thunderous testosterone roar. The guy with the shoulders was Trevor. Norman recognized him instantly. He could hardly recognize his daughter. Displaying your breasts to fifty thousand men and making them roar—was this the upshot of working in a home for the dying?

Norman drove home alone. Kimberley didn't call that night. He had a bad dream, in which his novel was published and all the reviews were torpedoes—"a fourth-rate pastiche of American minimalist fiction . . . has all the charm and sophistication of a handful of boogers"—and she didn't call the next morning. He called Mama in Lyon, and the phone rang twenty times before she picked up. *"Allo?"* She had been entertaining a gentleman from Chicago, she said, and now he was washing up. She couldn't talk long. They were going to Burger King. He said, "Mama, you've got to get out of the profession. It's too dangerous. AIDS, Mama. It sneaks up on you."

"I use condoms," she said. "I need sex, Norman. Your mama is not a nice person. If they wouldn't pay me, I would pay them."

"And you want to come and practice your trade in Des Moines, Mama? In my home?"

"I like Americans, they're so clean," she said. "And of course I would use hotels, my darling."

He said Kimberley was missing. "I'm not surprised she doesn't come back to your place," she said. "Not surprised at all. She's a healthy young girl."

He called the Humane Society. He said, "I've got some cats here I'd like to have picked up." The woman said the soonest pickup would be Tuesday.

The cats were all over him, purring, rubbing, for the next two days as he futzed with his sinking novel and waited for his lost daughter to call and thought of his mama shacked up with Chicagoans. The cats could feel betrayal in the air and they were trying to make him change his mind. They sat and looked him straight in the eyes, searching for clemency. Please, they were saying. Please. We're just cats, we're doing the best we can.

Finally, Tuesday morning, came the knock on the door. The cats looked at Norman in panic. They dove under the couch. A little guy in a trench coat, a wicker basket in his hand, stood at the door. "You the guy with the cats you want us to plant?" he asked, a cruel glint in his eye.

"Actually, they're my daughter's ex-boyfriend's cats."

"How long you had 'em?"

"Two weeks."

"You gotta have 'em a minimum of one month before you can have 'em iced," he said. "It's policy." He drove away.

Norman was relieved. He opened three cans of tuna to celebrate and then, bang, he had an idea for the novel.

The man in the novel would live alone, except with cats, and Bernardine would be the name of his favorite cat, an orange Persian. The man is devoted to these cats and gives them a beautiful life without fear or hunger or loneliness or discomfort of any kind. It's cat heaven. Big fans cool the cats in summer, and in winter they nest under down comforters. He is the cats' God, the Provider of All Good Things, who stands high above cat society and sees and knows all and bestows perfect harmony on those cats who obey and adore him. All goes well until one night, Bernardine speaks up and accuses him of making their lives empty and barren. "But you have everything you could possibly want!" He cries.

"How would you know?" she says.

"You do nothing but lie here and purr."

She tells him that purring is a language unto itself. Cats use it to express not only content but also depression, doubt, boredom, and the misery of stomach gas.

"You're not happy?" He asks, in tears.

"You're a sick man," she tells him. "You bring your sickness into our lives, we eat it with our breakfast. Everything you do, you do for yourself. You're sick."

"No! Not true!" He cries.

She accuses him of ruining their lives. So He kills her

and stuffs her body into the freezer compartment of the refrigerator. The next day, another cat looks up from the water dish and says, "You bumped off Bernardine last night, didn't you?" He denies it. The cat laughs. "You think we're stupid?" she says. "You think we don't notice that you're weird?" So He kills that cat and stuffs her in next to Bernardine. The next day, another cat walks into the bathroom while He's shaving and says, "Nazi creep. Murderer." He kills that cat. Now three cats are left. He lies awake at night, waiting for one of them to mouth off, but none of them says a word. Days go by. He can't sleep, can't eat. Finally, He turns on the cats and screams, "Go ahead! Say it! You hate me! Don't you! You think I don't know? I know! Go ahead! Get it off your chests!" And the neighbors hear him ranting and call the cops and He is hauled away to the loony bin. The man from the Humane Society comes to round up the cats. He chases them around the house and captures two of them, and the third hides behind the refrigerator. As he moves the refrigerator away from the wall, the freezer door comes open, and as he bends down to grab the cat he feels something cold on his neck. Something cold with sharp claws that rake the side of his head, digging deep into his brain.

Kimberley called. She and Trevor had gone to South Dakota for a biker rally and wound up in Montana and now she was in Minneapolis. She had quit her job at Oak Ridge. She was pregnant. Trevor was looking for a job. She was sorry about the trouble she had caused. All she wanted now was to settle down and have her baby and love her husband and do good things with her life.

"Husband?" asked Norman. Yes, said Kimberley, we decided to get married in Spearfish, so we did.

"Daddy," she said, "you've done so much for me, I could never ask another thing, but I really do need to borrow some money. We're broke. We owe two thousand dollars in rent and Trevor probably isn't going to be getting his first check for another month or so. I need to borrow three thousand from you. Maybe thirty-five hundred."

He wired her four thousand and wired two thousand to Mama, then he wrote three funny stories. One was about people who haul great big pieces of luggage onto an airliner and try to stuff them into the overhead compartments, and another was about bad haircuts and how barbers are descended from the barbarians who pillaged the coasts of Europe, and the third one was about the seven types of farts: slow leaks, barkers, whizzers, bangers, boomers, butt burners, and death farts. He got warmed up on the baggage and barber stuff and when he got to the gaseous explosions he was in full stride, the old master, easy and elegant as he had not been for months. The baggage one should fetch eight hundred dollars, the barber one about the same, and the fart one—well, including syndication, musical, and dramatic rights, it was sure to get five thousand at least, maybe much more, and it had rescued his mother and bailed out his daughter, and what good can a man do greater than that?

ZEUS THE LUTHERAN

I. Hera, Fed Up with His Philandering, Hires a Lawyer

Zeus the Father of Heaven, the Father of the Seasons, the Fates, and the Muses, the father of Athena and Apollo and Artemis and Dionysus, plus the father of Hephaestus by Hera, his wife, and of Eros by his daughter Aphrodite, was a guy who didn't take no for an answer. Armed with his thunderbolts, he did exactly as he pleased and followed every amorous impulse of his heart, coupling with nymphs or gods or mortal women as he desired, sometimes changing himself into a swan or a horse or snake or taking the form of a mortal so as to avoid detection. Once, he became a chicken to make it more of a challenge.

His wife Hera was furious and hired a lawyer, Alan, to talk some sense into him. The day before, she had heard that Zeus was involved with a minor deity named Janice, shacked up with her on the island of Patmos, riding around on a Vespa with her clinging to him like a monkey.

"Tail him," she said. "Track down the bastard and nail him to the wall and put the bimbo on a plane to Peru." Hera threw her great bulk into a chair and glared blackly out the temple window. "One of these days, I'll catch him when he has set his thunderbolts aside and I will *trap him!* And then—" she laughed, *ho ho ho ho ho.* "Then we will have the Mother of Heaven. The patriarchy will be put on the shelf once and for all. With Athena, the goddess of wisdom, on my right hand, and Artemis, the goddess of the moon, on my left, I will civilize this universe, this bloody hellhole that men have made. Find Zeus when he is in the throes of desire and we will overthrow him and change the world, Alan."

Alan picked up his briefcase. "Whatever you say. You're the client," he said, and got on a boat to Patmos.

When Alan spotted Zeus, sitting at a table in an outdoor cafe by the harbor, there was no bimbo, only the ageless gentleman himself in a blue T-shirt and white shorts, fragrant with juniper, the Father of Heaven nursing a glass of nectar on the rocks and picking at a spinach salad. Alan introduced himself and sat down. He didn't ask, "How are you?" because he knew the answer: GREAT, ALL-POWERFUL.

"I realize you're omniscient, but let me come right to

the point and say what's on my mind," he said. "Enough with the mounting and coupling. Keep it in your pants. What are you trying to prove? You're a god, for Pete's sake. Be a little divine for a change. Knock it off with the fornication, okay? Otherwise, Hera means business, and we're not talking divorce, mister. You should be so lucky. Hera intends to take over the world. She's serious."

"You like magic? You want to see a magic trick?" said Zeus. And right there at the table he turned the young lawyer into a pitcher of vinaigrette dressing and his briefcase into a pine nut and he poured him over the spinach salad and then Zeus waved the waiter over and said, "The spinach is wilted, pal. Take it away, and feed it to the pigs. And bring me a beautiful young woman, passionate but compliant, with small, ripe breasts."

That was his usual way of dealing with opposition: senseless violence followed by easy sex.

Hera was swimming laps in the pool at her summer house when she got the tragic news from Victor, Alan's partner. "Alan is gone, eaten by pigs," said Victor. "We found his shoes. They were full of salad dressing." She was hardly surprised; Alan was her six hundredth lawyer in fourteen centuries. Zeus was rough on lawyers. She climbed out of the water, her great alabaster rump rising like Antarctica, and wrapped herself in a vast white towel. "Some god!" she said. "Omniscient except when it comes to himself."

She had always been puzzled by Zeus' lust for mortal women—what did he see in them? they were so shallow, weak, insipid, childish—and once she asked him straight out: *Why fool around with lightweights when you've got me, a real woman?* He told her, "The spirit of love is the cosmic teacher who brings gods and mortals together, lighting the path of beauty, which is both mortal and godly, from each generation to the next. One makes love as a gift and a sacrament so that people in years to come can enjoy music and poetry and feel passion at the sight of flowers."

She said, "You're not that drunk—don't be that stupid."

Now she vowed to redouble her efforts against him, put Victor on the case. But the next day she was in Thebes, being adored, which she loved, and what with all the flower-strewing and calf-roasting, Hera was out of the loop when a beautiful American woman, Diane, sailed into the harbor at Patmos aboard the S.S. *Bethel* with her husband, Pastor Wes.

II. Bored, He Falls for an American

Wes and Diane were on the second leg of a two-week cruise that the grateful congregation of Zion Lutheran Church in Odense, Pennsylvania, had given them in gratitude for Wes's ten years of ministry. Zeus, who was drinking coffee in the same sidewalk cafe with the passionate, compliant woman and was becoming bored with her breasts, which now seemed to him slightly too small and perhaps a touch overripe, saw Diane standing at the rail high overhead as the *Bethel* tied up. The strawberry-blonde hair and great tan against the blue Mediterranean sky, the healthy American good looks made his heart go boom and he felt the old, familiar itch in the groin—except sharper. He arose. She stood, leaning over the rail, wearing a bright-red windbreaker and blue jeans that showed off her fabulous thighs, and she seemed to be furious at the chubby man in the yellow pants who was laying his big arm on her shoulder, her hubby of sixteen years. She turned, and the arm fell off her. "Please, Diane," he said, and she looked away, up the mountain toward the monastery and the village of white houses.

Zeus paid the check and headed for the gangplank.

The night before, over a standing rib roast and a 1949 Bordeaux that cost enough to feed fifty Ugandan children for a week, Wes and Diane had talked about their good life back in Odense, their four wonderful children, their luck, their kind fellow Lutherans, and had somehow got onto the subject of divine grace, which led into a discussion of pretentious Lutheran clergy Diane had known, and Wes had to sit and hear her ridicule close friends of his—make fun of their immense reserve, their dopey clothes, their tremendous lack of sex appeal, which led to a bitter argument about their marriage. They leaned across the baklava, quietly yelling things like "How can you say that?" and "I always knew you felt that way!" until diners nearby were studying the ceiling for hairline cracks. In the morning, Diane announced that she wanted a separation. Now

Wes gestured at the blue sea, the fishing boats, the mountain, the handsome Greek man in white shorts below who was smiling up at them—"This is the dream trip of a lifetime," he said. "We came all this way to Greece to be miserable? We could have done that at home! This is nuts. To go on a vacation trip so you can break up? Give me a break. Why are you so hostile?" And in that moment, as he stood, arms out, palms up, begging for an answer, the god entered his body.

III. In the Heat of Passion, He Converts to Lutheranism

It took three convulsive seconds for Zeus to become Wes, and to the fifty-year-old minister, it felt exactly like a fatal heart attack, the painful tightening in the chest—Oh, shit! he thought. Death. And he had quit smoking three years before! All that self-denial and for what? He was going to fall down dead anyway. Tears filled his eyes. Then Zeus took over, and the soul of Wes dropped into an old dog named Spiros, who lived on the docks and suffered from a bad hernia. *Arf,* said Wes, and felt a pain in his crotch. He groaned and leaned down and licked his balls, a strange sensation for a Lutheran.

The transformation shook Zeus up, too. He felt suddenly nauseous and clutched at the rail and nearly vomited; in the last hour, Wes had consumed a shovelful of bacon and fried eggs and many cups of dreadful coffee.

The god was filled with disgust, but he touched the woman's porcelain wrist.

"What?" she said.

The god coughed. He tried to focus Wes's watery blue eyes; there was some sort of plastic disc in them. "O Lady whose beauty lights the darkening western skies, your white face flashes when I close my eyes," he said in a rumbly voice.

She stared at him. "*What* did you say?"

The god swallowed. He wanted to talk beautifully, but English sounded raspy and dull to him, an inferior language; it tasted like a cheap cigar.

"A face of such reflection as if carved in stone, and such beauty as only in great paintings shone. O Lady of light, fly no higher, but come into my bed and know eternal fire."

"Where'd you get that? Off a calendar? Is this supposed to be a joke or what?" she said. She told him to be real.

All in all, Zeus thought, *I would rather be a swan.* The dumb mustache, the poofy hair around the bald spot on top, the heavy brass medallion with a fish on it, the sunken chest and wobbly gut and big lunkers of blubber on his hips, the balloon butt, the weak arms and shaky legs, and the poor brain—corroded, stuffed with useless, sad, remorseful thoughts. It was hard for Zeus to keep his mind on love with the brain of Wes thinking of such dumb things to say to her—"I'm sorry you're angry. Let's try to have a nice day together and see the town and write some postcards. Buy some presents for the kids, take some pictures, have lunch, and forget about last night."—Zeus didn't want to write postcards, he wanted to take her below and peel off her clothes and make love so that the *Bethel* rocked in her berth.

Just below, the dog sat on his haunches, a professional theologian covered with filthy, matted fur, and the remains of his breakfast lying before him, the chewed-up hindquarters of a rat, and the rest of the rat in his belly.

"Look. That sweet little dog on the dock," said Diane, who loved dogs.

Zeus cleared his throat. "When you open your thighs, the soft clanging of bells is heard across the valley, O daughter of Harrisburg. Come, glorious woman, and let us waken the day with the music of your clamorous thighs."

"Grow up," she said, and headed down the gangplank, smiling at the dog.

The god's innards rumbled, and a bubble of gas shifted in his belly, a fart as big as a child. He clamped his bowels around it and held it in; he followed her down to the dock, saying: "Dear, dear Lady, O Light of my soul—the cheerful face of amiable passion in a cold, dry place. To you I offer a thousand tears and lies, an earnest heart longing for the paradise that awaits us in a bed not far away, I trust. Look at me, Lady, or else I turn to dust." His best effort so far. But the language was so flat, and the voice of Wes so pompous.

"I could swear this dog is human," she cried taking

its head in her hands, stroking under its chin, scratching its tattered ears.

"Thank you, Diane," said the dog. "I don't know how I became schizophrenic, but I do know I've never loved you more." This came from his mouth as a whine, and then he felt a terrible twinge in the hernia and moaned. The woman knelt and cradled his head in her arms. She crooned, "Oh, honey, precious, baby, sweetness, Mama gonna be so good to you, little darling." She had never said this to him before. He felt small and cozy in her arms.

IV. The Great Lover Tries and Falls Short

The dog, the woman, and the god rode a bus three miles over the mountain to the Sheraton St. John Hotel, the woman holding the dog's head on her lap. She was thinking about the future: she'd leave Wes, take the kids, move to Philadelphia, and go to Bryn Mawr College and study women's studies—the simple glories of the disciplined intellectual life! what a tonic after years of slouching around in a lousy marriage. The god vowed to go without food until she surrendered to him. The dog felt no pain, but he hoped to find a cigarette lying on the floor somewhere, even a cigarette butt, and figure out how to light it.

The hotel room had twin beds, hard as benches, and

looked out on a village of white stucco houses with small gardens of tomato plants and beans, where chickens strolled among the vines. Brown goats roamed across the brown hills, their bells clanging softly. Diane undressed in the bathroom, and slid into bed sideways, and lay facing the wall. Zeus sat on the edge of her bed and lightly traced with his finger the neckline of her white negligee. She shrugged. The dog lay at her feet, listening. Zeus held her shoulder strap between his thumb and index finger. It was bewildering, trying to steer his passion through the narrow, twisting mind of Wes. All he wanted was to make love enthusiastically for hours, but dismal Lutheran thoughts sprang up: Go to sleep. Stop making a fool of yourself. You're a grown man. Settle down. Don't be ridiculous. Who do you think you are?

He wished he could change to somebody trim and taut, an athlete, but he could feel the cold, wiggly flesh glued on him and he knew that Hera had caught him in the naked moment of metamorphosis and with a well-aimed curse had locked him tight inside the flabby body, this clown sack. A god of grandeur and gallantry living in a dump, wearing a mask of pork. He could hear his fellow gods hooting and cackling up on Olympus. (The Father of Heaven! Turned Down, Given the Heave-Ho! By a Housewife!)

Zeus pulled in his gut and spoke. "Lady, your quiet demeanor mocks the turmoil in my chest, the rage, the foam, the wind blasting love's light ships aground. Surely you see this, Lady, unless you are the cruelest of your race. Surely you hear my heart pound with mounting waves upon your long, passive shore. Miles from your coast, you sit in a placid town, feeling faint reverberations from beneath the floor. It is your lover the sea, who can never rest until you come to him."

"I don't know who you're trying to impress, me or yourself," she said. Soon she was snoring.

V. The Husband (the Dog)
Takes the Long View

"This is not such a bad deal," said the dog. "For me, this could turn out to be a very positive experience in terms of making an emotional breakthrough in my life, bursting the psychological bonds of pastorhood and Lutheranness, becoming a fully functioning, loving, sensitive, caring human being. Becoming a dog would never have been my choice, but now that I am one, I can see that, as a man, my sense of self always was tied up with power and, in some sense, with being an oppressor, being dominant. In the course of following my maleness, as my culture taught me to think of maleness, I got separated from my beingness, my creaturehood. It is so liberating to see things from down here at floor level. You learn a lot about man's relentlessness."

They spent two sunny days at the Sheraton, during which Zeus worked to seduce Diane and she treated him like a husband. She laughed at him, not at his witty stories but at his ardor. The lines that had worked for him in the past ("Sex is a token of a deeper friendship, an affirmation of mutual humanity, an extension of conversation") made her roll her eyes and snort. She lay on a blue wicker lounge beside the pool—her caramel skin set off by two red bands of bikini, her perfect breasts, her long, tan legs with a pale-golden fuzz. Her slender hands held a book, *The Concrete Shoes of Motherhood*, and she read it as he spoke to her.

"Let's take a shower. They have a sauna. Let me give you a backrub. Let's lie down and take a nap," he said.

"Cheese it," she said. "I'm not interested. Beat it."

He lost eighteen pounds. He ran ten miles every morning and swam in the afternoon. He shaved off the mustache. She refused to look at him, but, being a god, he could read her thoughts. She was curious about this sea change in her husband, his new regimen, his amazing discipline. She hiked over the dry brown hills and he walked behind and sang songs to her:

> *Lady, your shining skin will slide on mine,*
> *Your breasts tremble with gladness.*
> *Your body, naked, be clad in sweet oils,*
> *And rise to the temple of Aphrodite,*
> *Where you will live forever, no more*
> *Lutheran but venerated by mortals. This I pledge.*

She pretended not to hear, sweeping the horizon with her binoculars, looking for rare seabirds. Zeus thought, *I should have been a swan. Definitely a swan.* The dog trotted along, his hernia cured by love. She had named him

Sweetness. "You go ahead and use my body as long as you like," he said to Zeus. "You're doing wonders for it. I never looked so good until you became me. No kidding. But when it comes to lyrics, you're no Cole Porter, pal."

VI. The Great Lover Tries Again

She wouldn't let him touch her until they got on the plane back to America and they had eaten the lasagna and watched the movie and were almost over Newfoundland. The *Fasten Seat Belts* signs flashed on and the pilot announced that they would be passing through a turbulent period and suddenly the plane bucked and shuddered in the boiling clouds, and Diane reached over and grabbed him as the plane tipped and plunged and rattled, and people shrieked and children cried. "If this is our time to die, then I want you to know that they were good years, they really were," Diane said, kissing him. "I love you, Wes. I'm crazy about you." Her kisses were hot and excited, and soon she was grabbing him and groping under his sportcoat, digging her sharp tongue into the corners of his mouth and writhing in his arms and groaning and saying his name, but Zeus was unable to respond somehow. His divine penis was as limp as an empty balloon. He tried to encourage it by thinking of smokestacks, pistols, pedestals, pole vaults, peninsulas, but nothing worked. Her hands reached for his zipper but he fought her off. "Not here, people are watching," he muttered, and then the plane hit the concrete at Kennedy and bounced and touched down and rolled to a stop, and Diane shuddered and said, "I can't wait to get you home, big boy."

In the terminal, Zeus felt so weak, he could not carry their bags through customs. They fetched the dog, who emerged from the baggage room dopey and confused and out of sorts. He bit Zeus on the hand. Zeus limped to the curb and collapsed into the back seat of a van driven by a burly man named Paul, who, Zeus gathered, was his brother. Paul and Diane sat in front, Zeus and the dog in back. "Wes is pretty jet-lagged," Diane said, but the man yammered on and on about some football team that Zeus gathered he was supposedly interested in. "Hope you had a great time," said Paul. Yes, they said, they had. "Always wanted to go over there myself," he said. "But things come up. You know." He talked for many miles about what he had done instead of going to Greece: resodding, finishing the attic, adding on a bedroom, taking the kids to Yellowstone.

Do we have kids? Zeus wondered. "Four," said the dog, beaming. "Great kids. I can't wait for you to meet them, mister." Then he dropped his chin on the seat and groaned. "The littlest guy is murder on animals. One look at me, he'll have me in a headlock until my eyeballs pop." He groaned again. "I forgot about Mojo. Our black Lab." His big brown eyes filled with tears. "I've come home in disgrace to die like a dog," he said. "I feed Mojo for ten years and now he's going to go for my throat. It's too hard." The god told him to buck up, but the dog was gloomy all the way home.

VII. *The Husband Disappears*

When Paul pulled up to the double garage behind the green frame house and Diane climbed out, the dog squeezed out the door behind her and tore off down the street and across a playground and disappeared. *"Sweetness!"* she screeched.

Paul and Zeus cruised the streets for half an hour searching for the mutt, Zeus with gathering apprehension, even panic. Without Wes to resume being Wes, he now realized, he couldn't get out of Wes and back into Zeus. There was, however, no way to explain this to Paul.

"You seem a little—I don't know—distant," said Paul.

"Just tired," said Zeus.

They circled the blocks, peering into the bushes, whistling for the dog, calling his name, and then Paul went home for a warm jacket (he said, but Zeus guessed he was tired and would find some reason not to come back). The god strode across yards, through hedges, crying, "Sweetness! Sweetness!" The yards were cluttered with machines, which he threw aside. Sweetness!

The dog was huddled by an incinerator behind the school. He had coached boys' hockey here for ten years. "I'm so ashamed," he wept. The god held him tightly in his arms. "To be a dog in a foreign place is one thing, but to come home and have to crawl around your own neighborhood—" He was a small dog, but he sobbed like a man—deep, convulsive sobs.

Zeus was about to say, "Oh, it's not all that bad," and

then he felt a feathery hand on his shoulder. Actually, a wing. It was Victor, Hera's lawyer, in a blue pin-striped suit and two transparent wings like a locust's.

VIII. The Lover's Feet Held to the Fire

Zeus tried to turn him into a kumquat, but the lawyer only chuckled. "Heh, heh, heh. Don't waste my time. You wanna know how come you feel a little limp? Lemme tell ya. Hera is extremely upset, Mr. Z. Frankly, I don't know if godhood is something you're ever going to experience again. It wouldn't surprise me that much if you spent the rest of recorded time as a frozen meatball."

"What does she want?"

"She wants what's right. Justice. She wants half your power. No more, no less."

"Divide power? Impossible. It wouldn't be power if I gave it up."

"Okay. Then see how you like these potatoes." And Victor snatched up the dog, and his wings buzzed as he zoomed up and over the pleasant rooftops of Odense.

"Wait!" the god cried. "Forty-five percent!" But his voice was thin and whispery. On the way home, he swayed, his knees caved in, he had to hang on to a mailbox.

IX. Trapped

For three days, Zeus was flat on his back, stunned by monogamy: what a cruel fate for a great man! The dog

Mojo barked and barked at him, and Diane waited on him hand and foot, bringing him bad food and despicable wine; wretched little children hung around, onlookers at the site of a disaster, children who he had to pretend were his own. They clung to him on the couch, fighting over the choice locations, whining, weeping, pounding each other. They stank of sugar and yet he had to embrace them. He could not get their names straight. Melissa and Donnie (or Sean or Jon), or Melinda and Randy, and the fat one was Penny, and the little one's name began with an *H*. He called him Hector, and the little boy cried. "Go away," the god snapped at them. "You are vile and disgusting. I'm sorry but it's the truth. I'm dying. Let me die in peace. Bug off." The older boy wept: something about a promise, a trip to see a team play a game, a purchase—Zeus couldn't understand him. "Speak up!" he said, but the boy blubbered and bawled, his soft lemurlike face slimy with tears and mucus. The god swung down his legs and sat up on the couch and raised his voice: "I am trapped here, a divine being fallen from a very high estate indeed—you have no idea—and what I see around me I do not want."

Everybody felt lousy, except Diane. "It's only jet lag!" she cried, bringing in a tray of cold, greasy, repulsive food, which he could see from her smile was considered a real treat here. He ate a nugget of cheese and gagged.

"You'll feel better tomorrow," she said.

From outside came a burst of fierce barks and a brief dogfight and then yelping, and Diane tore out the door and returned a moment later with her husband, wounded, weeping, in her arms. "Oh, Sweetness, Sweetness," she murmured, kissing him on the snout, "we'll make it up to you somehow."

Later, Penny, the fat girl, asked Zeus if Greece was as dirty as they said. She asked if he and Mom had had a big fight. She asked why he felt trapped. She wanted to hear all the bad news.

"I felt crazy the moment we landed in America. The air is full of piercing voices, thousands of perfectly normal, handsome, tall people talk-talk-talk-talk-talking away like chickadees, and I can hear each one of them all the time, and they make me insane. You're used to this, I'm not. What do you people have against silence? Your country is so beautiful, and it is in the grip of invincible stupidity. Your politicians are habitual liars and toadies, and the writers are arrogant hacks," he said. "The country is inflamed with debt and swollen with blight and trash and sworn to flaming idiocy, and there is no civility left except among drunks and cabdrivers."

"How can you say that, Dad?"

"Because I'm omniscient."

"You are?"

"I know everything. It's a fact." She looked at him with a level gaze, not smirking, not pouting, an intelligent child. The only one prepared to understand him.

"Do my homework," she whispered. So he did. He whipped off dozens of geometry exercises, algebra, trigonometry, in a flash. He identified the nations of Africa, the law of averages, the use of the dative. "You are so smart," she said.

X. *The Wife Courts the Lover While the Husband Watches*

Diane packed the kids off to bed. "Now," she said, "where's that guy I rode home with on the plane?"

How could she understand? Passion isn't an arrangement, it's an accident, and Zeus was worn out. Nonetheless, he allowed himself to be undressed and helped into bed, and then Diane slowly undressed, letting her white silk slip slide to the floor, unhooking her garter belt and stripping the nylons slowly from her magnificent golden legs, unsnapping the brassiere and tossing it over her right shoulder, and stepping out of her silver panties. Then, naked, she stood a moment for his admiration, and turned and went into the bathroom.

"Relax, she'll be in there fifteen minutes if I know Diane," said the dog, sitting in the doorway. "She likes to do her nails before making love, I don't know why. Anyway, let me give you a few pointers about making love to her. She comes out of the gate pretty fast and gets excited and you think you're onto the straightaway stretch, but you're not—she slows down at that point, and she doesn't mount you until you're practically clawing at the walls."

"She mounts *me?*" asked Zeus.

"Yes," the dog said. "She's always on top."

When Diane emerged from the bathroom, she found Zeus in the living room, fully dressed, trying to make a long-distance call to Greece. She wanted him to see a therapist, but Zeus knew he was going back to Olympus. He just had to talk Hera down a little.

XI. Last Chance

The next morning, Zeus drove to the church, with Penny snuggled at his side. The town lay in a river valley, the avenues of homes extending up and over the hills like branches laden with fruit. The church stood on a hill, a red brick hangar with a weathervane for a steeple, a sanctuary done up with fake beams and mosaics, and a plump secretary with piano legs, named Tammy. She cornered him, hugged him, and fawned like a house afire. "Oh, Pastor Wes, we missed you so much! I've been reading your sermons over and over—they're so spirit-filled! We've got to publish them in a book!" she squealed.

"Go home," said Zeus. "Put your head under cold water." He escaped from the sanctuary into the study and slammed the door. The dog sat in the big leather chair behind the long desk. He cleared his throat. "I'd be glad to help with the sermon for tomorrow," he said. "I think your topic has got to be change—the life-affirming nature of change—how it teaches us not to confuse being with having—the Christian's willingness to accept and nurture change. . . . I'll work up an outline for you."

"That's a lot of balloon juice," said Zeus. "If I weren't going home tomorrow, I'd give a sermon and tell them to go home and hump like bunnies." He caught a look at himself in a long mirror: a powerful, handsome, tanned fellow in a white collar. Not bad.

"You sure you want to leave tomorrow?" asked the dog.

"That's the deal I made with Victor. Didn't he tell you?"

"You couldn't stay until Monday? This town needs shaking up. I always wanted to do it and didn't know how, and now you could preach on Sunday and it'd be a wonderful experience for all of us."

"You're a fool," Zeus said. "This is not a long-term problem, and the answer to it is not the willingness to accept change. You need heart, but you're Lutherans, and you go along with things. We know this from history. You're in danger and months will pass and it'll get worse, but you won't change your minds. You'll sit and wait. Lutherans are fifteen percent faith and eighty-five percent loyalty. They are nobody to lead a revolt. Your country is coming apart."

The dog looked up at the god with tears in his brown eyes. "Please tell my people," he whispered.

"Tell them yourself."

"They won't believe me."

"Good for them. Neither do I."

"Love me," Diane told Zeus that night in bed. "Forget yourself. Forget that we're Lutheran. Hurl your body off the cliff into the dark abyss of wild, mindless, pas-

337

sionate love." But he was too tired. He couldn't find the cliff. He seemed to be on a prairie.

XII. *The Lover Leaves, the Husband Returns*

In the morning, he hauled himself out of bed and dressed in a brown suit and white shirt. He peered into the closet. "These your only ties?" he asked the dog. The dog nodded.

Zeus glanced out the bedroom window to the east, to a beech tree by the garage, where a figure with waxen wings was sitting on a low limb. He said, silently, "Be with you in one minute." He limped into the kitchen and found Diane in the breakfast nook, eating bran flakes and reading an article in the Sunday paper about a couple who are able to spend four days a week in their country home now that they have a fax machine. He brushed her cheek with his lips and whispered, "O you woman, farewell, you sweet, sexy Lutheran love of my life," and jumped out of Wes and into the dog, loped out the back door, and climbed into Victor's car.

"She'll be glad to hear you're coming," said Victor. "She misses you. I'm sorry you'll have to make the return flight in a small cage, doped on a heavy depressant, and be quarantined for sixty days in Athens, both July and August, but after that, things should start to get better for you."

XIII. How the Husband Saw It

At eleven o'clock, having spent the previous two hours tangled in the sheets with his amazing wife, Wes stood in the pulpit and grinned. The church was almost half full, not bad for July, and the congregation seemed glad to see him. "First of all, Diane and I want to thank you for the magnificent gift of the trip to Greece, which will be a permanent memory, a token of your generosity and love," he said. "A tremendous thing happened on the trip that I want to share with you this morning. For the past week, I have lived in the body of a dog while an ancient god lived with Diane and tried to seduce her."

He didn't expect the congregation to welcome this news, but he was unprepared for their stony looks: they glared at him as if he were a criminal. They cried out, "Get down out of that pulpit, you filth, you!"

"Why are you so hostile?" he said.

Why are you so hostile? The lamp swayed as the ship rolled, and Diane said, "Why so hostile? Why? You want to know why I'm hostile? Is that what you're asking? About hostility? My hostility to you? Okay. I'll answer your question. Why I'm hostile—right? Me. Hostile. I'll tell you why. Why are you smiling?"

He was smiling, of course, because it was a week ago—and they were still in Greece, the big fight was still on, and God had kindly allowed him one more try. He could remember exactly the horrible words he'd said the first time, and this time he did not have to say them and become a dog. He was able to swallow the 1949 wine, and think, and say, "The sight of you fills me with tender affection and a sweet longing to be flat on my back in a dark, locked room with you naked, lying on top, kissing me, and me naked, too."

So they did, and in the morning the boat docked at Patmos, and they went up to the monastery and walked through the narrow twisting streets of the village, looking for a restaurant someone had told them about that served great lamb.

XIV. *What the Lover Learned*

The lawyer and the dog rode to the airport in the limousine, and somewhere along the way Zeus signed a document that gave Hera half his power and promised absolute fidelity. "Absolute?" he woofed. "You mean 'total' in the sense of bottom line, right? A sort of basic faithfulness? Fidelity in principle? Isn't that what you mean here? The spirit of fidelity?"

"I mean pure," the lawyer said.

Zeus signed. The lawyer tossed him a small, dry biscuit. Zeus wolfed it down and barked. In the back of his mind, he thought maybe he'd find a brilliant lawyer to argue that the paw print wasn't a valid signature. He thought about a twenty-four-ounce T-bone steak, and he wasn't sure he'd get that either.